D0301603

Benefit Realisation Management

Reviews for Benefit Realisation Management
1st Edition

'What spurred me to open the book and delve into its contents was the fact I had heard Gerald Bradley speak at the BPPM summit at Heathrow earlier in the year and had found that talk both interesting and practical in providing a way into benefit management. I am pleased I made the effort. The book brings together in one place everything you might need to implement successful benefit realisation. It is easy to read and logically structured... Sometimes a book will be published that fills a need within the market. This book is one of those. It provides a master class on the subject, enabling understanding and providing the tools to allow project managers to implement practical and viable processes to identify, track and measure benefits. If you buy one book on benefit realisation management for your organisation then I suggest you buy this.'

Ed Burney-Cumming, *Project Magazine*

'I read the book with keen interest as somebody who has been heavily involved in bringing about change and ensuring benefits required by Directors are achieved. Whilst reading I have frequently said to myself "if only I had known, appreciated that at the time". The book is a source of many useful and practical insights for any individual or organisation really wanting to achieve the benefits they expect of their change initiatives. It is not a book of theory but one of practical application and how to overcome the inevitable pitfalls that will be experienced in successfully bringing about change. You might not agree with all the points Gerald makes but you will find his ideas and comments challenging and thought provoking. I thoroughly recommend the book for those facing the challenge of supporting their organisation in realising its goals.'

Brian Cowley, Head of Business Change, Friends Provident

'It is not just an investment in a management book, but this book is an investment in a technique that can be used, to add value to all the current and future change initiatives within an organization...More than just enjoyable for reading, this book is a complete tool kit for understanding and learning about the dynamics of change and for eliminating the frustrations associated with failure in achieving the desired results of any change initiative.'

VISION. *The Journal of Business Perspective*

Benefit Realisation Management

A Practical Guide to Achieving Benefits Through Change

Second Edition

GERALD BRADLEY

GOWER

© Gerald Bradley 2010

Reprinted 2013

All rights reserved. No part of this publication may be reproduced, stored in a retrieval system or transmitted in any form or by any means, electronic, mechanical, photocopying, recording or otherwise without the prior permission of the publisher.

Published by
Gower Publishing Limited
Wey Court East
Union Road
Farnham
Surrey
GU9 7PT
England

Gower Publishing Company
110 Cherry Street
Suite 3-1
Burlington
VT 05401-3818
USA

www.gowerpublishing.com

Gerald Bradley has asserted his moral right under the Copyright, Designs and Patents Act, 1988, to be identified as the author of this work.

British Library Cataloguing in Publication Data
Bradley, Gerald.
  Benefit realisation management : a practical guide for achieving benefits through change. -- 2nd ed.
  1. Organizational change. 2. Rate of return.
  I. Title
  658.4'063-dc22

  ISBN: 978-1-4094-0094-3 (hbk)
         978-1-4094-1086-7 (ebk)
         978-1-4094-5876-0 (ePub)

Library of Congress Cataloging-in-Publication Data
Bradley, Gerald.
  Benefit realisation management : a practical guide to achieving benefits through change / by Gerald Bradley.
       p. cm.
  Earlier ed. published in 2006.
  Includes bibliographical references and index.
  ISBN 978-1-4094-0094-3 (hbk.)
  1. Organizational change--Management. 2. Reengineering (Management) 3. Strategic planning. 4. Organizational effectiveness--Evaluation. 5. Cost effectiveness. I. Title.
  HD58.8.B714 2010
  658.4'06--dc22

                                                                     2009042617

Printed and bound in Great Britain
by MPG PRINTGROUP

Contents

List of Figures

Acknowledgements

This work is a synergistic product of many minds – colleagues and clients – which has developed and evolved over 25 years. I am thankful for the inspiration of friends and colleagues and the frequent encouragement to pioneer and pursue the subject of benefit realisation over this period.

For the development and production of the original version and this revision I am grateful to:

- those organisations who have applied successfully the concepts and many of the tools and techniques described in the book, in particular the Driver and Vehicle Licensing Agency (DVLA), the British Council and the Royal Borough of Kensington and Chelsea Council and for their willingness to allow their experiences to be included as case examples;

- colleagues and readers of the first edition for their encouraging comments and helpful suggestions;

- Pat for her painstaking editing and many improvements to the readability of the original version;

- my children and my mother for their inspiration and motivating interest, but most of all to my wife Rosemary for her long suffering, support and encouragement.

Glossary of Terms

Term	Definition	Elaboration
ABR	Active Benefit Realisation	This is the term used by Dan Remenyi et al. to describe BRM in their book *Achieving Maximum Value from Information Systems*
Activity	A task or piece of work with a defined timescale and resource requirement	It will normally be something for which someone can clearly be made responsible. Activities are normally grouped into work packages, projects and programmes
		Does wording start with the imperative form of verb? – e.g. investigate, create, design, implement, appoint, establish
Added value	Value which is additional to cost reduction	
Attribute of a benefit	A charateristic of a benefit (e.g. business impact, category, value type, value, expected time of realisation, beneficiary, accountable stakeholder, risk)	These are gathered together in a Benefit Profile
Balanced Business Scorecard (BBS)	A scorecard for monitoring business performance	This is normally divided into four quadrants – Customer, Development/learning, Internal improvement and Finance
Balanced Scorecard Category	A particular category or quadrant from the Balanced Business Scorecard	
Baseline	The value or trend line of a measure at a particular point in time	The point in time is normally during the planning/justification phase of a proposed investment in change.
		If the trend line is horizontal this equates to the value
BAU	Business as usual	The routine day-to-day activities of an organisation
BCM	See *Business Change Manager*	The person responsible for coordinating business change for a programme
BDM	See *Benefit Dependency Map*	
Beneficiaries	People who will feel or experience the value of a benefit	
Benefit	An outcome of change that is perceived as positive by a stakeholder	Typically these are outcomes which are valuable to the organisation and measurable.
		Does wording start with a change word? Would we expect the value to change gradually? Does it link to a programme objective? Could we identify one or more measures for the benefit?

Term	Definition	Elaboration
Benefit Dependency Map (BDM)	A Benefits Map with the addition of dependencies – enablers and business changes	A map which links primary objectives to the enabling technology and business change and so charts the activities on which the benefits depend
Benefit Distribution Matrix	The matrix which defines how the benefits (and disbenefits) are to be distributed between the stakeholders	This is a commonly-used instance of an Investment Assessment Matrix
Benefit Facilitator	A centre of expertise for BRM to support programmes with benefit realisation yet challenge benefit claims and Business Cases	The role should be a permanent role within an organisation sitting outside individual programmes

The role is probably best located in the Portfolio Management Office |
| Benefit Management | The name we previously used for BRM and still used by other organisations including OGC | |
| Benefits Management Strategy | A framework for realising benefits, a description of how, and at what level, BRM is to be applied | This should refer to the particular approach adopted by the organisation for applying BRM, and could include the plan for specific BRM activities, e.g. workshops

To avoid possible confusion with the Benefit Realisation Plan, 'Strategy for BRM' is a preferred title for this document |
| Benefit Maturity Index | An index indicating the maturity of an organisation with respect to benefit realisation | Levels range from 1 (low) to 4 (high) |
| Benefit Owner | A person responsible for the realisation of the benefit | |
| Benefit Profile | The template which contains the comprehensive description of a single benefit, including all its attributes and dependencies | It includes all the information – precise definition, attributes, system and business dependencies, measurement criteria – needed to aid realisation and so is also known as the Benefit Realisation Proforma

In paper format we suggest that this is contained on a single page. Suggested templates are available from **sigma** |
| Benefit Realisation Manager | The term used by MSP to describe a Benefit Facilitator | |
| Benefit Realisation Management (BRM) | The process of organising and managing, so that potential benefits, arising from investment in change, are actually achieved | It can be applied to a whole organisation, a portfolio of change initiatives, a programme or a project

It is a continuous process running through the whole change life-cycle and should be the central theme of any change initiative |
| Benefit Realisation Plan (BRP) | The document which shows how and when all the benefits, for a particular change initiative, are expected to be realised | The document would be the handbook of the sponsor and of value to stakeholders, the programme team and those accountable for the realisation of specific benefits |

Term	Definition	Elaboration
Benefit Tracking Report	A regularly produced report showing the values of the benefits and so tracking progress towards the ultimate goal and the fulfilment of the vision	
Benefit trajectory	A time sequence of benefits	A stream of expected benefits values
Benefits Bucket	A corporate or portfolio 'pot' for a particular type or category of benefit	This pot would be established corporately in the expectation that a number of programmes or projects will contribute to it This is not dissimilar to a benefit category or a KPI
Benefits Map	A network of benefits, usually linked to one or more of the primary investment objectives, which maps all the cause-and-effect relationships	Its status will evolve through: wish list, set of feasible paths, plan of selected options, visual for communicating intentions, benefit tracking mechanism
Best Value	A Government-introduced initiative to target the changes which would deliver best value	
Blueprint	A model of the future business environment needed to achieve the vision	A Benefit Dependency Map is an early and high-level view of a Blueprint
Boston Matrix	A 2x2 matrix used for assessing a portfolio of products	The quadrants are described as 'Problem Child', 'Star', 'Cash Cow' and 'Dog'
Bounding Objective	See *Primary Objective*	
BRAG Status	Like a RAG Status but including Blue for benefits not due to have reached their target	
BRM Process	The process for applying BRM. This is effectively the process for managing change	This is sub-divided into six phases with a recommended review point at the close of each phase It can be applied at any level within an organisation – corporate, divisional, programme or project
BRP	See *Benefit Realisation Plan*	
Business Case	The document used to justify investment in change. It is an evolving document with stages such as Strategic Outline, Outline and Full Business Case	It should describe and value the expected benefits, specify the costs covering enablers and business changes and include a map of how the change is expected to realise the benefits
Business Change	A change which occurs within the business/operational environment, often a new way of working or a new business state, which may utilise a new enabler	A task, process, piece of work, intended to produce a new business state or a benefit. It should be defined so that it could have definite start and end dates and someone responsible This should not be an ongoing or BAU process (e.g. decide whether to recruit or train) but an activity to bring about change. So we recommend that its descriptions start with the imperative form of verb – e.g. investigate, create, design, implement, appoint, establish

Term	Definition	Elaboration
Business Sponsor	See *Sponsor*	
Capability	This can refer to an enabler or to the integration of enablers and business changes – a sub-state of the Blueprint	For example: new staff (enablers) are trained and developed (business change) and become a skilled team (capability)
Case for Change	The initial case for proceeding with the proposed change	The Case for Change document is often referred to as the Programme Mandate
Change	Activity, within the organisation and sometimes outside the organisation, which creates new ways of functioning, new ways of working, new ways of communicating and new ways of making decisions	The set of actions by which the organisation moves from any current state to any desired state. This can apply at any level (i.e. a change can be a group of changes) Changes may also be grouped into work packages, projects, tranches and programmes
Change-action Plan	The template that lists the required changes and actions, grouped by change initiative, with owners, timescales and costs	
Change delivery mechanisms	A mechanism for delivering change – project, programme or work package	
Change initiative	A change delivery mechanism	
Change Lifecycle	The life-cycle of a change initiative	
Change-Benefit Impact	The impact of a particular change on a set of benefits and their measures expressed as percentage contributions	This can apply to both actuals and to targets The change referred to will often be a project or a programme
Communications Strategy	The strategy for communicating with all the stakeholders of a programme or project	This would normally be part of the Stakeholder Management/Engagement Strategy
Consumers	A person who consumes or uses a product	
Cranfield Grid	A variant of the Boston Matrix, developed by Cranfield University to assess a portfolio of programmes and projects	
CSF	Critical Success Factor	
Customers	Individuals and organisations that buy and/or receive products and services	
DCF	Discounted cash flow	A stream of future financial values – cost or benefits – discounted back to a common point of time (usually year 0) The discount factor may be a combination of inflation rate and the cost of borrowing
Deliverable	An output of a process or project	
Dependency	Anything subordinate or dependent	
Disbenefit	An outcome of change that is perceived as negative by a stakeholder	A disbenefit may be similar to a risk

Term	Definition	Elaboration
Driver	Some internal or external pressure or opportunity which is stimulating or driving the need for change	
Earned value	A measure of progress or percentage completion in the construction of an object, expressed as a percentage of the planned cost	
eBusiness, eCommerce	Business conducted electronically using the Internet	
Economic Value	A financial value estimated for a benefit using economic data	This is usually applied to benefits which are not truly financial or to consequential benefits
EFQM	European Foundation for Quality Management	A Total Quality Management (TQM) framework based on 9 criteria, 5 'enablers' and 4 'results'
Enabler	An enabler is something that can be developed/built/acquired normally from outside the environment in which it will be embedded and where the benefits will be realised	An enabler is normally costed, budgeted and formally planned, usually within a project or programme. It is typically within the space of the technical domains

Enablers include: IT Systems, Communications Systems, Buildings, Policies, Procedures, Skills |
Enabler Project Manager	A Project Manager responsible for the acquisition (or development) and implementation of an enabler	
End Benefit	An ultimate benefit of a programme or project	One of the set of benefits that together are equivalent to one of the bounding objectives of a programme or project
Forcible extraction	The process whereby projected benefits are extracted from budgets before they are generated or realised	
Full Business Case	The final stage of the evolving Business Case	This would be completed either at the end of Phase 3 or Phase 4 in the change life-cycle
Gateway Process	This is a process, instigated by OGC, of formal reviews or gates, to be applied at various stages of a programme or project	A project has six distinct gates, numbered 1 to 6, while a programme has a single Gate 0, which can be applied many times
Goal	A general term for the purpose of change which may be any combination of vision, objectives and end benefits	
Governance structure	The organisation and processes needed to govern a programme	
Gross Domestic Product (GDP)	The total value of goods produced and services provided in a country in one year	
IAM	Investment Assessment Matrix	
Initiation Workshop	A workshop with the senior stakeholder managers, including sponsor, to confirm investment scope and initiate the benefits work	

Term	Definition	Elaboration
Intermediate benefits	Benefits which will occur between the implementation of early changes and the realisation of the end benefits	
Investment Assessment Matrix (IAM)	A matrix of benefits used for checking balance and alignment and for optimising the worth of a programme	The axes of the matrix are benefit attributes taken from the Benefit Profile The visual nature of the matrix facilitates the required checks and balances
Issues Log	Used to capture and actively manage programme issues	This should be coordinated with the Risk Register
IT	Information Technology	
ITT	Invitation to tender	Request for a proposal for some products or services Sometimes referred to as an RFP (Request for Proposal)
KPI	Key Performance Indicator	A measure, usually tracked at a corporate level, to monitor overall performance
Lean Thinking or Lean Process	Is an approach designed to increase efficiency, reduce waste and focus on what is important	The approach has come from the manufacturing industry, particularly the car industry
Life-cycle	The sequence of events covering the complete life of a project or programme	
Map score	This is a score attached to an entity in a map, normally to objectives and benefits, to indicate their importance or weight relative to the other entities	If the paths of a map are given percentage weightings according to the significance of their contribution to the entity they feed, the scores are computed by giving the right most entity an arbitrary score (ususally a large round number like 1000) followed by a right to left calculation using the percentage weightings
MD	Managing Director	
Measure	The entity whose value is reported regularly to demonstrate the realisation of the benefit. A quantity, derived from a set of metrics, whose change in the desired direction would help to confirm that the related benefit is being realised	The measure is the thing that will be tracked and monitored (e.g. 'value of monthly sales') – it is not the value (e.g. £300,000) or the target (e.g. +30 per cent) or the means of measurement (e.g. quarterly financial review) or the benefit (e.g. more sales) A measure should start with words like – the average value of, percentage of, longest time taken to... Occasionally the measure may equal a metric. One benefit may have several measures
Measure Monitor	The role of gathering and consolidating the ongoing monitoring and reporting of the raw measurement data	
Measure Owner	A person responsible for the overall achievement of the measure's target	

Term	Definition	Elaboration
Measure value	The value of the measure at a particular point in time	These are of two types – actual or target It will be necessary to define: the mechanism and frequency of monitoring and to whom and by whom the measure will be reported
Measures Dictionary	A dictionary or register of measures for an organisation or a major part of an organisation	Each entry will hold – a description, how and by whom it will be measured, a series of historic values, forecast contributions from different change initiatives
Metric	A raw piece of data, often captured by a computer system, from which measures may be derived	This could be the basic statistics of each call made to a call centre or details of every sale
Milestone	A significant event or stage in a project	
Mission	The purpose for which the organisation exists	
MSP	Managing Successful Programmes (2007 edition)	A TSO Publication written by OGC giving guidance on Programme Management
NAO	National Audit Office	
NPV	Net Present Value	100 x (Benefits DCF – Costs DCF)/Costs DCF
Objective	An answer to the important 'why?' question which defines purpose, aim and direction	A major component of the transition from current state to blueprint expressed as an aim or purpose Wording to start with 'To'
OGC	Office of Government Commerce	
Optimisation	A process which is benefit driven which exploits all types of opportunity for increasing the value of an investment	
Orphan Benefit	A benefit arising from the changes planned for a programme, but which does not contribute to the programme's objectives	This applies both to planned and realised benefits
Outcome	The result of change	If the outcome is perceived as positive it is called a benefit if negative it is called a disbenefit
Outline Business Case	An interim version of a Business Case	
P3O	This is the OGC term for an office or an hierarchy of offices to support Portfolio, Programme or Project Management	
Performance Indicator	A measure or group of measures used to indicate performance	
Phase	One of the six subdivisions of the BRM/ Change Process	

Term	Definition	Elaboration
Portfolio	A collection of change initiatives	The portfolio may relate to the whole organisation or to a major subdivision. Ideally the mix of initiatives will be balanced in respect of size, complexity, risk, and reward
Portfolio Board	The senior-level board responsible for managing the whole change portfolio	Sometimes referred to as: Steering Group, Sponsoring Group or Change Management Executive
Portfolio Investment Matrices	Matrices used to aid the analyis of a portfolio of change initiatives	All the component change initiatives are positioned in the matrix according to criteria defined by the axes. Initiatives which are cause for concern are so highlighted
Portfolio Management Office	The office responsible for supporting the Portfolio Board in the managing of the whole change portfolio	The Benefit Facilitator Role fits comfortably into this office
Primary Objective	An end objective for a change initiative which helps to bound its scope	Ideally a single change initiative, such as a programme, should have no more than three primary objectives
Prince 2	A methodology for managing projects	Recommended and supported by OGC
Programme	A mechanism for managing large or complex changes in order to achieve a vision	The total investment or package of change (the fried egg) designed to achieve the primary objectives, and the related benefits, in support of the vision
Programme Board	A group of senior stakeholder representatives, responsible for providing leadership and direction for the programme	This Board would normally be chaired by the SRO
Programme Brief	A document that builds on the Programme Mandate to make the case for progressing from Phase 2 to Phase 3	
Programme Definition Document	The document that fully defines the programme, especially what is necessary to deliver the Blueprint and to mitigate the risks	
Programme Director	A senior Programme Manager	For very large programmes it may be helpful to have a Programme Director and Manager
Programme Manager	The person responsible for the effective fulfilment of the programme, including the realisation of benefits	This person manages the programme, normally in a full-time capacity, ensuring the smooth integration of enabler implementation and business change and the consequential realisation of benefits

This person works on behalf of the SRO and Programme Board, to whom they report |
| Programme management | The process of managing a programme | |
| Programme Mandate | The document that makes the case for progressing from Phase 1 to Phase 2 | An alternative name is Case for Change |

Term	Definition	Elaboration
Programme Sponsor	The person who sponsors the programme, which may include the commitment of the required funds	The person ultimately responsible and accountable for the effective fulfilment of the programme, including the realisation of benefits This is usually the more general term for SRO, though SROs are not always responsible for the provision of the funds
Project	A mechanism for the acquisition/creation and perhaps implementation of an enabler	
RAG Status	Red, Amber, Green Status	Green – on or close to target; amber – a wider deviation from target; red – well off target Tolerances may be precisely defined depending on the situation
Realisation	Conceiving as real, understanding clearly, making realistic, achieving and perhaps converting to money	
Requirement	A need – something that is required in order to achieve a benefit	This is normally a feature of an enabler but could apply to a business change These may be subdivided into 3 levels: key requirements, user requirements and system requirements
Requirement Analysis	A formal process for analysing requirements, usually for a computer system	The creation of a BDM is a good example of initial 'requirements analysis'
Requirement specification	A detailed description of the requirement	Used for specifying technology functionality
RFP	Request for a proposal – for products or services	Sometimes referred to as an ITT (Invitation to tender)
Resources	People, equipment, money	
Risk Log or Register	A register of potential risks, normally associated with a programme or a project, but could be related to the complete portfolio of changes	The characteristics of each identified risk include: description, probablity of occurrence, impact on the programme particularly the realisation of benefits, proximity and owner
ROI	Return on Investment	The return for a particular investment, usually expressed as a percentage of the outlay
Root Cause Modelling	A methodology for assessing the cause of problems and identifying remedial actions using a mapping process	
Score	A value or relative weight attached to an entity, usually a benefit, from applying weights to the paths of a map	See also *Map Score*
Senior Responsible Owner (SRO)	A more formal definition of sponsor, introduced by OGC in MSP	An SRO has the ultimate accountabiity for benefit realisation They should be appointed by the Portfolio Board of which they are likely to be a member

Term	Definition	Elaboration
Sigma Grid	A variant of the Boston Matrix, developed by sigma to identify and assess the set of benefits for a particular programme or project	The four quadrants are defined as 'speculative', 'strategic', 'key-operational' and 'support'
Sigma Value Types	A classification of benefit values, developed by sigma and subsequently adopted by MSP in 2007	The classification has 6 tangible classes – definite, expected and logical for both financial and non-financial – and an intangible class
		The classification is very useful in Business Cases, for setting realistic expectations regarding measurements and predicted values
Six Sigma	A disciplined and data driven approach and methodology for eliminating defects	From manufacturing to transactional and from product to service
Sponsoring Group	The group of senior managers who will sanction, monitor and generally oversee the orgnisation's portfolio of programmes and projects	This is an MSP term which is synonymous with Steering Group and Portfolio Board
SRO	See *Senior Responsible Owner*	
Stakeholder	Any individual, group or organisation who will be affected by, or have influence over, the proposed investment	Stakeholders should normally include customers and suppliers (internal or external)
		Anyone who can throw a spanner in the works
Stakeholder Management Strategy/Plan	The strategy/plan for managing/engaging the stakeholders of a programme, covering involvement and communication	
Stakeholder Profile	The template which details all the expected impacts, from the portfolio of changes, on a single stakeholder or stakeholder group	It includes the changes, benefits and disbenefits they are likely to experience, and the changes and benefits for which they are responsible
		In paper format we suggest that this is contained on a single page. Suggested templates are available from **sigma**
Steering Group	The senior management group which oversees a portfolio of programmes and projects	This is often referred to as the Portfolio Board
		Responsiblities cover the selection, monitoring and termination of change initiatives in the portfolio and the creation of an environment in which the portfolio will thrive
Strategic Outline Case	The first of three stages of a Business Case according to OGC	An alternative name for the Programme Brief
Strategy	The plan of action or management mechanism needed to achieve an objective or vision	
Strategy Map	A map linking objectives in 'cause and effect' relationships	This normally relates to a programme but could be applied at organisational level
		The term comes from the work of Kaplin and Norton – see *Bibliography*

Term	Definition	Elaboration
Strategy Score	A map score which is computed for a programme, rather than a single map, by giving the initial arbitrary number to the right most objective in the Strategy Map	
Target, Predicted Value	A defined end point, normally expressed as a numeric value	This is generally applied to objectives, benefits and measures
TOR	Terms of Reference (e.g. for job roles)	
Value Management	A style of management aimed at maximising the overall performance of an organisation	This approach is particularly dedicated to motivating people, developing skills and promoting synergies and innovation

Also called 'value engineering' |
| VFM | Value for Money | |
| Vision, Vision Statement | A concise description/picture of the desired future state of an organisation or organisational unit, resulting from planned change | The planned change may be managed as a portfolio of programmes, a single programme, a project, a work package or a combination of these

The vision provides the basis for communicating and encouraging buy-in from stakeholders |
Weighted paths	A map path which has been weighted (usually as a percentage) relative to other paths to signify its relative importance for further investment	
Work Package	A piece of work, which has clear outputs or deliverables (and therefore a start and finish), but which doesn't merit formal management structures and/or governance mechanisms	This is in contrast to a project or programme which require formal management processes and structures
Yield	The annual return from an investment	

Preface

This book explores the drivers, concepts and principles underpinning successful benefit realisation and describes in detail a proven, comprehensive and practical approach to benefit realisation referred to as Benefit Realisation Management (BRM).

The roots of interest in BRM in the 1980s were fed by a need to understand 'What is our Return on Investment (ROI) from Information Technology (IT) spend?' Time and experience have shown that IT is merely a catalyst for change – the real challenge is centred on change itself, not on any particular technology. The approach described here, which covers any type of investments in change, irrespective of whether IT is one of the enablers, has seen effective application in a wide variety of circumstances within a diverse range of organisations, both private and public.

BRM can be used to maximise the return from a specific project or programme, to optimise and balance a portfolio of projects or programmes or to determine and manage effective business strategy. It has equal applicability to public and private sector organisations. BRM offers an opportunity for substantial improvement in business performance; however implementing BRM is a challenge, requiring funding, skills and commitment.

The book is based on a solid body of benefit realisation expertise, built up over 25 years, combined with the practical experiences of the benefit-realisation consultants from **sigma**, a company specialising in benefit realisation, founded and now chaired by the author. Its purpose is to help organisations to change, by harnessing the enormous potential of BRM to improve performance and deliver value to stakeholders.

Where appropriate the book refers to aspects of various related disciplines, especially programme management as advocated by the Office of Government Commerce (OGC) in their latest edition of *Managing Successful Programmes* (MSP).[1] Though this book has been extremely successful in putting benefit realisation on the management agenda, it suffers from having multiple authors and limited practical track record on which to rely.

In spite of all the good efforts of OGC and the publication of MSP, I believe the big challenge for the public sector is to create a focus on benefits which is rooted in a desire to achieve them. The existing strong culture of 'we will do benefits because we need a Business Case to secure the funding, and/or because OGC or the Treasury say we must and we have to face a series of Gateway Reviews' is narrow and restrictive.

The current focus within both public and private sectors on implementing enablers, rather than on realising benefits and achieving the vision or end goal, is so widespread and deep rooted that it needs a clear process and sustained effort to change. I hope this book may

---

1   Managing Successful Programmes published by TSO in September 2007.

make some contribution towards changing this culture by providing a holistic, cohesive, practical and proven process.

One of the Critical Success Factors (CSFs) for benefit realisation is quality communication which requires clear and precise use of language and visual support. So we encourage extensive but selective use of pictures, diagrams, charts and maps. In our practical work with clients we also use colour to facilitate communication and consistency. I am therefore delighted that, in response to readers' requests, colour has now been included in this revised version of my book, showing clearly the colour conventions which we normally adopt. The colour conventions used throughout this book are given in the table below (Figure P.1)

	Stakeholders
	Vision
	Objective
	Bounding objective
	End benefit
	Intermediate benefit
	Consequential benefit
	Orphan benefit
	Disbenefit
	Measure
	Benefit Realisation Management
	Enabler
	Business Change
	Portfolio
	Programme
	Reviews and Governance
	Document

Figure P.1   Colour convention recommended for BRM and adopted throughout the book

Effective use of language requires clear and consistent definition of terms and so each key term introduced is accompanied by a suggested definition. These definitions are mutually consistent, have generally stood the test of time (20+ years of practical use), and as far as possible are consistent with the spirit (if not the exact words) of definitions used in related documents, such as MSP. They have also been tested through the rigours of software development. A complete set of terms is given in the Glossary.

Ideally this book should be read sequentially; however its logical structure, with a small amount of repetition in content, should enable the reader to gain value from dipping into chapters of their choosing. It is divided into four parts:

Part I – Fundamentals and Foundations of Benefit Realisation – Chapters 1 to 7

Part II – The Application of BRM to Programmes and Projects – Chapters 8 to 23

Part III – The Application of BRM to Portfolio Management – Chapter 24

Part IV – Embedding BRM within an Organisation – Chapters 25 to 31.

After reading the overview of BRM in Part I, readers may wish to treat the remainder of the book as a reference document, where further detail can be obtained as required.

BRM is not about ticking boxes or validating past decisions; it is an active, dynamic process for maximising future returns. BRM provides the management information for change, removing the smoke screens from the tough decisions without making them for you. My wish is that, after reading this book, many will apply the principles and techniques described and experience a consequential and dramatic improvement in benefit realisation and in the effectiveness of portfolios, programmes and projects.

Before reading the book you may like to apply a simple health check. Consider each of the following 15 statements, score 2 if you strongly agree, 1 if you mildly agree and 0 if you disagree, and compute your total score. Calculate a similar score for your organisation, based on your assessment.

1. The primary purpose of benefits is to justify a proposed investment.

2. If the enabler (for example, computer system) is specified and delivered correctly then we will definitely get the benefits.

3. A shared vision/end goal is a luxury we can postpone or dispense with.

4. BRM is secondary to the task of delivering the programme – the enabler(s).

5. Benefit identification is the responsibility of the Programme Team.

6. Disbenefits may be an inconvenience but they should never kill a project.

7. Maps such as a Benefits Maps are complicated and unnecessary.

8. A good Business Case is one which just shows that the anticipated return is worth the proposed outlay.

9. Senior managers don't need to bother about benefits or understand BRM.

10. At the end of the day stakeholders will just have to do what they are told.

11. Measurement is for the benefit of managers, to justify their decisions.

12.   You only need to measure and report key (usually end) benefits.

13.   The only benefits that count are hard financial ones.

14.   BRM is too bureaucratic and at best is only applicable to large programmes and projects.

15.   We don't really have a problem as we have always done a cost-benefit analysis and then taken what has been claimed from future budgets.

If your personal score is greater than 5 or your organisation's score is greater than 10, then I recommend that you read the whole book.

Fundamentals and Foundations of Benefit Realisation

In seven chapters, Part I examines the fundamentals of benefit realisation, providing a good overview of Benefit Realisation Management (BRM). The chapters cover:

- Today's Biggest Challenge

- Stakeholders

- Benefit Realisation

- Overview of BRM

- Project and programme fundamentals

- Key BRM roles and responsibilities

- Planning and preparing for success.

The remainder of the book expands this summary, providing elaboration and detail, especially in respect of some of the specific BRM techniques, such as:

- Mapping

- Identifying, classifying, validating and profiling benefits

- Measure identification

- Documentation

- Governance

- Process

- Portfolio Management

- Stakeholder engagement.

Today's Biggest Challenge

1

'If you don't know where you're going, any path is as good as another... but you won't realise you're lost, you won't know what time you'll get there, you might unknowingly be going in circles, and others won't understand how they can help. And, since you could pass right by without knowing it, you won't get the satisfaction of having arrived!.'

(Lewis Carroll: *Alice in Wonderland*)

1.1   Recent Industry Performance

Each year, UK industry invests around £100bn on change, presumably in order to improve business performance. Individually, organisations are usually unsure how much return they receive from this investment. Collectively, if we measure the return based on Gross Domestic Product (GDP), the yield is negative, at around minus 6 per cent; based on shareholder value over a ten-year period, even before the impact of the 2009 credit crunch, the yield is still negative at around minus 4 per cent.

In terms of specifics, Professor Clegg of the University of Sheffield collected data drawing on the experiences of around 14,000 UK companies investing in new information and communications technologies. He found that performance goals were frequently not set and often not carefully evaluated. However, his conclusions were that around 10–20 per cent of such investments can be counted as outright successes – they met their objectives. About 40 per cent were outright failures and a waste of money, time and energy. A further 40 per cent were deemed as partial successes, meeting some but not all of their goals. These conclusions were consistent with other data, for example the report published by the Royal Academy of Engineering and the British Computer Society in 2004.

sigma's[1] experience indicates that only 10–25 per cent of potential benefits are usually achieved from investment in change. This shortfall, or waste (which is what it is), is estimated to cost the UK over £50bn per annum.

So it may seem surprising that organisations continue to invest in change. The dilemma is that change in the external environment will probably continue to accelerate, so without internal change many organisations will die. This is particularly true in periods

---

1   **sigma** is the Strategic Management Consultancy organisation founded by the author.

of recession such as we experienced in 2009–2010. Like death and taxation, change is one of the certainties of life, or as Alvin Toffler put it: 'Change is not merely necessary to life – it is life.'

1.2   So Why Endure the Pain of Change?

Avoiding change is not a viable option. The challenge is to develop an effective and timely method of determining the optimum set of proactive changes, and to manage them, so that stakeholder resistance is overcome and defined performance goals are achieved. Change can be a source of tremendous business potential. When the worldwide customer base was growing and the average demand from each customer was also growing and developing, change was necessary to meet demand in an efficient and competitive manner. When global demand is falling change becomes all the more important – it is in fact the life blood of survival. So effective management of this change becomes even more critical and involves doing the 'right' things and doing them 'right'. Benefit Realisation Management (BRM) is a process that addresses both of these challenges – creating and maintaining a portfolio of the best change initiatives and then ensuring each one delivers maximum value. There is no doubt that the organisations that will survive and even thrive in a recession will be those that adapt, managing change innovatively and effectively.

A major hindrance to the achievement of potential is a dominant focus on delivering capability – brainwave solutions looking for problems. The real need is for solutions, carefully constructed as a response to clear objectives, which have been determined, owned and established by the organisation. Here it is useful to distinguish between the change which is acquiring and implementing a capability, and the change which embeds this capability into the working practices of the organisation.

I refer to the first change as enabling change, or simply an *enabler*, which is defined as 'something that can be developed/built/acquired normally from outside the environment in which it will be embedded and where the benefits will be realised', and the second as *business change*, which is defined as, 'a change which occurs within the business/operational environment, often a new way of working or a new business state, which may utilise a new enabler'. This distinction between the two types of change helps to:

- highlight the importance of both, including the need to cost, budget and plan for both;

- acknowledge that they may be funded and managed differently;

- ensure that business change is neither neglected nor squeezed, especially when budgets are tight or later reduced.

One reason why business change is often the poor relation in this pair is a prevalent myth that enablers, such as systems, technology and buildings, generate benefits of themselves and so have intrinsic value or even equate to value. This is evidenced by the technique named *Earned Value*. Earned Value is used in construction type activities in order that progress can be assessed against a time schedule or an expenditure schedule. So if a building, which is expected to cost £4m, is 25 per cent complete, then its earned value is £1m, whereas expenditure to date might be £1.3m. The merits of this analysis are clear – it is a useful technique; but the name[2] is unfortunate though revealing, implying that an enabler such as a building, or even worse part of a building, equates to some value. Value is only achieved when the enabler is put to appropriate use and benefits are realised – which is certainly impossible if an enabler is still being built. In fact an enabler, complete or not, has no value – earned or otherwise.

We recently had a new kitchen, costing £8,000, which was scheduled to be installed in four days. At the end of the first day the installation was 30 per cent complete. The old kitchen had been removed, and in its place were partly assembled new cabinets, plenty of sawdust, exposed electric cables and piping and no running water. If the fitter had decided at that stage to quit, with a request for just £2,000 of the £2,400 earned value, I think I would have had great difficulty in getting my wife excited about the £400 we would then supposedly have just gained.

Figure 1.1   Cart before the horse

1.3   Cart Before the Horse

I continue to be surprised at how often organisations 'put the cart before the horse' by focusing too early on enablers, without being clear about the end goal. The idea of a cart pulling a horse is almost too absurd to imagine, yet in reality this is what frequently happens with benefit realisation.

A cart with no horse is easier to imagine. But without a horse to pull it and steer it towards its intended destination, a cart will either not move at all or will start to drift, taking

2   Perhaps for the above reason some now refer to Earned Value as Cost Schedule Performance.

the easiest path – downhill – accelerating under its own momentum, completely out of control.

How often is change just like this? Is it because many managers find it more stimulating to generate the adrenaline rush from what seems like innovative and sometimes frenzied activity, rather than to increase shareholder value by a carefully planned and methodical approach to change, driven by a clearly defined and appropriately shared goal?

A classic illustration is the Millennium Dome, an impressive technological achievement, delivered within budget and on time, yet with unclear objectives and dubious benefits, especially for UK taxpayers. In December 1999, Tony Blair hailed it as a 'triumph of confidence over cynicism' yet only 4.5m of the predicted 12m visitors materialised, over £250m of lottery rescue grants were needed to keep the venture solvent, and five years on the Dome was still standing empty, costing the taxpayer almost £190,000 a month for maintenance and security.[3] Is this another instance of a dominant focus on a sophisticated deliverable without any clear sense of purpose or end goal? Were initial construction costs budgeted, while whole life costs were not considered? Was there no overall long-term vision?

Perhaps the Dome's rebranding as The O2 has at last put the horse before the cart?

1.4   What UK Managers Say

Groups of managers from over 200 of the UK's larger public and private sector organisations[4] have, over the past five years, invariably identified as the top three hindrances to successful investment in change:

- lack of commitment by senior managers;

- vision/objectives that are unclear;

- stakeholders who have not bought in to the change.

These are very similar to the top three independently identified by the National Audit Office (NAO) and the Office of Government Commerce (OGC).Without a clear vision and agreed objectives it is not surprising that senior managers show little commitment – worse still, that commitment may be wrongly focused and of limited duration.

1.5   The End in Mind

For success, organisations need clearly defined end goals and then a properly planned route to reach them, milestones along the way to mark progress, and criteria (for example,

---

3   *Daily Mail*, 4 February 2005.

4   The managers were surveyed by **sigma** during one-day seminars on BRM.

defined targets) against which to report success. Such goals may be defined in terms of a vision, a set of objectives or a group of end benefits and will be elaborated in Chapter 8.

In Stephen Covey's widely acclaimed book *The 7 Habits of Highly Effective People*, which is recognised as having applicability for addressing personal and professional challenges, the second habit is 'Begin with the end in mind'. This is not only required for effective living but also for effective benefit realisation and so I have taken this as a fundamental thread that you will see runs through the whole of the book.

It would be wrong to imply that organisations never know the destination they seek. Mostly they have some kind of vision or end goal, however this goal:

- is often expressed in terms of delivering or implementing capability, rather than fulfilling business objectives or realising benefits;

- is seldom adequately shared and owned;

- is frequently unrealistic with no defined or documented 'route map';

- often requires a leap of faith, and patient waiting for the 'hoped for' miracle to happen.

A good example of a vision was the Americans' vision, in the 1960s, to put a man on the moon and bring him safely back again by the end of the decade. This was simple to understand, valued by the American people, shared by all those involved and was easily measurable. With such a clear and appropriately shared end goal, it was not too difficult to define and document the path to get there. Public communication was primarily about the vision and not about the spacecraft and how it would be built.

One utility company with which we worked, had, in a typical back-to-front approach, determined a solution to a particular problem, costing it at £25m. In order to justify this expenditure, they started to identify benefits, at which point they sought help from **sigma**. Applying the approach described in this book, beginning with the identification of some clear objectives, they fairly soon realised that they could achieve over 80 per cent of the benefits they sought, using a solution costing around £5m.

1.6　Stakeholder Commitment

This back-to-front approach to change and benefits – that is, where the target benefits have been determined to justify the proposed investment, rather than vice versa – frequently fails to generate the required stakeholder commitment as illustrated below:

In Company A the Sales Director is targeted by her MD to increase sales by 5 per cent. In response she commissions a programme of change supported by a new sales system to enable her to achieve this target. She is, and feels accountable, for achieving this 5 per cent increase.

In Company B the IT function comes across some new sales software, whose implementation they believe will lead to a 5 per cent increase in sales. After appropriate analysis to confirm their belief, they persuade the Sales Director to sponsor the necessary investment. Will this Sales Director be accountable for the 5 per cent increase in sales? I certainly doubt it.

1.7   Other Reasons to Start from the End – Become Outcome Driven

A company which focuses on customers, customer service and on beating the competition, experiences fewer internal squabbles, politics and practices such as cross-charging. In a similar way, where investments are driven by desired outcomes and end benefits, the likelihood of competing initiatives and the need to agonise over attributing benefits to a particular enabler/investment are reduced.

I heard recently of a large three-year project, whose primary purpose was to eliminate the need for a particular business unit. The project was making steady progress, successfully achieving intermediate milestones. About six months before benefits were due for delivery, they were in effect stolen by another group, who had implemented some process and organisational changes which eliminated the need for the unit and generated the primary benefits planned for the original project. Whether or not the second initiative was a deliberate internal competitive strike, there was an indisputable waste of investment – of both energy and funding. This waste would probably have been avoided, had the organisation started with some agreed desired outcomes and then selected the best set of options to deliver them.

This lack of focus on outcomes is prevalent throughout UK society and can even affect how we think about people and their jobs. For example, we may think of a person as a bus driver rather than as someone who serves the community by getting people to their destination comfortably and on time. In contrast, successful organisations focus not only on delivering good products but equally on providing quality service and ensuring that their customers achieve the value they are looking for.

1.8   Change Doesn't Have to be Like This

The good news is that change doesn't have to be like this. An increasing number of organisations are using the approach and many of the techniques described in this book to reverse the downward trend in performance, creating genuine success stories. Carts are at last being pulled by horses to well-defined destinations, creating great rewards for organisations and for the myriad of stakeholders involved.

> **BRM, the process which can deliver this success, is not about ticking boxes or validating past decisions; it is an active, dynamic process for maximising future returns.**

Stakeholders

'All of us perform better and more willingly when we know why we're doing what we have been told or asked to do.'

(Zig Ziglar)

'Tell everyone what you want to do and someone will want to help you do it.'

(W. Clement Stone)

2.1 Stakeholders – What or Who are They?

A stakeholder, as the name suggests, is someone who has a stake in something. Their stake may be financial, practical or emotional and in the context of benefit realisation the 'something' is likely to be an investment in change. So my definition for *stakeholder* is 'any individual, group or organisation who will be affected by, or have influence over, the proposed investment in change'. Another definition of stakeholder, which highlights one good reason for taking them seriously, is 'anyone who can throw a spanner in the works'.

If the proposed change includes implementing new enablers, such as systems, technology and new buildings, the users of these enablers will all be stakeholders; however, the full set of stakeholders will generally also include many people who are not users.

Any list of stakeholders should normally include customers. Most processes have customers – internal or external – and so any change is likely to affect them. Customers are generally considered to be individuals and organisations that buy and/or receive products and services. It is important not to forget that some do this very indirectly. For example, most citizens, through the payment of taxes, are buying services such as healthcare, a national road network and protection from terrorists, and are therefore customers.

Sometimes you will need to include customers' customers and customers' relatives. For example: a project to change Air Traffic Control systems and procedures should not only see the airlines as stakeholders but also the airlines' passengers and the passengers' relatives and friends.

Some years ago, before the advent of mobile phones, I was due to fly back one evening from a business trip to Milan. Unfortunately all flights were grounded due to fog and eventually a coach took us to another airport about two hours' drive away. After significant further delays we boarded a flight for the UK. At this point we were asked by the cabin crew if we had any messages which we wanted passed on to family or friends. I was encouraged by this recognition of the wider group of stakeholders and duly gave the member of cabin crew a message for my wife to inform her of the delay. I knew I did not need to let my taxi driver know as he regularly checked flight arrival times and would discover the change of flight and my new arrival time.

I discovered later that this recognition of the wider group of stakeholders was not shared throughout the airline. My wife never received my message. My taxi driver checked his usual information sources, made countless phone calls, which included being forwarded to a call centre in the USA who could not help him, and made two trips to Heathrow. Eventually he discovered what had happened, used his initiative to call and inform my wife, and was waiting to meet me at 2 am when I arrived back.

This wider group of second-level stakeholders, which also exist in other industries, should be taken more seriously. Within the NHS, a patient's relatives and friends, who are often more concerned about the patient's health and well-being than the patient themselves, are important stakeholders.

2.2   The Importance of Considering Stakeholders

In Chapter 1 I shared the top three hindrances to success, from my survey of managers from large UK organisations. These were:

- lack of commitment by senior managers;

- vision/objectives that are unclear;

- stakeholders who have not bought in to the change.

The second of these was discussed in Chapter 1 and is more fully addressed in Chapter 8, and the other two both relate to stakeholders.

Stakeholders are extremely valuable for their experience and their creativity yet their worth is often undervalued and sometimes not recognised at all. Have you ever heard a project manager say, when asked how their project is progressing, that everything would be fine if it were not for people? I have heard this and similar statements many times.

People are often seen as the problem yet people can be a major part of the solution. In most change initiatives, benefits arise as people behave differently:

- customers buy more;

- suppliers delivery sooner;

- staff take on new responsibilities;

- people communicate more effectively;

- managers make better decisions.

The challenge is to equip and motivate people to behave differently. This generally requires engaging and involving them so that their ideas are heard and considered, and they buy in to the change.

Change is rarely successful without the involvement and commitment of stakeholders – from senior managers to users. Without this commitment a project may deliver a capability – a new system, some technology, a new office block – but is unlikely to deliver anything of significant worth to the business – that is, business benefits.

Stakeholders' involvement should cover:

- creating the vision;

- agreeing the objectives;

- identifying the benefits;

- determining the dependencies – enablers and changes;

- selecting from among the solution options;

- developing the Business Case;

- acceptance testing the new capabilities;

- implementing the changes;

- determining the measures;

- tracking the benefits.

2.3   Identifying and Classifying Stakeholders

In order to engage and involve stakeholders you first need to identify them. So an early part of any change process is the identification of potential stakeholders. I say potential because at an early stage in any change life-cycle, while the vision is still being established and the scope defined, the stakeholder population may be a little fluid. The process may therefore need to be iterative.

When identifying stakeholders it may be helpful to first determine the most relevant dimensions – for example, organisational unit, process, function, job role, geographic area.

Don't forget those stakeholders who are external to the organisation, including partners, suppliers, customers, customers' customers, consumers and those who would wish they were not stakeholders, such as victims of crimes.

I remember one programme where the programme team had identified about 160 stakeholders. With such a large number, the benefits process can become very complex and bureaucratic. For manageability I would recommend a granularity which results in between 6 and 15 primary stakeholder groups. This may involve grouping together those stakeholders who are likely to be affected in a similar way from a benefits or a change perspective – for example, in certain situations: Treasury, NAO and OGC may be grouped as External Governance. Sometimes it may be helpful to subdivide a stakeholder – for example, customers might be divided into existing customers and new customers.

A possible representation and grouping of stakeholders is illustrated in the mind-map in Figure 2.1.

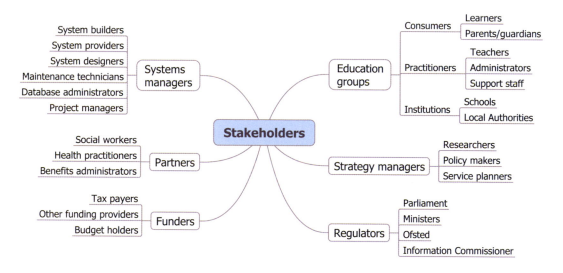

Figure 2.1   Mind-map representation of stakeholders and their grouping hierarchy

2.4   Stakeholder Commitment

Achieving successful change is much easier if all stakeholders are committed and the earlier this commitment is accomplished, the smoother the path to a successful outcome.

Generally this commitment is closely related to the degree of understanding as to why the change is happening. Change that is just imposed on people, with no explanation of the reason why, generates the greatest resistance. Success is much more likely when stakeholders are engaged in formulating the vision. or at least influencing the shape of the change and where they can see clear value, either for themselves or for the whole organisation, or for the organisation's customers.

Some time ago I was working in a large pharmaceutical company helping to apply BRM to a large programme. One day I was introduced to Susan, a project manager from a different area, who was seriously struggling and seeking help. Although Susan thought her problem had nothing to do with benefit realisation management, she wondered whether I might be able to help. She explained that her project involved implementing a new computer system which mainly affected three internal stakeholder groups – I will refer to these groups as A, B and C. Group A, the smallest of the three groups was very enthusiastic about the project, Group B was reluctant and Group C was strongly opposed. Susan felt that Groups B and C were not very computer literate and that this was why they were resistant to the new system.

I said I would see what I could do and offered to talk to key representatives from the different groups. I quickly appreciated that they were all very busy people, and that Group A were primarily technology enthusiasts who revelled in new kit, especially if it had fancy bells and whistles. When I spoke to Groups B and C, I was surprised to discover that they were not intrinsically opposed to the project; they just wanted to understand the business reasons for doing it and what the benefits would be, and no one had communicated this information. There had been no attempts to engage stakeholders or involve them in setting objectives or identifying benefits. As soon as they understood the value of the project to the business, and appreciated the potential improvements to their own activities, they became very committed. Ironically, as the project progressed, Susan found that the majority of her problems lay with Group A, who were more interested in technology features than business benefits.

Unfortunately political considerations can introduce bias in the assessment of stakeholder needs and wishes, especially in the public sector, when stakeholders are voters.

2.5   Stakeholder Engagement

To ensure that stakeholders become committed, it is important to engage them effectively, throughout the complete change life-cycle. This is best achieved through a carefully planned combination of two-way communication and involvement. However, engagement is often difficult and requires recognition of the different backgrounds and cultures of the stakeholders.

In my experience most stakeholders welcome the opportunity to help formulate the shape and direction of the change, contributing from their experience and exercising creativity. However, this requires investment in time and in consequence some stakeholders occasionally prefer to be presented with a fait accompli or at least to start with a straw man rather than a clean sheet.

A very effective way to engage stakeholders is through well-structured and facilitated workshops. For these to achieve their full potential it is important to secure the participation of appropriate representatives from the key stakeholder groups. In the early stages of a change life-cycle, this usually means senior managers – people who shape direction and strategy and who can commit resources and are able to influence other programmes.

Unfortunately many senior managers are reluctant to make the time commitment, perhaps because they do not fully appreciate the importance of BRM or the value of the workshop process. I wonder whether these managers are either not really serious about achieving benefits, or just naïve in their understanding of what is required.

A good benefit realisation workshop process normally encourages stakeholder engagement by:

- producing consensus information on benefits and/or changes;

- generating enthusiasm for the change initiative;

- generating enthusiasm for BRM;

- moving the focus from technology to change and benefits;

- identifying necessary business changes not envisaged;

- making people feel they are contributing and being listened to;

- helping multiple stakeholders to understand how their needs and difficulties overlap, and how they can work together to minimise difficulty and gain maximum advantage;

- generating commitment to some immediate changes.

Customers are often recognised as key stakeholders, yet unfortunately they are rarely involved in the workshop process, especially if they are external customers.

Workshops, valuable as they are, form only part of the engagement process – a single benefits workshop early in the life-cycle will never be sufficient. Ensuring that stakeholders remain positive requires ongoing, dynamic engagement and communication, since the environment may be frequently changing and relationships decay without good communication.

Communication, which should always be two-way, is a line management responsibility, and should start at the most senior appropriate level and then cascade down through the line.

Bringing together stakeholders from different environments can be very rewarding, as they begin to appreciate one another's viewpoints and likely future expectations. I remember running one particularly enjoyable workshop which included representatives from the police, criminal justice, fire service, primary health care and the local authority. Apart from the immediate value they gained from getting to know and understand one another, it also led to beneficial ongoing working relationships. Such workshops can make a very effective contribution to joined-up working, which is often vital for achievement of global objectives and the realisation of benefits for stakeholders such as customers and the public.

2.6   The Workshop Process

For workshops to be successful they need a number of essential ingredients:

- clear objectives;

- the right participants;

- some pre-workshop scene-setting for participants;

- the right starting point;

- some explanation of BRM;

- a conducive environment, preferably away from the office;

- sufficient time;

- a structure designed to match purpose and objectives;

- strong but flexible facilitation;

- appropriate processing and timely feedback of outputs.

The objectives for the workshop are likely to be some combination of the following:

- to understand the aspirations and anxieties of the stakeholders;

- to gather necessary information to define the purpose of the envisaged change and the pathway to success;

- to gain buy-in to the change initiative, to the BRM process and to the benefits being identified.

When identifying the most suitable workshop participants, there are several important considerations, including:

- Are several workshops likely to be required in order to achieve the required coverage and ensure quality outputs?

- Within the organisation's culture, are workshops recognised as valuable?

- Will participants contribute freely if working with colleagues who are several levels more or less senior?

- How knowledgeable are the participants about the current organisation and any plans for its future?

- How knowledgeable are the participants about the area of focus of the workshop?

In the early stages of a project for the UK arm of an American oil company, initiated to improve procurement, four initial objectives were identified and the main stakeholders determined. The matrix in Figure 2.2 was then constructed, where the ticked cells indicated that the particular stakeholder had relevant knowledge, which would be useful when considering the corresponding objective.

Stakeholder Group Initial objectives	Procurement specialists	Production	Suppliers	Logistics	ICT	Accounts
To increase procurement speed and quality	✓	✓	✓	✓		
To reduce cost of goods and services purchased	✓	✓				
To reduce the cost of the procurement process	✓		✓		✓	✓
To leverage corporate procurement expertises	✓					

Figure 2.2   Information gathering – sources and areas of focus

Several workshops were required, and so an early question was whether they should be structured around stakeholders or around objectives. Each has different merits and risks: structuring around stakeholders provides for more effective information gathering, whilst structuring around objectives achieves greater shared understanding and buy-in. Often it is useful to organise the initial information-gathering workshops around stakeholders, then to structure any feedback sessions around objectives, which is what we did in this instance.

This approach turned out to have an added advantage. When we ran the workshop for Production, whose function was the production of gas from the southern North Sea, it soon became clear that an important objective had been missed from the earlier stage. For Production it was far more important to improve procurement in order to have rapid access to reliable spare parts, to minimise any possible rig downtime. Had we run cross-functional workshops focused on one of the four initially identified objectives, this might not have surfaced.

The diagram can also help to sequence workshop agendas. In the above case, expertise to consider the fourth objective was perceived to be only available from the procurement specialists. So it was important that the workshop for this group considered this objective early in the day, while the group was still fresh, rather than last, when it might have been squeezed off the agenda if other activities had overrun.

2.7   Influencing Stakeholders Beyond the Control of the Change

In many large change initiatives, stakeholders, whose behaviour may need to change, are often outside the control of the change team, especially when an initiative is set up and sponsored by a central corporate or government function. In such cases, benefits, and the dependent changes in processes and practices, usually lie outside this central organisation. They may span sites throughout the organisation and sometimes beyond. Private sector organisations may include branches throughout the UK or sites across the world. In the public sector this could include other departments or agencies which may be spread throughout the UK. Usually problems arise less from geographic spread than from the fact that different management structures and sometimes cultures are involved. Such problems may be eased by creating a programme, which contains the change, but has much wider scope. This programme could relate to the overall vision and include all the necessary business changes, but would need the involvement of representative business managers from across the organisation.

Achieving such company-wide scope can be more challenging in the public sector than the private requiring, as it does, well-planned concerted influence and involvement, often between diverse major organisations.

In assessing a situation it can be helpful to map stakeholders on to an Influence-Attitude Grid, like the one illustrated in Figure 2.3.

External customers, and some internal customers, lie beyond the control of the change activity. 'Customers' therefore, form a special group of stakeholders who are given further consideration in Section 2.9.

2.8   Communications Strategy and Stakeholder Engagement

More and more organisations are recognising stakeholders as key to successful change, and are acknowledging the importance of quality two-way communication and stakeholder

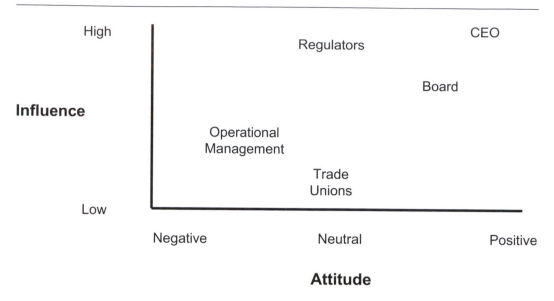

Figure 2.3   Influence-attitude grid

involvement throughout any change life-cycle. Consequently many approaches to managing change now include, as specific activities:

- the creation of a *Communications Strategy* early in the life-cycle; and

- active stakeholder engagement throughout the life-cycle, including the production of a *Stakeholder Engagement Strategy* and *Plan*.

This strategy and plan is often under the heading of stakeholder 'management' rather than 'engagement'; however most stakeholders, particularly customers, cannot be managed, at least in the traditional sense, so engagement is a more appropriate term.

For details of this strategy and plan see Chapter 20.

2.9   Special Stakeholders – Customers

The 'customers' group of stakeholders may include customers who pay indirectly for products or services – for example, customer's customers, consumers, NHS patients, criminal offenders, victims, citizens, taxpayers and the public at large. Such stakeholders are special for a variety of reasons, including:

- for many change initiatives they are the primary stakeholders;

- they can rarely be managed in the traditional sense of management;

- they are seldom involved in shaping or managing the change or in participating in benefits workshops;

- their interests are often dependent on a collaborative contribution from several departments or organisations;

- their requirements are frequently and frustratingly passed between some of the other stakeholders.

Examples of customers requiring a collaborative response, instead of being painfully passed between other stakeholders are:

- a customer with a faulty product, passed backwards and forwards between supplier and manufacturer;

- a customer seeking to find out how his order is progressing, passed between sales, order processing, stock control and logistics;

- a patient passed from the Ambulance Service to Accident and Emergency;

- a prisoner released into the community without any monitoring or support.

Such pain is usually a consequence of the other stakeholders not communicating or not being 'joined up'. The recent drive towards more joined-up government should improve matters in the public sector. In a benefit realisation context, once the vision recognises the customer as a primary stakeholder, the scope of the change should include all stakeholders who need joining up. This concept is more fully discussed in relation to specific situations in later chapters.

Effectively engaging stakeholders, including those who can throw a spanner in the works, can be stimulating and energising and will make vision achievement more likely.

3

Benefit Realisation

'The only limit to our realisation of tomorrow will be our doubts of today.'
(Franklin Roosevelt)

'There are some people who live in a dream world, and there are some who face reality; and then there are those who turn one into the other.'
(Douglas Everett)

3.1   Different Meanings of Realisation

The *New Oxford Dictionary* gives several meanings for the word realise, which, in the order they are listed, are:

- be fully aware, conceive as real;

- understand clearly;

- make realistic;

- convert into actuality, achieve;

- convert into money.

Each of these definitions is applicable to benefits, and the sequence matches the logical stages through a typical change life-cycle. The benefit is first conceived as real, though at this stage only aspirational and probably lacking detail; next understood clearly – the detail is probed; next made realistic through the mapping of its dependencies – earlier benefits and required changes; next achieved as the changes are implemented; finally converted into money in certain situations. I recommend caution before converting benefits to money (see Section 9.6 and Chapter 27).

3.2   Realisation – Not Forcible Extraction

A few years ago I met a manager who claimed that his organisation did not have a problem with benefit realisation. Whatever benefits were claimed for a project, he said, were immediately removed from the establishment or budget of the relevant organisational unit, for the following financial year.

I believe this approach revealed a naïve lack of understanding of benefit realisation. Firstly, it assumed 'benefit' to be synonymous with 'headcount' or 'cost reduction' and that only benefits to be realised within the next financial year are worth considering. Secondly, he seemed to assume that claiming a benefit ensured its achievement.

Changes must be properly designed and managed so that the benefits are genuinely generated. I refer to benefits not generated, but nevertheless removed from budgets or headcount numbers, as 'forcibly extracted'. Forcible extraction is not realisation. In fact it may lead to situations worse than receiving no benefits. For instance, if headcount is forcibly reduced, without genuine benefit realisation, the remaining staff will find themselves working under increased pressure, often resulting in reduced customer services and/or increased staff sickness and attrition.

3.3   Realisation – A Team Effort

Although primary accountability for the realisation of a benefit may reside with a single individual and the ultimate accountability with the sponsor or Senior Responsible Owner (SRO)[1] – see Chapter 6, achieving benefits and agreed targets needs team effort – as when Roger Bannister, having run the first mile in under four minutes, said he could not have done this without those who ran with him, striving to achieve the same target.

The longer the course the more important others become. In running a marathon, participants are responsible for their own performances, yet the sheer volume of runners alongside, pursuing the same goal, provides a sense of support and encouragement, and team spirit helping runners to penetrate their individual psychological barriers.

3.4   Benefits – What are They?

Before proceeding further, we must examine what we mean by a benefit. I frequently come across narrow views of a benefit, as something that can be directly related to a cost reduction or increase in revenue. Such narrow views generally stem from the idea that the primary purpose of a benefit is to justify some proposed expenditure.

A broader view results from recognising that the primary reason for considering benefits is to realise them, enabling stakeholders to experience beneficial outcomes from planned change. The *New Oxford Dictionary* defines a *benefit* as 'an advantage on behalf of ...' highlighting its relative nature. Whether a particular outcome is a benefit depends on the outlook of the person considering it.

---

1   Senior Responsible Owner (SRO) is the term used by OGC to describe the sponsor.

My preferred definition of a *benefit*, which has stood the test of 23 years' consultancy work, is: 'an outcome of change which is perceived as positive by a stakeholder'. This makes explicit the relative nature of a benefit and highlights an important distinction between the outcome and the change. **Disbenefits** are outcomes seen as negative. A particular outcome may be a benefit to one stakeholder and a disbenefit to another.

This definition is short and memorable but contains all the key elements. Firstly, it distinguishes the benefit itself from the change which gives rise to it. This distinction is important as it helps us to understand that benefits (for example, improved image, increased customer satisfaction, more sales, faster regulatory approval of new pharmaceutical products), cannot directly be made to happen. Whereas the changes, which should logically lead to the realisation of the benefits, can be managed (made to happen), while the benefits can be tracked (measured and reported). Success depends on identifying and managing the right set of changes which logically should generate the desired set of outcomes.

Changes consume resources, cost money and need managing. Benefits are the outcomes, which cannot be directly made to happen and have no direct cost. However, you would normally want to measure them, checking that they have been achieved.

Secondly, this definition acknowledges the importance of the stakeholder perspective for the word 'perceived' in the definition, far from being vague, simply recognises that value or worth is in the eye of the beholder. The same outcome may be perceived differently by different stakeholders. A colleague tells of the time he first started to receive itemised telephone bills – he perceived these as valuable, his teenage daughter at the time had a totally opposite perception.

3.5   Route Map to Realisation – The Benefits Map

The realisation of a benefit is frequently dependent on the earlier realisation of other benefits. For example, the benefit 'less frustration for customers' may be dependent in part on the benefit 'fewer errors', so until the benefit 'fewer errors' has been achieved, the benefit 'less frustration for customers' can never fully be achieved. Similarly, 'improved image' is dependent on 'improved customer service' which is dependent on 'less frustration for customers'. Dependencies like these are best represented visually so that the 'cause and effect' relationships are easily seen, as in Figure 3.1.

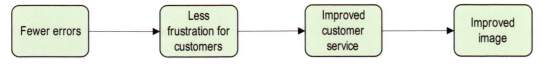

Figure 3.1   A simple benefit linkage

Usually the route to an ultimate benefit involves many of these 'cause and effect' linkages, related together in a single route map, known as a **sigma Benefits Map**. Figure 3.2 shows the fuller Benefits Map, which includes the above linkage.

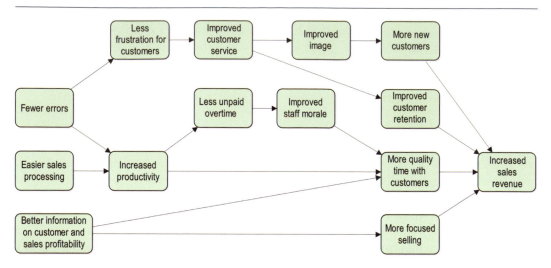

Figure 3.2   Benefits Map to achieve 'increased sales revenue'

A fuller discussion of this map is given in Chapter 15 under Benefit Tracking. Route maps are a critical part of benefit realisation and the **sigma** approach uses three types of map:

- Strategy Maps of linked objectives;

- Benefits Maps as illustrated in Figure 3.2;

- **Benefit Dependency Maps (BDMs)** which are Benefits Maps with the dependent enablers and changes added.

The status of Benefits Maps will progressively alter through the change life-cycle. Changing from a wish list, through a set of feasible options, a prioritised set of options, a plan (as some paths are chosen and others rejected), a vehicle for communicating expectations, eventually becoming a report of actual progress towards achievement of the vision.

sigma's Maps are extremely useful for:

- providing the basis for identifying the dependent changes;

- assessing the impact of unexpected changes – internal and external;

- communicating expectations;

- tracking benefits:

- avoiding double counting of benefits;

- attributing benefits to their source;

- maximising benefit realisation.

Benefits Maps are more fully considered in Section 9.5, and are used for illustration in several other places.

3.6   Basis for Benefit Realisation – People Doing Things Differently

In implementing and managing change, benefits are realised as people do things differently, as they change:

- their attitudes;

- the way they work;

- the way they communicate; and

- the way they make decisions.

So benefits are primarily a business rather than a programme responsibility.

3.7   Responsibility for Benefit Realisation – Benefit Owners

The ultimate accountability for benefit realisation lies with the sponsor of the change, who may delegate responsibility to the Programme Director/Manager. This is explicit in OGC's *Managing Successful Programmes* (MSP), which states that 'the Senior Responsible Owner (SRO)** is ultimately accountable for the overall realisation of benefits from the programme';[2] also according to MSP, the SRO will usually be a member of the sponsoring group,[3] and normally the chair of the Programme Board.

Although overall accountability for benefit realisation, related to a single change initiative, may rest with a single individual, such as the sponsor of the change, responsibility for benefits is likely to be spread across a number of stakeholders groups, to specific individuals who are generally called **Benefit Owners**; many of them may be responsible for a single benefit. Often the majority of benefits will be realised in the operational units of an organisation, where much of the change should occur. The managers of these business units will be Benefit Owners.

Benefit Owners will not necessarily experience and savour the benefits – this is for the '**beneficiaries**'. When an owner is also a beneficiary, there is added motivation to ensure that the benefit is realised. So, for instance, it is helpful if the sponsor, or SRO, is a senior representative of the stakeholder group who will receive the most benefits.

Benefit Owners are frequently responsible for benefits, dependent on changes which are outside their direct control. So the Benefit Owner must understand these dependencies,

---

2   MSP 2007 Section 4.6.

3   MSP 2007 Section 4.5.

be aware of all the details relating to each benefit for which they are responsible. They should know who to chase and influence. This information, for a single benefit, is normally contained in a single page document, the Benefit Profile.

3.8 Benefit Profiles

A *Benefit Profile* is 'the template which contains the comprehensive description of a single benefit including all its attributes and dependencies' – a repository of all relevant information which would aid realisation. It would normally include:

- identifier information – number, title and perhaps fuller description;

- its impact and contribution to business/programme vision, objectives and goals;

- categorisation(s) to check for balance and alignment;

- dependencies both internal and external to the particular change initiative;

- stakeholder information, including beneficiaries and owners;

- measures and measure attributes, including baseline, target, realisation timescales, measurement frequency and reporting mechanism;

- assumptions and risks related to the realisation of the benefit.

A fuller description and an example are given in Sections 9.9 and 18.2.

A complete set of Benefit Profiles covering all the benefits for a programme could be regarded as the database of benefit realisation information. From this core repository key benefit-related documents can be generated including:

- the Benefit Realisation Plan (BRP);

- the framework for benefit tracking reports;

- much of the information required for a Business Case (project cost and resource information come from elsewhere).

3.9 Benefit Realisation Plans (BRP)

The *BRP* is 'the document which shows how and when all the benefits, for a particular change initiative, are expected to be realised'. It will draw on information contained in Benefit Profiles, (the full set of profiles may appear as an appendix). It should include a full set of Benefits Maps and a summary trajectory showing when the benefits are expected to be realised. Benefit trajectories combined with cost trajectories form a key part of the justification section of a Business Case (see Section 22.7).

The BRP should also include details of all dependencies – these are usually best presented in the form a BDM – see Section 11.2. It should also describe the mechanism to be employed for tracking and reporting benefit realisation.

Finally, the BRP should define accountabilities and responsibilities relating to benefit realisation, naming specific individuals, possibly including signatures confirming acceptance of responsibility for specific benefits.

A fuller description of this plan is given in Chapter 19.

3.10   Rewarding Benefit Realisation

Many organisations reward those who deliver enablers on time and to budget – or conversely penalise them if they are late, over budget or not up to specification. Far fewer reward achievement of benefits.

I believe more should be done to reward staff, and sometimes suppliers, for the realisation of benefits, though it can be more difficult than rewarding for the delivery of enablers – such as computer systems or new buildings. The three main difficulties with this suggestion are:

- It is often less easy to be sure that the outcome has been achieved or is attributable to the change undertaken.

- Achievement of benefits is usually dependent on several parties working together. So is it reasonable to link payments to suppliers, to the realisation of benefits, when realisation is not only dependent on the enabler from the supplier, but also on changes in attitudes and working practices by some of the staff?

- Linking rewards or penalties to inappropriate targets can encourage behaviours which are completely contrary to the spirit of the vision, as was seen in Primary Care in 2006 when many GP practices introduced systems allowing patients to book appointments only up to 48 hours before the required appointment. This theoretically showed that no patients had to wait more than 48 hours to see their GP – it did not record the many patients who were then unable to see their GP at all.

Although these difficulties are real they are not insurmountable and techniques for overcoming them are dealt with in later chapters.

Quality Benefits Maps, rigorously built and owned by stakeholders, can remove realisation limits, eradicate doubts and turn dreams into realities.

4

Overview of Benefit Realisation Management (BRM)

'Benefit realisation management is common sense but not common practice.'
(Gerald Bradley)

'We need the courage to let go of the old world, to relinquish most of what we have cherished, to abandon our interpretations about what does and doesn't work.'

(Margaret Wheatley)

4.1   Definitions and Scope

sigma defines *Benefit Realisation Management* (BRM) as 'the process of organising and managing, so that potential benefits, arising from investment in change, are actually achieved'.

In 1986 **sigma** originally named the process *Benefit Management*, but in 2003 switched to what was felt to be the more meaningful title of *Benefit Realisation Management*. MSP use both titles interchangeably, while others split the process into two parts – *Benefit Management* and *Benefit Realisation*, though it is difficult to see how this distinction works. Other terms used include *Active Benefit Realisation* (ABR).[1]

The OGC definition[2] highlights that BRM is a continuous process running through the complete life-cycle. It should be the core process of any change initiative, the backbone of any programme, involving far more than a few benefit events early in the process.

MSP 2007 highlights the centrality of BRM (see Figure 4.1), especially that it should be the driver for all change and programme activities including:

- providing the mechanism for engaging stakeholders;

---

1   ABR is the term used by Dan Remenyi in *Achieving Maximum Value from Information Systems*.

2   'A continuous management process running throughout the programme' (MSP 2003).

- defining requirements and acceptance criteria;

- helping establish and maintain the Blueprint;

- determining project and programme boundaries;

- developing programme and project plans;

- identifying risks;

- informing the Business Case;

- ongoing monitoring and reviews.

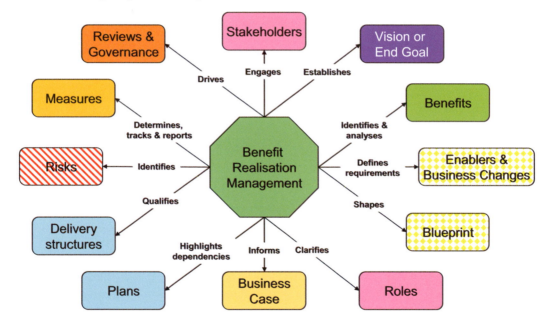

Figure 4.1   BRM – key driver for change

BRM recognises the starting position (current status, drivers for change, stakeholders and cultural factors); next through active engagement with the business, articulates and establishes the end point (vision supported by objectives and benefits). Then, and only then, BRM determines the changes required to achieve this goal – enablers and business changes (see Figure 4.2).

The BRM process can be applied to individual projects and programmes, portfolios of projects and programmes, or to business strategy. When we first started applying BRM, in the late 1980s, it was normally to specific projects, usually at a fairly late stage in their life-cycles, often subsequent to the implementation of some technology or a new system. While this remains a worthwhile activity, our involvement has gradually moved to

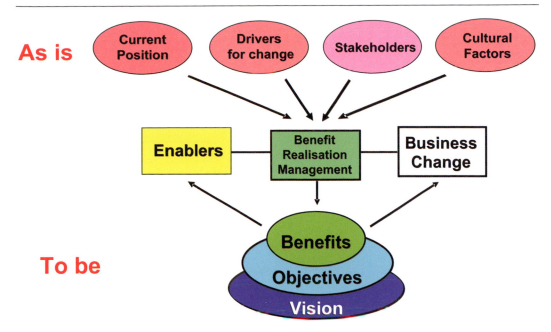

Figure 4.2   Focus on the real goal – the end point

earlier more strategic levels with strong focus on programmes, but embracing the whole spectrum from projects to business strategy.

Application of BRM should prove particularly fruitful in the area of 'mergers and acquisitions', where recent analysis[3] has revealed that:

- 83 per cent of mergers fail to achieve announced expectations;

- nearly a half of all acquisitions are divested within five years.

The only valid reason for investing in change is to generate benefits. Benefits may be of value to the organisation making the investment, its staff, its customers, or even other parties; but without generation of benefits for at least one group of stakeholders, there is no justification for investing in change.

So benefits are the ultimate deliverable and BRM should be the central theme or core of any change initiative. It should lay the foundations for Project or Programme Management rather than being, as so often, the afterthought.

Sometimes people ask whether BRM is yet another new management fad. Their concern arises from the fact that their organisation is already overwhelmed with different approaches, such as European Foundation for Quality Management (EFQM), Balanced Business Scorecard (BBS), Prince 2, Best Value, Value Management, Lean Thinking and Programme Management. Although BRM is relatively new, elements are found in many

---

3   www.mapartners.net (August 2005).

other management approaches, and it is much more than a mere fad. It is probably the approach for which all the others have been waiting, bringing meaning and purpose to activities such as change management, requirements analysis, project management (for example, Prince 2) and programme management (for example, MSP). And as one manager rather succinctly put it, BRM is the glue that binds together all the other management techniques (see Figure 4.3).

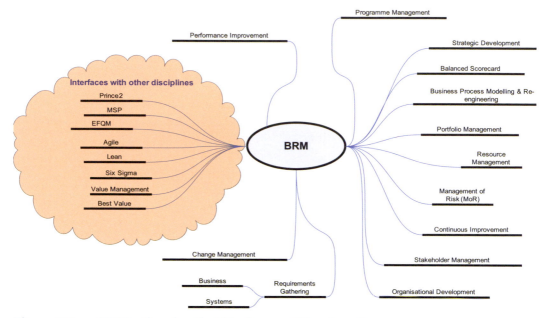

Figure 4.3   BRM – the glue that binds everything together

BRM is also central to other recognised disciplines connected with change, as illustrated in Figure 4.4.

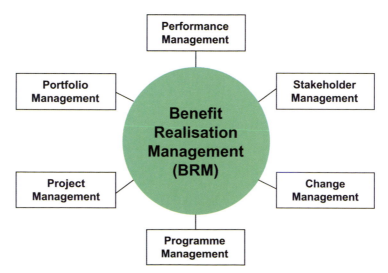

Figure 4.4   The relationship between BRM and other management disciplines

Once, at the end of an executive briefing on BRM for directors of a UK high street bank, the MD, having asked his colleagues for their reactions, said in his summing up –'this isn't just about projects, it's about everything that we do'. How right he was.

4.2   Why BRM is of Increasing Importance

There are many reasons why BRM is of increasing importance today. In the last few years there has been a noticeable increase in the attention given to benefit realisation by management at all levels. In particular the UK Government now puts a strong emphasis on benefits, which is being channelled directly to government departments, but also indirectly through the Treasury, the NAO and the OGC. In the private sector, chief executives, managing directors and other senior managers are mandating the application of BRM to programmes and projects, demanding increased quality and rigour in business cases – and more meaningful benefit tracking and reporting.

This top level drive has probably arisen as a consequence of two factors:

- In an increasingly competitive global economy, organisations cannot afford to continue wasting costly investment. Organisations must expect benefits from change and ensure that these expectations are fulfilled.

- Business environments, both private and public, are increasingly complex and changing rapidly, making benefit realisation more difficult. This is evident from a historical perspective. The diagram below (Figure 4.5) traces the development of computing in business over five decades.

	Driven by	Used by	Opportunity	Benefits
1960s	IT	IT	Automation of clerical processes	Reduced Costs
1970s	IT	Business	Transaction processing	
1980s	Business	Business & 3rd Parties	Management Information, Systems Integration	
1990s	Business & 3rd Parties	Business & 3rd Parties	Executive Info.Systems, Process Re-engineering	Added Value
2000s	Senior Management	Senior Management	Knowledge Management Teamworking, eBusiness	

Figure 4.5   How the decades of computing have impacted benefit realisation

Between 1960 and 1980, changes were largely initiated by IT functions, not by business units. This is still true in some organisations today. In the 1960s, benefits were predominantly 'reduced costs' from automating clerical processes, such as payroll and accounting, whereas today the majority of benefits are aspects of 'added value'.

In many cases, the IT project team was made responsible for identifying the benefits, making the Business Case, and (if the organisation bothered to check whether they had been achieved) for tracking and reporting the benefits. I believe this responsibility was wrongly placed, though in the 1960s it was usually effective for the following reasons:

- the nature of the benefits – reduced costs from automating clerical processes – could be analytically determined and IT people are good at analysis;

- since the majority of benefits were financial, the justification for inclusion in the Business Case was easy to construct;

- the majority of benefits would have been realised soon after implementation, while the project team was still around to verify their realisation.

This is inadequate for many of the changes undertaken today, for example the move to eBusiness and eCommerce. In these situations:

- benefits will not be fully identified without adequate engagement of the business community;

- business cases will be more complex with justifications often dependent on non-financial benefits;

- the majority of benefits will be realised after the project team has moved on.

In the 1960s and 1970s, projects were frequently sponsored and funded by a single business department, within which the change occurred and where the benefits would be realised. In contrast, today's change initiatives, especially the larger ones, involve a wide range of stakeholders, crossing functional and sometimes organisational boundaries.

A further complicating factor is the speed of change. In the 1960s, the internal and external environments would have been similar at the beginning and at the end of a two-year project, the goalposts remaining unmoved. Today these factors will have changed even during the life of a six-month project.

4.3   Common Issues Addressed by BRM

Many problem situations may be solved, or at least alleviated, by BRM. Some may appear to have little to do with benefits, and more to do with change or project management. But since the only meaningful reason for change and for projects is the realisation of benefits, BRM has a much wider impact than many people appreciate.

The table in Figure 4.6 lists many of the problem situations addressed by BRM with a brief indication of how it helps, and the section/chapter(s) in which the issues are addressed:

	Situation	How BRM helps	Section
1	Management are not committed to benefit realisation	BRM is helping to change management attitudes, but it may take time	26
2	It is difficult to get the staff time for BRM activities	BRM can show why this time investment is vital if historic bad performance is to be changed	4.5
3	The vision or end-goal is difficult to define	BRM process includes structures techniques for moving from drivers to vision & objectives	8.6
4	Stakeholders do not own the vision	Use of the workshop process and vision/objective setting techniques	2.6, 8.7
5	Stakeholders are not engaged effectively	The BRM Methodology and the related workshop process facilitates stakeholder engagement	2.5, 2.6
6	Portfolio of programmes not aligned to organisation's mission	BRM is strong on alignment but also prefers to start with the organisation's Mission or Strategy	8, 24
7	The dominant focus is on technology - enablers	BRM is excellent at shifitng the focus from technology to business change and benefits	1.3-1.7
8	The life-cycle is long (e.g. greater than 4 years)	BRM's use of maps with intermediate milestones enables progress to be steadily monitored	9.5, 15
9	There are dependencies between projects	Mapping techniques can show dependencies and indicate programme boundaries	8.7
10	There are dependencies between programmes	Benefit Profiles and Maps can register dependencies and create prompts to monitor dependent activity	13
11	Benefits are dependent on several projects	BRM will treat these as programme benefits and manage accordingly	2
12	Business Cases are difficult to write	BRM produces a Benefit Realisation Plan which is often one of the most difficult elements of a case	19
13	There is complexity or large-scale change	BRM ensures that change is identified and managed with the same importance as enablers	5.1, 11, 12.3
14	Resources are scarce	BRM helps to focus available resources on areas of greatest need or impact	14.6
15	Business change is not driven by benefits	BRM's Maps and Investment Assessment Matrices use benefits to drive change	11, 13
16	There is resistance to change	Through Benefit Distribution analysis BRM can help to anticipate and overcome resistance	9.4a, 14.6
17	Communication is poor or difficult	BRM's use of pictures, maps, matrices, charts and use of colour significantly aids communication	13
18	There is lack of trust	BRM's maps make implicit assumptions explicit and so increases transparency and trust	9.6
19	There are many options for rolling-out the solution	Benefit considerations should drive implementation and so maximise the overall investment return	14.5
20	Measuring benefits is difficult	This can be for a variety of reasons but often because BRM has not been applied from the start	4.8
21	Benefits are intangible	The Sigma Value Types framework shows that most benefit are in fact tangible	9.4d
22	It is difficult to attribute the benefits to the change	Monitoring benefit achievement through a Benefits Map increases confidence in respect of attribution	15.2
23	The same benefit is claimed by more than 1 project	Use Benefits Maps to avoid double counting and Measures Dictionary to apportion between projects	9.1
24	Benefits are not adequately tracked or reported	Benefit measurement is an intrinsic part of BRM but BRM first lays the necessary foundations	15
25	Benefits are not being realised	The whole BRM process works towards benefit realisation and can sometimes be applied retrospectively	23

Figure 4.6   How BRM helps in 25 problem situations

4.4   How Different Stakeholders can Benefit from BRM

The many stakeholders are likely to be affected in different ways by BRM. The table in Figure 4.7 shows how the benefits and disbenefits of BRM relate to some of these stakeholders.

Key Benefits and Disbenefits by Stakeholder	Board	Sponsor (e.g. SRO) & Programme Board	Programme Director/Manager	Business Change Manager	Programme Team	Enabler Project Teams	Business Manager	Business User
Benefit								
More optimum programme portfolio	X	X					X	
Earlier recognition of ineffective programmes	X	X						
Improved stakeholder engagement			X	X	X		X	X
Clearer sense of direction			X	X	X		X	X
More effective programme management			X	X	X			
Better use of resources		X	X		X			
Improved management of risk		X	X		X			
Reduced Enabler costs		X	X	X		X		
More financial benefits realised	X	X	X	X				
More non-financial benefits realised		X	X	X			X	X
Greater visibility of realised benefits		X	X	X				
Improved Programme image			X	X	X			
Disbenefit								
Extra effort by the business							X	X
Slower start to the programme					X	X	X	X
Enabler project targets threatened						X		

Benefit	(green)
Disbenefit	(red)

Figure 4.7   Benefits and disbenefits of BRM by stakeholder

This table, generally referred to as a **Benefit Distribution Matrix**, is a common deliverable from the early stages of the BRM Process.

4.5   The Return on Investment from BRM

The Return on Investment (ROI) generated by BRM stems from the following:

- elimination, or reduction in the number, of wasted investments;

- earlier realisation of benefits;

- increased realisation of benefits;

- sustained realisation of benefits.

The ROI has two main components – an improved return from each investment (doing things right), and a contribution from an improved investment portfolio (doing the right things).

IMPROVED RETURN FROM EACH INVESTMENT

Without a structured approach, such as BRM, most organisations probably achieve between 10 per cent and 25 per cent of potential benefits from any significant change initiative.[4] With BRM these results can usually be trebled. Since the cost of BRM, for a particular investment, is typically between 4 per cent and 6 per cent of total investment costs,[5] the ROI from BRM is likely to exceed 1000 per cent, *provided* it is applied from the earliest possible stage of the investment life-cycle. For example: an investment, of say £1000, where the benefits are expected to equal the costs (hopefully worse case scenario), is likely to realise benefits of less than £250 without BRM, and greater than £750 with BRM. If the cost of BRM is 5 per cent then the ROI is 1000 per cent; if it is only 4 per cent then the ROI from BRM is 1250 per cent.

If BRM is introduced late in the change life-cycle, the return, though much lower, is usually still good. The diagram below (Figure 4.8) illustrates how the ROI is likely to vary depending on when BRM is first applied.

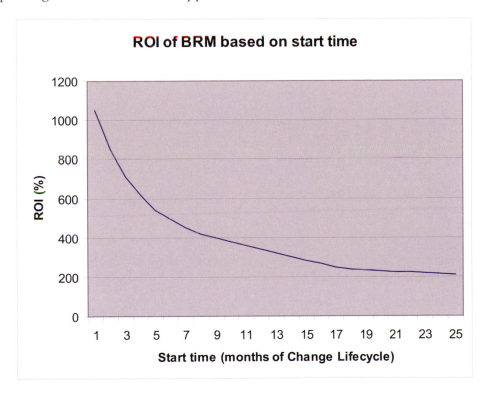

Figure 4.8   ROI of BRM based on start time

---

4   This cannot be scientifically proved, but is based on **sigma**'s experience over 20 years. It has also been confirmed many times during the past six years, by the views of managers participating in **sigma**'s management seminars on BRM.

5   Based on **sigma**'s experience.

Note how the ROI of BRM falls significantly if it is not applied from the earliest point. A common nightmare is being asked to help with BRM in situations where the programme organisation is already set in stone and the poorly expressed Vision Statement is considered immutable!

IMPROVED RETURN FROM AN OPTIMISED PORTFOLIO

In addition to improving the return from each investment, BRM can be used to create and continuously refine the complete portfolio of investments in change. In this situation the potential improvement depends on the quality of the starting portfolio and the processes employed to improve and maintain the portfolio. Depending on the organisation's success in these areas, the improvement from the application of BRM will vary, probably between 25 per cent and 100 per cent. Chapter 24 describes how BRM can be used to create and maintain a high value portfolio.

4.6   The Process for BRM

sigma's approach to BRM puts particular emphasis on:

1.   identifying and engaging potential stakeholders;

2.   establishing a clear vision and objectives which are owned by key stakeholders;

3.   identifying a comprehensive set of realistic benefits, which support the objectives and are owned by the relevant stakeholders;

4.   relating these benefits in 'cause and effect' Benefits Maps, providing intermediate milestones and ensuring improvements in end benefits are attributed to the programme;

5.   identifying the details of the required enablers and changes using Benefit Dependency Maps (BDMs);

6.   prioritising paths in the maps in order to focus investment, resources and activities;

7.   determining the most effective way to procure the enablers and implement the changes, either through existing initiatives or by creating new ones;

8.   justifying and establishing new initiatives such as projects and programmes;

9.   using Investment Assessment Matrices (IAM) to check alignment and balance, to manage expectations and to communicate significant messages;

10.   using measures to track performance, throughout and beyond the programme life-cycle, to demonstrate success, and to take corrective action if intermediate targets are not fully achieved.

This approach can be organised in six consecutive phases as represented in Figure 4.9 below:

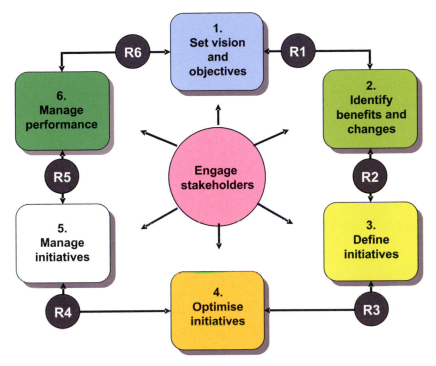

Figure 4.9   The high-level change process

The process is cyclical – it can be entered at any phase – though starting at Phase 1, setting vision, would be the optimum entry point. This flexibility allows for the application of BRM to initiatives which are well under way. Engaging stakeholders throughout the change process is a critical success factor.

It is also iterative, enabling return to a previous point. This is useful since more detailed analysis frequently prompts refinement of earlier definitions and plans. A change in the external environment may also require a return to and re-work of earlier phases.

It is also applicable at any level within an organisation – for example at:

- corporate or group level to determine business direction and strategy;

- divisional level to determine the optimum portfolio of change investments;

- programme level (within a single division or cross-divisional);

- project level.

A slightly modified version of this diagram forms part of MSP guidance in MSP 2007 Figure 6.1.

4.7   Phases Within the BRM Process

PHASE 1 – SET VISION AND OBJECTIVES

Initially a vision, followed by supporting objectives, should be established, ideally with no preconceived ideas about solution (enablers and business changes, or delivery mechanisms, such as programmes or projects). In this situation, no Programme or Project Managers having been nominated, the ideal person to facilitate this initial activity is a **Benefit Facilitator** (if such a role exists – see Chapter 6.13 for a definition) or a Business Change Manager with BRM skills and experience.

With continued stakeholder engagement, supporting objectives are then established, related in a Strategy Map, and then analysed to determine two or three primary or bounding objectives. Bounding objectives are end objectives for the programme, which bound its scope, and are ideal for communicating programme purpose to a wider audience. They also provide a solid basis for building Benefits Maps.

An example of an Strategy Map with three primary or bounding objectives (darker blue), linked to a vision, is given in Figure 4.10.

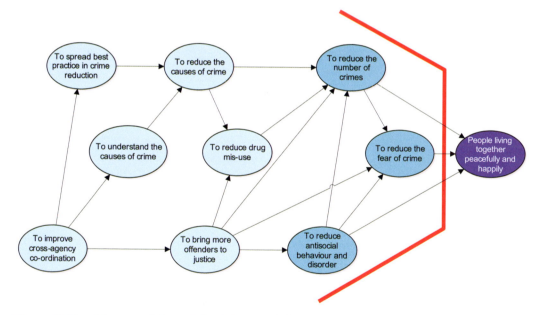

Figure 4.10   Strategy Map with vision and three bounding objectives

This phase must achieve four principal aims:

- to clarify and capture the pressures and opportunities (drivers) which have triggered the need for change;

- to determine or clarify a vision for the investment, which will successfully address all the drivers;

- to derive a set of objectives or measurable end goals, which fully support the vision, and then to select a sub-set of these objectives to bound a feasible change initiative;

- to check that senior stakeholders have agreed to the vision and are committed to achieving the selected objectives.

In some situations, particularly at programme and project levels, a vision may not be considered necessary; however a set of clear objectives will always be required.

PHASE 2 – IDENTIFY BENEFITS AND CHANGES

Working back from these primary objectives, from right to left, deriving routes to reach the agreed destination, first a set of end benefits, and later a whole network of intermediate benefits are determined. This is best undertaken in a workshop involving key stakeholders and facilitated by an experienced BRM practitioner.

The complete network is a Benefits Map, which should contain the full set of benefits, all linked to one of the primary objective(s), in cause-and-effect relationships. Sometimes it is helpful to have a separate Benefits Map for each primary objective; sometimes it is more useful to combine them in a single Map.

To illustrate the approach I have applied it in a domestic situation to the objective 'to reduce carbon footprint'. The corresponding Benefits Map is given in Figure 4.11.

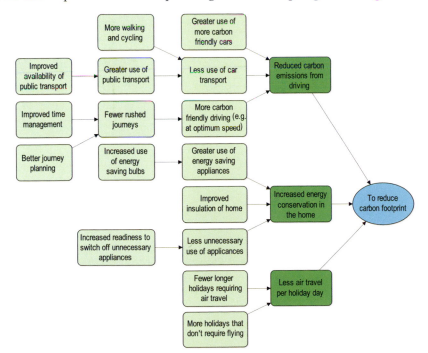

Figure 4.11   Benefits Map for 'To reduce carbon footprint'

Once the Benefits Map(s) have been refined and agreed, benefits may be scored using a weighting algorithm, beginning with the primary objectives. Scoring processes are fully described in Section 9.7 and provide a structured process for capturing priorities. Subsequently the weighted paths and benefit scores can be used to prioritise investment in enablers and business changes.

The result of applying weights and then calculating scores, for the above Benefits Map, is given in Figure 4.12.

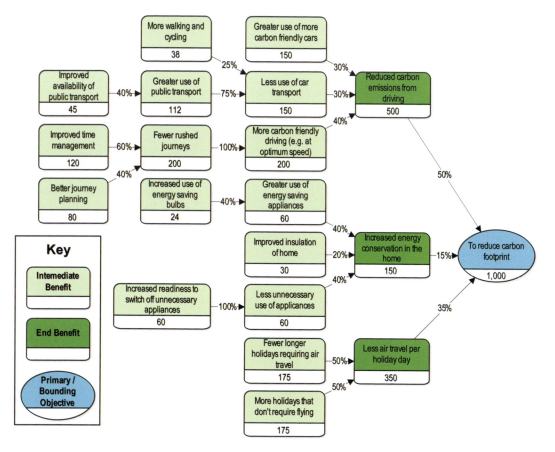

Figure 4.12   Benefits Map for objective: 'To reduce carbon footprint' with weighted paths and benefit scores

The Benefits Map, with or without the benefit scores and path weightings, is then used to identify required enablers and business changes, this time using a left to right process. The resulting map, referred to as a **Benefit Dependency Map (BDM)**, is in effect an early component of the Blueprint for the Vision. Using the above example a partially developed BDM is shown in Figure 4.13.

Finally within this phase, one or more measures and a first estimate of target values are identified for each benefit.

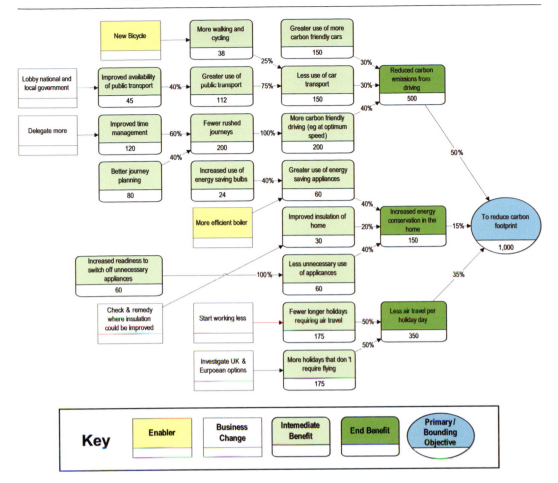

Figure 4.13   BDM 'To reduce carbon footprint' with weighted paths and benefit scores

PHASE 3 – DEFINE INITIATIVES

The required enablers and changes, identified in Phase 2, are then processed and analysed including:

- categorising them to facilitate the identification of duplicate changes, and consolidating those identified;

- checking whether they are already planned as part of an existing project or programme;

- determining likely costs, resource requirements and timescales for any changes not already planned;

- relating these costs to the BDM, preferably with benefit scores and weighted paths, to prioritise and evaluate options and to commission potential change;

- packaging changes together into projects and programmes, and securing the necessary resources and funding;

- establishing the most appropriate organisation, management and governance structures.

PHASE 4 – OPTIMISE INITIATIVES

Irrespective of whether Phase 3 results in a single programme – including projects, a portfolio of projects or a portfolio of programmes – there are usually opportunities to optimise the combination in order to maximise benefit realisation.

One of the tools available to support this optimisation is the Investment Assessment Matrix (IAM) (see Section 13.3). It can also be valuable for checking alignment and balance and to test for serious gaps.

Earlier realisation of the higher-value benefits is often achieved by using benefits to plan, sequence and drive implementation and roll-out.

PHASE 5 – MANAGE INITIATIVES

Programmes and projects commissioned in Phase 3 are then managed and monitored with particular attention to the management of business change, optimised roll-out and the overcoming of any stakeholder resistance.

The BDM remains useful for steering the overall activity.

Milestones, for a mixture of completed enabler and change activities and the realisation of early benefits, will be used to monitor progress.

PHASE 6 – MANAGE PERFORMANCE

In this phase benefit realisation is monitored and reported, contributions for multiple programmes and projects are consolidated, and appropriate actions to compensate for shortfalls in target achievement are initiated.

Although progress towards the vision is assessed in this phase, measuring and tracking benefits should have begun as soon as the measures were identified – in Phase 3 or possibly Phase 2.

STARTING POINT

I have already indicated that the optimum entry point into this process is Phase 1 – Set Vision and Objectives, but because the process is flexible and scalable, it is possible to begin with another phase. The brief description given above assumes starting with a clean sheet and some clear drivers for change or an agreed or embryonic vision. If a programme has already been set up and some projects are already in place, then the starting point may be Phase 3. In this case, some of Phase 1 and 2 activities should be undertaken in Phase 3.

4.8   Managing BRM Information – Key BRM Documents

A considerable amount of information is required to enable the programme team to manage benefit realisation and the dependent changes, some of which will be required by decision-making bodies involved in governance and review. A single repository for all this information is desirable, from which extracts can easily be made to satisfy particular needs; ideally this would be an integrated electronic database with a powerful reporting capacity (for the specification of such a system see Chapter 29). If an electronic system is not available, a set of Benefit Profiles might provide the appropriate repository.

There is a plethora of recommended documents for BRM, which relate either directly to benefit realisation or to the management of dependent changes, including programme, project and stakeholder management. Most methodologies specify as mandatory a large number (sometimes more than 20) of these documents, occasionally including several versions of the same document such as a Business Case.

Because in these circumstances a programme manager may feel overwhelmed, separation may develop between the documents used for governance and those used for managing the programme, with the consequent risk that governance and management are based on different sets of information. **sigma** has therefore sought to rationalise the number of documents around five themes, as described in Chapters 18–22, resulting in the following key documents:

- A Benefit Realisation Plan (BRP) describing all the benefits with their measures and targets, including how, when and where their realisation is expected;

- Stakeholder Management Plan describing how stakeholders are to be engaged throughout the life-cycle;

- Blueprint or business model describing the planned integration of enablers and business changes;

- Business case;

- Programme Management Strategy.

4.9   Is There an Alternative to BRM?

Some Frequently Asked Questions:

- Is it important to apply the whole BRM process?

- Can we just use a few of the techniques?

- Is it important to start at the beginning?

For effective benefit realisation, I believe it is essential to apply all steps of the BRM process. But since it is a scalable process, the particular tools and techniques, employed at each stage, may depend on the size and nature of the proposed change, and on the type and culture of the organisation.

Most organisations already apply some of the suggestions made in this book. But unless these are applied as part of a sequential and comprehensive process, their effects are likely to be limited, possibly even negligible. This is borne out by the fact that many organisations seem dissatisfied with their current benefit realisation performance.

People often say that they particularly want help with the measurement of benefits, as it is this that they find most difficult. Measurement may be difficult and there are many factors to consider (see Chapters 10 and 15), but investigation often reveals that difficulty with measurement is largely a symptom of deeper problems. If solid foundations have been laid, construction of the finishing touches is inevitably easier and potentially more valuable.

When I have probed this particular concern about measurement, the responses have often followed a similar pattern, ultimately leading to the root cause that BRM has been applied either not at all or too late. The diagram below (Figure 4.14) illustrates the pattern of analysis which often emerges.

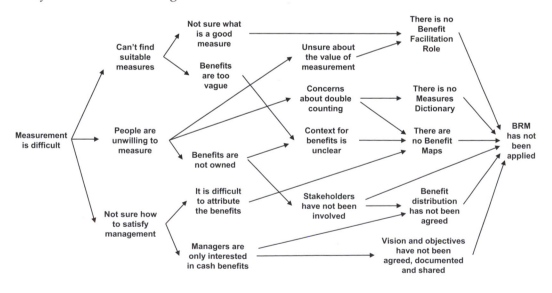

Figure 4.14   Why measurement can be difficult

Therefore there is no sensible alternative to BRM! This is a conclusion supported by the diagram's logic and illustrated by the following Benefit Management fable, used by **sigma** in its marketing literature for several years:

> *A farmer once planted a vineyard. He prepared the ground with care, and devoted much time to choosing the best vines, planting and nurturing them lovingly, using the best methods available. As the grapes began to form he worked long and hard trimming the bunches to the most beautiful shapes and sizes.*
>
> *Then he sat back pleased that his work was done.*
>
> *He made no plan for harvesting or processing his crop. Although a few bunches were picked and eaten and a neighbour made good wine with a few that overhung his fence, most of the grapes rotted on the vines, and disease set in which reduced their fruitfulness next year.*

Apply BRM and make common sense common practice. Map a clear path to bridge the gap from where you are to your vision of where you want to be.

5

Project and Programme Fundamentals

'Whatever you dream, you can do. Begin it.
Boldness has genius, power and magic in it. Begin it now.'

(Goethe)

'Life consists not in holding good cards but in playing those you hold well.'
(Josh Billings)

5.1   Change Delivery Mechanisms

A benefit is an outcome of change perceived as positive by a stakeholder, and to achieve benefits the necessary changes must be identified, funded, resourced and managed. The mechanism used will vary, depending on the characteristics of the change, the sourcing of resources and funding and the range of stakeholders impacted.

Small changes, which impact only stakeholders from within a single business unit, are probably best managed internally, as part of good management practice, improving the business-as-usual situation. I refer to the mechanism for managing these changes as a *work package* – 'a piece of work, which has clear outputs or deliverables (and therefore a start and finish), but which doesn't merit formal management structures and/or governance mechanisms'. It could be the responsibility of a single individual, who also does most of the work. Funding will often come from the business unit where the change needs to occur and most of the benefits will be generated.

If, however, the change is characterised by one or more of the following:

- is a significant or even radical step change;

- affects multiple stakeholders;

- requires major internal resources;

- needs substantial investment in procurement;

- is likely to be spread over several years;

then it is almost certainly best managed using a formal structure – a programme or a project.

Another important characteristic of a change delivery mechanism is the way in which it is defined. A mechanism may be narrowly defined in terms of the outputs it is intended to produce, for example:

- the acquisition and implementation of enablers; and/or

- the management of specific business changes.

Or it may be described in terms of the outcomes it is intended to generate – vision, end goals and benefits. I would prefer to see all change mechanisms defined in terms of outcomes – the benefits which support the vision – since the only justification for any change should be the achievement of benefits. However, the acquisition or construction of some enablers are enormous activities in their own right and so may require a formal delivery mechanism such as a project.

A practical compromise, which is consistent with the way the terms 'programme' and 'project' are now being used in many organisations, is to define a *project* as 'a mechanism for the acquisition/creation and perhaps implementation of an enabler' (which would be defined in terms of the expected outputs), and a *programme* as 'a mechanism for the achievement of a vision' (which would be defined in terms of expected outcomes – that is, benefits).

5.2   Projects, Programmes and the Essentials of Successful Change

So a project or a programme is generally required to manage large or complex changes especially where multiple stakeholders are impacted. In particular, transformational change needs to be managed as a programme. Projects and programmes are change delivery mechanisms which share the following characteristics:

- they require a formalised management structure usually headed by a full-time manager or director;

- they need clear success criteria;

- they need funding beyond what is normally available in an operational or revenue budget – that is, an investment budget – which should be formally justified, usually through a Business Case;

- they need a definite plan with start and end times and intermediate milestones.

Projects have been used for many years to manage the delivery of complex enablers, in fields such as highway and building construction, engineering, systems development and process re-engineering. Success has generally been associated with delivering on time, within budget and to specification. Project management is now a well-established discipline, supported by several specific and widely recognised methodologies, such as Prince 2, with training on offer from a large number of organisations.

A general weakness in the planning and execution of projects is that the Business Case, which justifies the investment, needs the realisation of the claimed benefits, yet the projects themselves often focus on the delivery, and/or implementation, of enablers. The business change, which is generally an essential prerequisite to the achievement of the intended benefits, is frequently ignored and rarely managed with the same care and precision given to the creation of the enabler.

The message that enablers must go hand in hand with business change and that only when these are integrated in a cohesive whole is there a realistic basis for benefits, is highlighted using the analogy of a fried egg, where the yolk represents the enabler and the white the business change[1] – see Figure 5.1.

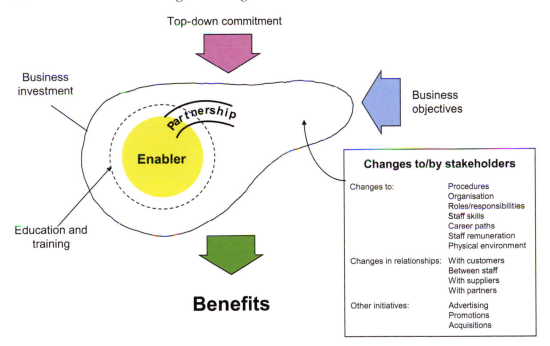

Figure 5.1   Basis for benefits – the whole business investment

This illustration highlights the fact that an enabler/capability (IT system, a new building or a redesigned process) is not, in itself, a benefit and does not, of itself, deliver benefits. An enabler must be supported by education and training (where training answers the

---

1   The analogy of the fried egg originated about 23 years ago while using diagrams to describe the relationship between enablers and business change. The resulting picture looked like a fried egg and the imagery was adopted. Some love the analogy, some hate it, most remember it!

question 'how?' and education answers the question 'why?') and integrated with business change in order to produce benefits.

Enablers must be embedded, via business change, into the culture, working practices and stakeholder behaviours of an organisation to give improved performance. If this total change (enabler plus business change) is appropriately determined, effectively managed and sensitively implemented, it should give rise to the required benefits.

When a change, involving say a new computer system, is rolled out across a number of company sites (such as the branches of a retail banking network), the enabler – the computer system – is likely to be identical in each branch. But the business changes needed to embed this system within the practices and behaviours of the branches are likely to vary depending on variables such as the number and skills of staff within the branch, its physical layout and the nature of its customer base (in the analogy of the fried egg, the yolks are consistently circular while the whites vary in shape).

If a 'project' is the mechanism for delivering the enabler (the yolk) and a 'programme' is the mechanism for delivering the whole business investment (the whole fried egg) in support of a business objective, then it is the programme and not the project that delivers the benefits. Of course projects may be defined differently but I believe the above distinction is helpful and in line with recent industry and government documents, including MSP.

When these definitions for project and programme are adopted, the frequently expressed concern that *'projects deliver capability rather than business improvement'* ceases to be an issue. Projects can rightly be seen as delivering capability, provided the organisation embraces a programme framework within which the projects fit, in order to generate the required benefits. A programme rather than a project would then be the mechanism for realising benefits.

This makes sense, because often benefits can only be realised from a combination of projects. Business change, which is often ignored at project level (or in the worst cases, made the responsibility of an Enabler Project Manager with neither capacity nor authority to effect it) is often best managed at a higher (for example, programme) level. A programme is often the best mechanism for managing multiple interdependencies between component projects which might otherwise be difficult to handle.

To reinforce this framework and increase focus on benefit realisation, we recommend that programmes should be named to indicate clearly their primary purpose or benefits, (for example, 'the customer relations improvement programme' or 'the crime reduction programme'). In contrast we have frequently encountered programmes named after the dominant enablers, resulting in an unhealthy focus on the capability – often a computer system – and not on the purpose for the change.

Some organisations use the term **'business project'**, to distinguish it from an enabler project, when describing a change delivery mechanism which is more narrowly defined than a programme but includes business change and benefit realisation.

5.3   More Complex Situations

Although the analogy of the egg highlights the fundamental principle that benefits are the result of a cohesive partnering of enabler and business change, most initiatives do not fit the simple model of a single egg with a single yolk. Most change initiatives usually have three or four objectives and many enablers, and require multiple eggs, sometimes with multiple yolks to represent them

Figure 5.2 illustrates this more complex situation for a programme which was contributing to improved community life.

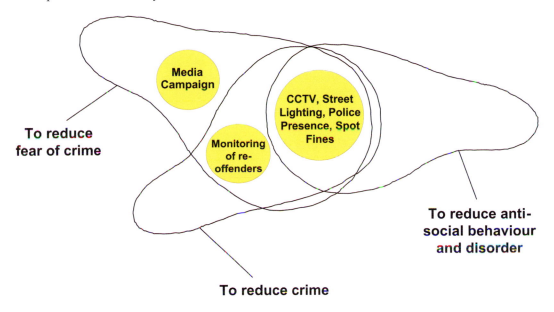

Figure 5.2   Multiple yolked eggs – how enablers support three related objectives

Whether or not you like the analogy of the fried egg, the concept of the diagram can be a wonderful aid for improving communication. The visual nature of the above diagram easily communicates the overall purpose and main characteristics of the programme, but also includes additional useful detail. For instance the diagram shows that the enablers: CCTV, street lighting, police presence and spot fines support all three objectives; whereas the monitoring of reoffenders supports the reduction in crime and the reduction in the fear of crime; while the media campaign supports only the objective 'to reduce the fear of crime'.

In addition to the given enablers, changes will be needed within public services (for example, the police), voluntary organisations and the community as a whole. These changes are indicated by the whites of the eggs, though they are not specified.

The fried egg diagram, whether for single or multiple objectives, gives a high-level picture of the integration of enablers and business change, so it is often the first representation of a Blueprint (see Chapter 21).

5.4   Justification, Success Criteria and Timescales

Using the definitions for project and programme given in Section 5.1, Business Cases for projects cease to have much meaning, but the Business Case for the programme becomes paramount. In practice, especially in the public sector, far more attention and urgency is given to the business cases for projects, while those for programmes seem almost optional. This may be because projects generally involve significant investment in procurement and are easier to define precisely. Programmes on the other hand tend to be complex, more open-ended and are sometimes introduced at a late stage to gather together a set of already well-established projects. This may result from belated and/or unclear recognition that the desired business benefits will require significantly more management effort than initially anticipated.

Project success is usually assessed in terms of time, cost and quality and the project plan will have definite dates when the enablers are to be delivered and implemented.

Programme success is measured in terms of the achievement of a vision and the realisation of benefits; dates and timescales are likely to be more fluid. A programme may take on projects throughout its life-cycle, as it steers a course towards the achievement of the vision, adapting in response to a bombardment of external changes.

5.5   Types of Programme and Project in Relation to BRM

Common variants on the above definitions for projects and programmes are:

VISION PROGRAMME

This is the type of programme described in 5.2 and 5.3, set up to achieve a vision, normally through a transformed way of working made possible through the creation of a changed environment. The new environment is frequently described in a Blueprint and so this programme is sometimes referred to as a Blueprint Programme.

It is likely to contain a variety of projects whose deliverables will be integrated into the operational environment through managed business change. Success will be measured by the achievement of the vision within an acceptable timescale and budget. Since this is usually a long-term aim, often requiring several years, intermediate milestones are vital, to track progress against expectations. Some will relate to the completion of change activities, others to the achievement of intermediate benefits.

PORTFOLIO PROGRAMME

This is a collection of separate projects grouped as a single entity for management or administrative purposes. The rationale for grouping them may be any of the following:

- they all have the same source – supplier or internal unit;

- their outputs are being delivered to the same, or similar, stakeholders;

- there may be some linkage between deliverables;

- as an administrative convenience, or for the economy of resources.

Any necessary business change is likely to be managed within the separate projects and the total benefits will be the sum of the benefits from all projects. Success will be the sum of the successes of the separate projects, including whether the deliverables were on time and to budget and whether the benefits were achieved.

BUSINESS PROJECT OR MINI-PROGRAMME PROJECT

This is a mechanism for managing change which is the integration of enabler delivery and implementation of business change, in the expectation that defined business benefits will be achieved – in my analogy a single fried egg. It has many characteristics of a Vision Programme but is probably being managed as a project, because it is well defined and not particularly large or complex.

Often a collection of projects of this type are managed within a Portfolio Programme.

SUPER PROJECT

This is a set of projects forming a single entity, which is itself being managed as a project. The set is being managed as a single entity because there are major interdependencies between the projects; there is often a single output or deliverable.

MSP 2007[2] defines three types of programme – Vision-led, Emergent and Compliance. Vision-led programmes correspond to Vision Programmes. Emergent Programmes are often Portfolio Programmes but where there is sufficient synergy for the programme to evolve into a Vision Programme. Compliance Programmes are 'must do' programmes driven by external events such as legislative change.

RELATIONSHIP TO BRM

Of the above four programme types, the Vision Programme has the greatest affinity to the BRM approach described in this book, and similarly is the best candidate for the application of MSP, so this is the implied model when 'programme' is subsequently referred to. Notwithstanding this, the process, tools and techniques of BRM can readily be adapted to support other programme models, especially the Business Project.

---

2   MSP 2007 page 6.

5.6   Attributes of a Successful Programme

In summary, the attributes of a successful programme are:

- it is focused on a clear vision or end goal which is shared and owned by key stakeholders;

- its backbone or core theme is a set of maps graphically outlining the campaign plan for vision achievement;

- dependent requirements – enablers and business changes – have been identified, starting with Benefits Maps, through the creation of BDMs;

- it includes responsibility for the coordination and oversight of the component, often interdependent, projects, which have been set up to deliver the new requirements;

- it includes a clearly defined mechanism for engaging stakeholders and managing the necessary business changes;

- the governance framework is focused on the monitoring of benefits at least as much as on the delivery of change and the tracking of costs.

5.7   Programme Themes and Structure

So for a programme, and any project which is not part of a programme, to be successful, there will be five themes for activity. These are:

- *Benefit Realisation* – to maintain the focus on the vision or end goal and to ensure the realisation of the benefits including all the intermediate benefits along the path.

- *Stakeholder Engagement* – to ensure stakeholders are engaged and involved so that their ideas are incorporated, they buy in to the vision and the required changes, and take responsibility for some of the benefits.

- *Solution Management* – to design, build/acquire and implement the solution, which will normally be an integration of enablers and business change.

- *Programme Management* – to coordinate the other themes, managing resources and risks and providing overall leadership.

- *Governance* – to provide senior level or independent oversight of the programme, ensuring availability of funds and resources and monitoring progress towards the vision including the realisation of benefits.

Although these inevitably overlap, I believe they are sufficiently distinct and important enough to warrant highlighting them as separate themes. This distinction has also been helpful in categorising and grouping the plethora of documents referred to in Programme and Project Management methodologies (see Section 18.1).

These themes are likely to vary in size, with Solution Management requiring the greatest resources and funding. So there is not a simple mapping between the five themes and an effective organisational structure for the programme. The themes which could most easily be combined are the last two as they share a similar purpose.

A programme's organisation and structure will vary depending on programme size, complexity and the degree of challenge for business change. Different models will be discussed in Chapter 12, after the consideration of roles and responsibilities in Chapter 6.

> **Organise with the vision in mind, such that required business change will be identified, owned and facilitated, and the focus on benefits will never be lost.**

6

Some Key Benefit Realisation Management (BRM) Roles and Responsibilities

'When it's all over, it's not who you were. It's whether you made a difference.'
(Bob Dole)

'The greatest things are accomplished by individual people, not by committees or companies.'
(Alfred A Montapert)

6.1   The Goal for BRM

The goal for any business investment must be the achievement of an appropriate, ideally maximum or optimum, return relative to outlay and risk. Whether expressed in financial or non-financial terms this goal should be SMART – Specific, Measurable, Achievable, Realistic and Timely.

In a business world where typical returns from change are often less than 25 per cent of those achievable, it is important to name those accountable for producing returns. However agreeing accountabilities is frequently fraught with problems, including: finding the right people, establishing targets and timescales, and overcoming resistance.

Resistance generally stems from:

- lack of involvement;

- lack of clarity regarding the nature of the accountability;

- lack of confidence in the realisation of the targets;

- attempts to pin accountability before establishing the real possibility of achievement.

But perhaps most of all:

- a back-to-front approach to programmes and benefits – that is, target benefits have been determined to justify the proposed investment instead of the proposed investment being determined to generate the required benefits.

Before agreeing accountabilities, an organisation must understand the outcomes for which those named will be held accountable, the process by which they will be achieved, who else will be involved, and how success will be defined and monitored.

So before discussing accountabilities further we will reconsider some fundamental issues relating to benefit realisation. It is also important to recognise that problems often arise because organisations hold people accountable for outcomes without granting them the necessary authority and empowerment.

6.2   Benefits and BRM

A benefit has been defined as: 'an outcome of change which is perceived as positive by a stakeholder'. The distinction between the change and the outcome is very important as it helps us to understand that benefits (for example, improved staff morale, more sales) cannot usually be made to happen. Changes which should logically lead to the realisation of the benefits must be managed (made to happen) and benefits must be tracked (measured and reported). Success depends on identifying and managing the right set of changes (that is, those that logically should generate the desired set of outcomes).

BRM is 'the process of organising and managing, so that potential benefits arising from investment in change, are actually achieved'.

As stated in 4.1, BRM recognises the starting position – current status, drivers for change, stakeholders and cultural factors, then, through active engagement with the business, articulates and establishes the end point – vision, objectives and benefits; *then and then only* BRM determines the changes required to achieve this goal – enablers and business changes. See Figure 6.1.

Any accountability for benefits must therefore include accountability for dependent changes – enablers and business changes.

6.3   Benefit Accountability

So who will be accountable for delivering the ultimate prize: producing the planned return? The ultimate accountability for benefits lies with the Programme Sponsor or SRO which may be devolved to the Programme Director/Manager who is also responsible for the change. Some responsibility can however be devolved further to those responsible for managing change (often the managers of the business units where the changes are to occur); this spread of responsibility must take careful account of the BDM – the route map.

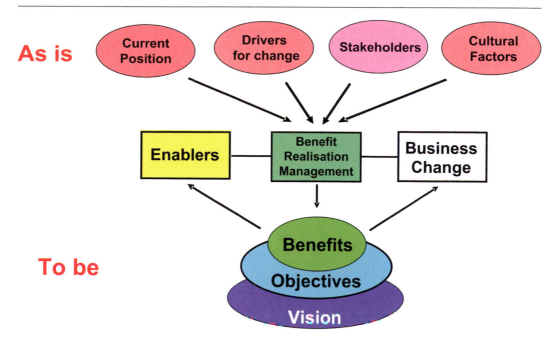

Figure 6.1   Focus on the real goal – the end point

Although responsibilities may be delegated, SROs can never lose their accountability for benefits.

So the Programme Director/Manager, on behalf of the sponsor, will be accountable for the whole programme – enablers, business changes and benefits. Responsibility for enablers will be devolved to Enabler Project Managers, responsibility for business change to the relevant Business Unit Managers, perhaps coordinated and supported by a **Business Change Manager**. At a simple level the diagram in Figure 6.2 illustrates the relationships between these roles.

In one sense all stakeholders share in the achievement of benefits – from those who work in the business units, to those who manage them, to the Programme Director who brings it all together, coordinating the integrated delivery of enablers and business changes. The Programme Director should also ensure that there is an agreed mechanism for tracking, consolidating and reporting benefits.

Organisations are sometimes slow to grasp the significance and the practical implications of these roles. Accountability for benefits may be a new responsibility about which people feel uncomfortable, often because there is little understanding of the issues or appreciation of some of the tools available to help them.

To support these roles and to increase confidence in benefit realisation, I strongly advocate an additional role – the 'Benefit Facilitator' (Figure 6.3).

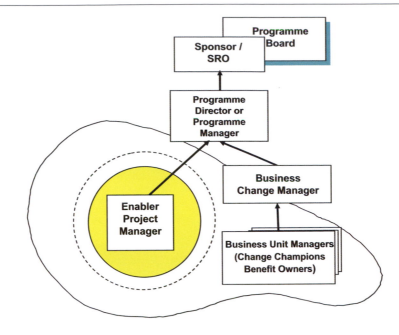

Figure 6.2　　Roles and structure for benefit realisation

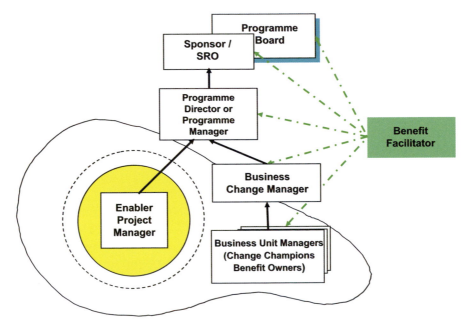

Figure 6.3　　The Benefit Facilitator role

The purpose of the **Benefit Facilitator** role is to provide support and challenge to Portfolio Boards (Sponsoring Groups), Programme Boards and Programme Teams throughout the area of benefit realisation. In my experience establishing such a role within an organisation is a critical success factor for effective benefit realisation.

It should be a permanent role and ideally not part of a specific programme. This separation enables facilitators to provide independent challenge (for example, of business cases and of reported benefits), to support sponsors, programme managers and business unit managers, often across several programmes at once and to be the 'centre of expertise' for BRM.

The advantages, which arise from locating the Benefit Facilitation function outside any particular programme, include:

- its challenge will be more objective;

- it can support several programmes at the same time, especially if they are at different stages in their life-cycles;

- it can more easily capture and disseminate 'best practices' in benefit realisation;

- it exists before a programme comes into being and so is an ideal resource for undertaking an initial appraisal of new ideas;

- it will continue to function after a programme is completed and the team has disbanded, and so can monitor/audit the ongoing reporting of benefits, perhaps long after most of the key players have moved to new roles.

Requirements are:

- good interpersonal skills;

- credibility with senior and middle business management;

- a thorough understanding of BRM concepts, process, tools and techniques;

- ability and experience to facilitate benefit mapping workshops;

- political sensitivity.

Finding people with these skills is rare and good facilitators command a high premium. Good training will help but may not be the answer as many people do not have the aptitude to become good facilitators, particularly of mapping workshops. I sometimes come across the belief, which I challenge, that accountants should make good BRM facilitators. Recently someone told me that their Board had questioned why they needed to hire BRM expertise as they already had 700 qualified accountants in the organisation. The same Board should have questioned why therefore their track record with benefit realisation was so poor.

Ideally the Benefit Facilitator role should sit within the business rather than within ICT or Programme Management. An excellent position would be within the Portfolio

Management Office if one exists. Aternative locations could be Performance Improvement, Business Change or Business Development functions.

It should not sit within a finance function, which could lead to an undervaluing of the non-financial benefits. Non-financial benefits are frequently stepping stones to financial benefits, so location within finance can reduce the probability of realising either type.

Many organisations with whom we have worked have set up such a role but they have rarely used the title Benefit Facilitator. Titles such as Benefit Manager and Benefit Realisation Manager[1] are frequently used, probably because the word 'Manager' adds prestige and clout to the role; unfortunately this encourages those who should have responsibility for benefit realisation to wash their hands of it. Others have used the title Business Change Manager; and while there is much value in emphasising the required, yet often ignored, business change, this title tends to dilute the significance of and effort required for benefit realisation.

6.4   Making the Roles Effective

An effective role will be:

- scoped in relation to *purpose*;

- located in the most appropriate *organisational position*;

- given appropriate *authority and accountability*;

- resourced with the right *skills and experience*;

- invested with sufficient *time commitment*.

These facets are considered in the following sections for each of the key benefit realisation roles listed below:

- Steering Group or Portfolio Board

- Programme Board

- Sponsor/SRO

- Programme Director

- Programme Manager

- Enabler Project Manager

---

1   This is the title used in MSP 2007 where the role is now recommended – pages 35 and 77.

- Business Change Manager

- Business Unit Manager

- Benefit Facilitator

- Benefit Owner.

6.5   Portfolio Board

PURPOSE

The Portfolio Board/Steering Group/Sponsoring Group is responsible for the active management of the portfolio of change initiatives. Responsibilities include:

- Evaluating and, where appropriate, sanctioning proposed new investments. The evaluation will include assessing the justification, ensuring alignment with the organisation's mission and direction, checking balance with the portfolio of existing initiatives.

- Regular monitoring of the whole portfolio, perhaps on an exception basis.

- Shelving or terminating current investments as circumstances dictate.

- Encouraging and stimulating an organisation-wide culture in which the portfolio will thrive.

ORGANISATIONAL POSITION

This Group should comprise senior representatives of the organisation and may be its main Board or a sub-committee of this Board. This Portfolio Board (or Sponsoring Group) is likely to include many of the SRO's of the major programmes.[2]

AUTHORITY AND ACCOUNTABILITY

Group members should have sufficient authority to commit the necessary funding and perhaps other resources, and to champion required corporate changes, especially those affecting culture. Group members should have sufficient 'teeth' to terminate non-performing or under-performing programmes and projects.

SKILLS AND EXPERIENCE

Technical skills would not normally be a requirement, but a good knowledge of the business is essential and some understanding of BRM is desirable.

---

2   'The Sponsoring Group will appoint the SRO, who as part of the SPonsoring Group, is likely to be a peer of other members of the Sponsoring Group.' (MSP 2007, Section 4.5, page 29).

TIME COMMITMENT

Sufficient time, depending on size and complexity, is required to monitor regularly the complete change portfolio. The role is never full time but commitment would rarely be less than two to three hours per month.

6.6   Programme Board

PURPOSE

Board members should own the vision for the Programme, ensure provision of the necessary resources (especially the contribution from their own business areas), and provide leadership and direction, particularly in the area of change.

ORGANISATIONAL POSITION

The Board should comprise senior representatives of the key stakeholders for the Programme. Key stakeholders are those who will receive a significant proportion of benefits or on whom a significant proportion of benefits depend.

AUTHORITY AND ACCOUNTABILITY

Board members should have sufficient authority to commit the necessary resources (especially from their own business areas) and to champion the changes within their business areas, ideally leading by example.

SKILLS AND EXPERIENCE

Technical skills would not normally be a requirement. However a good knowledge of the business is essential and an understanding of BRM highly desirable.

TIME COMMITMENT

Sufficient time is required to have some degree of involvement; this will vary depending on the nature of the programme. The role is never a full-time role but commitment would rarely be less than three to four hours per month.

6.7   Business Sponsor (or Senior Responsible Owner)

PURPOSE

The Business Sponsor, referred to as SRO by MSP, is the single person who is ultimately accountable for the success of the Programme; 'success' means the achievement of all the benefits.

This person should secure the necessary funding, provide overall direction, maintain focus on the vision and alignment with the organisation's mission and direction, and manage key risks, ensuring that necessary business change is adequately managed.

ORGANISATIONAL POSITION

The Sponsor should be a business manager generally responsible for the area of the business where most benefits are likely to arise or most change is likely to occur. Sponsors would own the vision for the Programme and normally chair the Programme Board and so they should be above or at the same level as the other Board members. The sponsor will often be appointed by the Portfolio Board/Sponsoring Group.

AUTHORITY AND ACCOUNTABILITY

The Sponsor should have sufficient authority to commit the necessary resources and to arbitrate on any differences between Programme Board members and would commission and chair reviews and interface with any key stakeholders not represented on the Programme Board.

SKILLS AND EXPERIENCE

Technical skills would not normally be a requirement. However a good knowledge of the business is essential and an understanding of BRM is highly desirable.

TIME COMMITMENT

Sufficient time is required to have a serious degree of involvement; this will vary depending on the nature of the programme. The role is never full time, but commitment would rarely be less than one day per month. I recommend that nobody should be SRO of more than two major programmes at any one time.

6.8   Programme Director

PURPOSE

The purpose of this role is to establish the programme, actively plan and direct, on behalf of the Sponsor, the integration of capability delivery and business change, so as to ensure the achievement of the planned benefits.

ORGANISATIONAL POSITION

The Programme Director will report to the Business Sponsor/SRO and Programme Board and would normally be ex officio a member of the Programme Board.

AUTHORITY AND ACCOUNTABILITY

The Programme Director will direct the programme within the strategy, plan and budget set by the Portfolio Board under guidelines agreed by the Programme Board. The Programme Director will direct and support the Programme Manager, especially in the wider issues of business change where they impact organisational groups outside the direct influence of the programme.

SKILLS AND EXPERIENCE

Programme Directors should come from the business community – ideally one of the key stakeholder areas – and have credibility with both the business and programme communities. The Programme Director must have strong leadership and influencing skills preferably with programme management training and/or experience. A good understanding of BRM is invaluable. In practice such people are hard to find and a compromise may be necessary. The degree of compromise should be weighed carefully against the significance or business impact of the programme.

TIME COMMITMENT

The time commitment will depend on the size and complexity of the programme but is likely to be full time for most programmes.

6.9   Programme Manager

PURPOSE

The purpose of this role is to manage actively, on behalf of the Programme Director and sponsor, the integration of capability delivery and business change, so as to ensure the achievement of the planned benefits. For programmes with limited business change or where the change is largely under the direct influence of the programme, the roles of Programme Manager and Programme Director can be combined.

ORGANISATIONAL POSITION

The Programme Manager will report to the Programme Director and Programme Board, and may be ex officio a member of the Programme Board. Those responsible for implementing capabilities (generally Project Managers) and for leading and coordinating change (the Business Change Manager) would usually report to the Programme Director/ Manager.

AUTHORITY AND ACCOUNTABILITY

The Programme Manager will manage the programme under the direction of the Programme Director, following guidelines agreed by the Programme Board. He or she will manage the Programme Team and (directly or indirectly) all suppliers of enablers/

capabilities, and will coordinate and monitor the business changes required in the affected business units. The Programme Manager's ultimate accountability is the realisation of benefits.

SKILLS AND EXPERIENCE

Programme Managers should come from the business community – ideally one of the key stakeholder areas, different from that of the Programme Director – and should have programme management training and/or experience with some knowledge of project management. A good understanding of BRM is essential. They must be able to develop and maintain effective relationships with senior managers, other members of the Programme Management Team, project teams and third-party providers. In practice such people are hard to find and a compromise may be necessary. The degree of compromise should be weighed carefully against the significance or business impact of the programme.

TIME COMMITMENT

The time commitment will depend on the size and complexity of the programme but is likely to be full time for most programmes.

6.10   Enabler Project Manager

PURPOSE

The prime purpose of this role is to deliver the capability as specified and agreed. It is not meaningful for the role to be responsible for benefits, though awareness of BRM is useful.

ORGANISATIONAL POSITION

Enabler Project Managers should report to the Programme Manager, irrespective of whether they are internal or external and should not be a member of the Programme Board, though they might attend occasional meetings for specific discussions. This helps to ensure that the primary focus of the Board is on benefit achievement and not on enabler delivery.

AUTHORITY AND ACCOUNTABILITY

The Enabler Project Manager is responsible for delivering the enablers within the agreed budget and timescales, with the functionality defined by the Programme to enable the required benefits. They will be assessed on time, cost and quality. Even when these enablers are managed as separate projects, the same recommendations apply.

SKILLS AND EXPERIENCE

Project Management experience, with sufficient technical skills to oversee the creation or acquisition of the required enablers.

TIME COMMITMENT

This will depend on the number, size and complexity of the enablers and whether they are being acquired off-the-shelf or built from scratch.

6.11   Business Change Manager

PURPOSE

The primary purpose of the role is to plan and coordinate the necessary business change (and in this capacity the Business Change Manager (also known as BCM) will be one of the architects for the Blueprint), and then ensure that it is implemented effectively. Change will be undertaken in the relevant business and operational units, both within and outside the organisation, and is the responsibility of the various Business Unit Managers. The Business Change Manager will therefore need to influence, persuade, coordinate and support these managers, monitoring progress against plan, on behalf of the Programme Manager.

Since there is a strong link between business change and benefit realisation, some organisations have merged the roles of Business Change Manager and Benefit Facilitator. It usually works better if these sizeable roles are separated, the Benefit Facilitator sitting outside the Programme while the Business Change Manager sits within it. MSP gives the Business Change Manager responsibility, on behalf of the SRO, for working with the stakeholders to identify and quantify benefits, assessing progress towards realisation, and achieving measured improvements with at least a dotted line reporting to the SRO. I have not seen this work effectively in practice, possibly because in this situation, the Programme manager becomes merely a very senior Project Manager.

ORGANISATIONAL POSITION

I recommend that the Business Change Manager reports directly to the Programme Director, or to the Programme Manager if the programme does not have a Programme Director. If significant change is required beyond the control and influence of the programme, then the Business Change Manager might report directly to the Programme Sponsor, whose senior status could enable him/her to exert the necessary influence on remote groups, where change is needed. If, contrary to recommended good practice, the sponsor is sponsor for several large programmes at the same time, it is unlikely that the sponsor will be able to give the Business Change Manager adequate support – another reason for the Business Change Manager to report directly to the Programme Director/Manager.

Where change needs to occur in many different business areas, MSP advocates a team of Business Change Managers, one for each business area. In this case an overall Business Change Manager should be appointed to coordinate the work and monitor progress. To distinguish between these two levels of Business Change Managers I prefer to refer to the Business Change Managers within the business areas as Change Champions, especially as they are likely to be very part-time compared to the BCM.

AUTHORITY AND ACCOUNTABILITY

The role is largely facilitative and will involve persuading, motivating and encouraging people to work and behave differently.

SKILLS AND EXPERIENCE

The requirements are:

- good interpersonal and listening skills;

- credibility with senior and middle business management;

- practical experience of managing change;

- a reasonable understanding of BRM;

- experience of business analysis;

- sensitivity.

TIME COMMITMENT

This role is likely to be full time during of most of the programme life-cycle.

6.12   Business Unit Manager

PURPOSE

The primary purpose of the role is to manage, on a day-to-day basis, the business unit for which they are responsible. If, however, the business unit needs to undergo change in order that benefits are realised, the Business Unit Manager must also ensure that change is managed effectively and the expected benefits are realised.

ORGANISATIONAL POSITION

The Business Unit Manager is not primarily a programme role, and fits wherever it has been positioned within the organisation's operational structure.

AUTHORITY AND ACCOUNTABILITY

The manager of a Business Unit will be ultimately responsible for all change and the realisation of related benefits within the unit. This responsibility does not, of course, preclude obtaining assistance from professionals experienced in change management and benefit realisation – Business Change Managers and Benefit Facilitators.

SKILLS AND EXPERIENCE

Skills additional to those required for the day-to-day job are not essential, though it is highly desirable that some appreciation and understanding exists of both change management and benefit realisation.

TIME COMMITMENT

This will depend on the amount of change required within their business unit. Business Unit Managers will need to make time for this activity alongside the day-to-day management of the business unit.

6.13   Benefit Facilitator

This role was introduced and discussed in Section 6.3. It has now been adopted as good practice by MSP[3] though unfortunately called a Benefit Realisation Manager.

ORGANISATIONAL POSITION

This role should sit outside the programme so the Benefit Facilitator should not report to the Programme Sponsor/SRO or the Programme Director/Manager. We also recommend that Benefit Faciliatators do not report to the Finance Director. Ideally he or she would report to a director responsible for Strategy, Performance Improvement, Business Development, Change Management or the whole change Portfolio.

AUTHORITY AND ACCOUNTABILITY

The role is probably 80 per cent facilitation and support and 20 per cent challenge. It should therefore be empowered with sufficient authority to challenge effectively the sponsor, the Programme Director/Manager, the BCM, and the Business Unit Managers.

SKILLS AND EXPERIENCE

The requirements are:

- good interpersonal skills;

- credibility with senior and middle business management;

- a thorough understanding of the concepts, process, tools and techniques of BRM;

- skills in facilitating mapping workshops;

---

3   MSP 2007 pages 35 and 77.

- political sensitivity.

TIME COMMITMENT

This would normally be full-time in support of a set of programmes or potential programmes. The time commitment for any particular programme will vary depending on the size, complexity and phase of the programme. A typical effort profile over the life of a programme is shown in Figure 6.4.

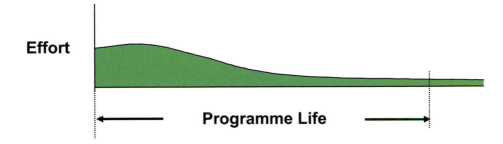

Figure 6.4   Profile of BRM effort over programme life-cycle

6.14   Benefit Owner

PURPOSE

This role is responsible for the realisation of the benefit(s) which they 'own'.

ORGANISATIONAL POSITION

This is not an organisational role, in the sense that the previous roles are. It relates to a particular responsibility rather than an organisational position. Occupants of some of the previous roles, especially the Business Unit Manager, will be Benefit Owners.

SKILLS AND EXPERIENCE

A good understanding of BRM is helpful, especially the ability to use the profile(s) for the benefit(s) they own.

TIME COMMITMENT

This is unlikely to be a full-time role and the time required is likely to fluctuate through the change life-cycle.

6.15 Summary of Relationships Between Roles and Functions

The matrix in Figure 6.5 shows a typical mapping of roles to functions for an organisation. Though this is likely to need adaptation for any particular organisation it should provide a good starter for ten.

	Portfolio Board	Sponsor/SRO	Benefit Facilitator	Senior Business Managers	Senior Stakeholders	Other stakeholders	PMO/PSO	Programme Manager	Business architect - blueprint developer	Enabler Project Managers	Business Change Managers	Measure Monitor
Portfolio Management	A	C	F				F	C		C		
Benefit accountability		A			C	C		A			C	
Visioning, objective setting		A	F	C	C							
Benefit identification & mapping		C	F		A	A						
Change identification & BDM			F		A	A						
Programme Management								A	C	C	C	
Change / enabler specification						A		C	C	A		
Change Management		F		F				C	C		A	
Measure determination			F		C	C	C	A				C
Baselining			F			C	C	A				C
Target setting		C					C					C
Benefit Realisation Plan	R	A	F		C	C		A	C		C	
Business Case	R	A	C		A			A		C		
Benefit tracking			R			C	R	A			C	A
Benefit consolidation & reporting	R	A	R	R			A	A				A
Benfit realisation	R	R		R	R	R						
Accountable A		Contributor C		Facilitator F		Recipient R					

Figure 6.5   Relationships between BRM functions and organisational roles

> **Mobilise a complementary team, with clear roles and responsibilities, focused on the end goal and empowered to make a difference.**

Planning and Preparing for Success

'By failing to prepare, you are preparing to fail.'

(Benjamin Franklin)

'The wise man bridges the gap by laying out the path by means of which he can get from where he is to where he wants to go.'

(John Pierpont Morgan)

7.1   The Importance of Preparation and Planning

In his book, *Making it Happen*,[1] Sir John Harvey-Jones describes two project teams – British and Japanese – working on equivalent projects. They started at the same time, but in the early months the British team moved rapidly ahead of the Japanese. Nine months later the Japanese team had overtaken the British and completed their project. This somewhat surprising outcome is explained by the fact that the Japanese team had spent time at the start preparing, establishing and gaining wide agreement to the purpose of the project, and then meticulously planning every step.

Some years ago I heard of a Japanese car manufacturer that was planning to open a production facility in the UK. Unsurprisingly the manufacturer's plans covered the design and building of the new plant; what was surprising was that they also included detailed proposals for the celebration to mark the millionth car off the production line.

These two examples highlight the importance of thorough preparation, not just for the building of the enabler – for example, the manufacturing plant – but for the ultimate achievement of the vision or the end goal being sought. Preparation and planning will inevitably be concentrated in the early stages making progress seem slow, and creating resistance from onlookers – managers and users – who want to see visible evidence of rapid progress. Unlike the Japanese, the British team bowed to this pressure in the comparative challenge described above.

In a similar way, BRM involves significant early planning which often arouses resistance in those responsible for delivering the enablers. Despite a strong drive within one large organisation to adopt a more structured approach to benefit realisation, such as BRM, a project team to deliver the anticipated enablers was established before the BRM activity

---

1   *Making it Happen*, John Harvey-Jones (Collins – 1988).

was under way. It took several weeks to confirm the objectives, to identify, map and value the benefits, and to determine the required enablers and business changes for this large and complex programme. During this period the Enabler Project Team became frustrated with waiting and prevailed upon the Programme Director to impose unrealistic timescales on the BRM activity, with consequent compromise of quality.

7.2   Recognising the Starting Point for BRM

If preparation is to be appropriate and adequate, it must start at the right point. For BRM this is the earliest possible point – ideally the idea stage, while the vision is still being shaped. This will give the greatest return on the investment in BRM – see Section 4.5.

Unfortunately many individuals and organisations believe the primary purpose of benefits to be justification of a proposed investment. Even those who have moved their focus from 'justification' to 'realisation' may imagine that all that is necessary is to measure the benefits. I hope I put this myth to bed in Section 4.9.

BRM is a comprehensive process running continuously through a change life-cycle. Every change life-cycle should start with BRM. It can help establish the vision, confirm and optimise the objectives, and identify the end benefits and ultimate goal. Until this is achieved there should be no programme, project or related change. Establishing a Programme Team before the benefits work is fairly well advanced is wasteful and often counter-productive, as illustrated above.

People often claim they are too busy, with one or more of the following, to spend time on BRM:

- scoping the programme;

- creating the Programme Brief;

- setting up the programme organisation;

- writing the Business Case;

- obtaining the required resources;

- negotiating with suppliers;

- designing the solution;

- sorting technical problems;

- preparing for implementation and roll-out.

They intend to apply BRM when they have surmounted their current crisis. They fail to realise that none of the above can be done effectively without applying BRM. Often these people, six months later and soon after they have started to apply BRM, will say 'if only we had started to do this six months earlier, everything would have gone so much more smoothly and the results would have been better'. Hindsight is a wonderful thing.

Encouragingly, this situation is changing. Fifteen years ago, people who looked at benefits beyond the Business Case usually saw a challenge, yet felt the challenge was in the measurement and tracking of benefits, post-implementation. This was reflected in the fact that most of **sigma**'s consultancy assignments at that time were focused on post-implementation problems (entry point 4 in Figure 7.1). Since then requests for help have steadily shifted focus to earlier stages of the life-cycle. Currently we frequently facilitate workshops to confirm vision, optimise objectives and identify benefits and subsequently the changes on which the benefits depend (entry point 3). We are also often involved in shaping the portfolio (entry point 2), and occasionally in reviewing and influencing business strategy (entry point 1).

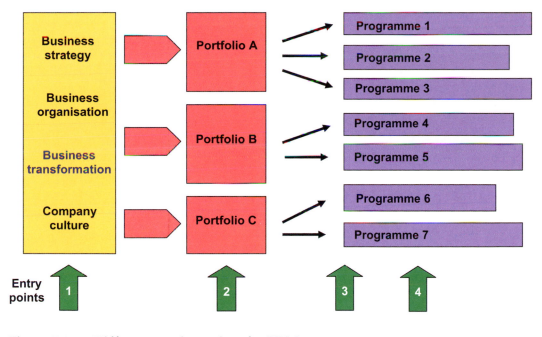

Figure 7.1   Different starting points for BRM

7.3   Budgeting for BRM

Organisations are increasingly recognising that BRM is vital for success. No doubt the same organisations also recognise that it doesn't come free. BRM requires skills and resources and consumes the time of business or operational staff, and so has a cost. Nevertheless, whenever I have asked managers if they have budgeted for the cost of BRM, the answer is always 'No'. I hope this situation will soon change, with BRM regularly built into project and programme budgeting.

In terms of amount to budget, I suggest as a rule of thumb, between 4 per cent and 6 per cent of total costs. This may seem a high figure; however, viewed in relation to the value it delivers – see ROI from BRM in Section 4.5 – it should actually seem a relatively small investment. Of course, if budgets have not provided for BRM, and the funding has to be taken from elsewhere, it may seem large.

BRM not only increases substantially the realised benefits, it can also reduce costs. Towards the end of Section 1.5, I mentioned the utility company that planned to spend £25m on technology to achieve certain end benefits. However, in the early stages of the application of BRM, it was discovered that only £5m needed to be spent on technology, thus saving £20m of project costs.

7.4   The Environment in Which BRM Will Thrive

BRM, a proven process for effective benefit realisation, is outlined in Section 4.6 and is described in detail in Chapters 8 to 23. Although the process can be applied at any level within an organisation – business strategy, portfolio, programme or project – much of this book focuses on its application to a single change initiative, such as a programme, which may contain several projects. Chapter 24 considers the application of BRM to a portfolio of programmes.

Irrespective of the level of application, effective benefit realisation requires more than a good process, the right starting point and a suitable budget. Ideally several foundational elements should be in place before starting to apply BRM. These include:

- customisation of the BRM Process, including its integration with existing related processes and practices;

- documentation of the agreed customised process;

- an organisational culture which is at least supportive of BRM (see Chapter 26);

- staff skilled and experienced in BRM;

- a Centre of Expertise for BRM (for example, the Benefit Facilitator function);

- a governance structure that is focused on benefit realisation;

- software to support BRM at organisational, portfolio, programme and project levels.

Acquiring these components and embedding them within the culture and practices of an organisation is not trivial. It involves not only adapting and documenting the methodology, and acquiring and maintaining the necessary skills, but also (and crucially) winning the hearts and minds of at least a majority of key stakeholders. For most organisations this represents a significant change and so we recommend establishing a programme to bring about this transition – see Chapter 25.

The eight essential components required for effective benefit realisation are listed in the table shown in Figure 7.2 with cross-references to their related sections in the book.

	Essential requirements for effective benefit realisation	Part1	Part2
1	A robust proven process - a methodology as described in this book	Ch. 4	Ch. 8-22
2	Customisation, documentation and the integration of this process with related disciplines	Section 7.5	Ch. 25
3	A supportive culture with senior managers demanding BRM and leading by example	Section 7.6	Ch. 26
4	A BRM Centre of Expertise / Benefit Facilitator Function	Sections 6.14, 7.9	Section 12.3
5	Change delivery mechanisms, such as projects and programmes	Ch. 5	Ch. 12
6	People with the required skills, experience, and empowerment and who are appropriately positioned within the organisational structure, to 'make it happen'	Ch. 6 and Section 7.7	Ch. 12
7	A governance structure which secures and releases funding and which reviews and assesses progress to ensure effective business change and realised benefits	Section 7.8	Ch. 17
8	Software to support the handling of information, the evaluation of options and the generation of review documents, in an efficient and consistent manner	Section 7.9	Ch. 29

Figure 7.2   Essential components to support the application of BRM

Components not already considered in Part 1 are briefly outlined in the remainder of this chapter. All eight components are then more fully described in Part 2, together with a programme to bring about the transition (Chapter 25).

7.5   Adapting the BRM Process to Fit the Organisation

To facilitate the acceptance of a new methodology it is important that it:

- is easy to understand;

- interfaces well with related processes and practices;

- fits with and is supported by appropriate roles and responsibilities.

So even a proven methodology, such as that described in this book, will need to be customised and embedded. Customisation may involve little more than a few changes in terminology to fit with the local language, and a reordering of activities to fit with any existing methodologies for managing change. Embedding addresses interfaces which may result in further customisation of the BRM Process, and also changes to existing practices, processes and sometimes policies. Some responsibilities will also require change, and certain new roles (for example, Benefit Facilitator) will have to be established.

The adapted process needs to be agreed as widely as possible, and certainly at senior levels, and then documented. It is preferable to have a single process for BRM within an organisation.

7.6   Encouraging a Supportive Culture

For optimum results a culture supportive of BRM is necessary (see Chapter 26). Achieving the necessary culture change will probably require at least a three- to five-year programme. The timescale will be shorter if the change starts with senior management commitment, which should be built on understanding and engagement.

In the past few years we have encountered several organisations in which senior managers have mandated the application of BRM to all large projects and programmes; unfortunately in most instances these managers had little understanding of BRM and did not appreciate the implications of this policy for:

- project and programme budgets;

- skill requirements;

- engagement of business staff;

- early timescales;

- pet projects.

As a result, project and programme managers and other practitioners, who did understand the implications of the policy, felt they had been set an impossible task.

In contrast, the Board members of an insurance company with which we have been working have not only endorsed the approach but are leading by example, using Benefits Maps at Board meetings and actively participating in benefit workshops.

It is important that this longer-term goal of a 'more benefit focused culture' is not ignored but is vigorously addressed alongside the shorter-term activities of applying BRM to programmes and business projects and to portfolio management.

Applying BRM in a limited way to a few selected projects without addressing the wider cultural and organisational issues generally leads to frustration and certainly misses the big prize.

7.7   Acquiring Skills and Establishing an Appropriate Organisation

In the same way that BRM does not come for free, it isn't an activity that just anyone can do. BRM needs people who are skilled and experienced in this relatively new discipline. Unfortunately such people are in short supply and although more and more people are becoming trained and skilled, I believe that demand may outstrip supply for several years to come.

I am frequently asked by business managers and by MBA and MSc students to point them to articles and books which would expand their understanding of benefit realisation, but I find there is very little to offer them, though have included a few suggestions in the bibliography.

The latest version of MSP (2007 edition), provides a very useful contribution to the subject, but I find that:

- its existence is little known among private sector managers;

- many of the public sector managers who know of it and use it, feel that it still has a few gaps and inconsistencies;

- it contains mixed messages about the significance and position of BRM. In the benefit chapters it emphasises that BRM should drive all aspects of a programme (see Figure 4.1) but this is not reflected in the content of the other chapters nor by the position of the benefits chapters in the book – since benefits should be the starting point for any change shouldn't the first chapter in the book be about BRM?

- it focuses more on what to do rather than how to do it.

The original edition of *Benefit Realisation Management* helped to fill this void and I hope this revised and updated version, with the addition of colour for the diagrams, will provide further insight into this challenging subject, together with more practical help with the how.

In Chapter 6 we considered some of the key roles and responsibilities needed for effective benefit realisation. Filling these roles is not an easy task, as relevant skills are in short supply and some senior managers do not yet recognise the need for all the roles. So in trying to move from where you are to where you would like to be, the following guiding principles may be useful:

1.   Scarce BRM expertise should be utilised where it will have the greatest impact and will generate the greatest return.

2.   In most organisations, valuable effort will be wasted if the BRM activity is not understood and endorsed by more senior managers.

3.   If new roles are introduced, such as Benefit Owners and Benefit Facilitators, it should be absolutely clear what responsibilities they carry and what lies outside their scope.

4.   Some BRM roles (for example, Business Change Manager) will sit within the change delivery mechanism, while others (for example, Benefit Facilitator) will sit outside it (see Figure 6.3).

5.   Consistency of roles across the organisation, in line with the use of consistent language, will contribute to a successful outcome and may also facilitate the filling of the roles.

6.   Organisations need, but often lack, an established role and clear process for handling new ideas. The Benefit Facilitator can very effectively undertake this role.

7.8   Review Points – Gates

Any investment in change should have a series of review points to check whether the change is on track and still valuable in the light of perhaps changed circumstances. In many project and programme methodologies these review points are often referred to as gates or gateways.

Most managers with whom I have talked, lament the fact that in their organisations, projects, once started, are virtually impossible to stop. This seems to be because there is no formalised and effective process for initiating a project, and any gateway process for ongoing review and assessment is limited in scope or lacks 'teeth'.

Even today, in many organisations, a project can be set up and make considerable progress before there is any formal approval or justification for its existence. In these situations any subsequently created Business Case may be seen as a response to some procedural requirement, so that the appropriate box can be ticked, rather than as a key decision-making document.

A review process should consider the following questions:

1.   Is the change (still) in line with the vision and the organisation's mission and direction?

2.   Is the change on track – are milestones being achieved according to the plan and in the expected timescales?

3.   Are the benefits on track – are measure targets being achieved in the planned timescales?

4.   Is good practice being followed, in particular how well is BRM being applied?

5.   Have circumstances, external to the change initiative and perhaps external to the organisation, altered in such a way that the value of continuing is now in question?

These five aspects of the review process are all-important and should be used to provide ongoing guidance but, ultimately, to assess the justification for continuing with the investment. If this were done effectively, many more projects would be stopped and resources saved for possible reinvestment on higher value initiatives, and the projects that continued would deliver increased value.

One hindrance to an effective review process, often particularly in the public sector, is the simultaneous operation of several different review mechanisms. Different review boards meet at different times and focus on different aspects of the review, such that the above five questions are rarely all answered at the same time by the same body. Splitting the review responsibility, in this way, also carries the risk that one aspect might fall through the cracks and become overlooked completely.

You should instigate a formal review after each of the six phases of the BRM Process, as indicated in Figure 7.3 below. This will help to ensure that the overall quality of the portfolio of change initiatives is high and that each initiative is more successful. More detail on reviews is given in the next section on BRM documents, in the chapter on Governance, Chapter 17, in the chapter on the Business Case, Chapter 22 and in the chapter on Portfolio Management, Chapter 24.

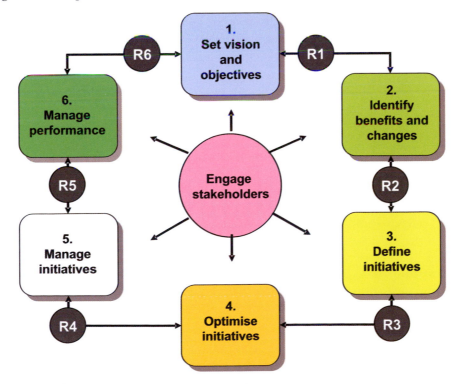

Figure 7.3   Change process with review points

In some situations you may wish to combine reviews R1 and R2, and for large programmes or those with long duration, it may also be useful to repeat some of the reviews, especially R5.

One popular review process is the Gateway Process, instigated by OGC. This is a valuable formalised process with independent assessment, which uses a different structure and content, depending on the particular gateway being reviewed. The independence is good but currently too few reviewers are sufficiently experienced in BRM to provide the necessary challenge. I am also concerned that the review report is confidential to the SRO and recommendations do not always get shared or actioned.

7.9   Practicalities Including Software to Support BRM

In addition to, and in support of, the BRM Process with its tools and techniques, there are some practical aids which are extremely useful and, for larger programmes, virtually indispensable. These include:

- a centre of expertise for BRM – a dedicated person or team experienced in BRM, such as a Benefit Facilitator;

- workshop tools to encourage stakeholder participation, to engender creativity, and to support the construction of Strategy, Benefits and Benefit Dependency Maps;

- an integrated software tool to manage the volume of data, to support the mapping process, to facilitate analysis, including the consideration of options, and to monitor progress, including milestone and benefit tracking.

Some might disagree that an integrated software tool is an essential component, and certainly for a single small- or medium-sized project it is possible to be successful using a standard desktop product, such as MS Project.

For large programmes, with multiple stakeholders, perhaps several Benefit Dependency Maps, where you may want to track in excess of 30 benefits – several with multiple measures – and where the number of change components may run into hundreds, it is very difficult to see how the volume of data can be effectively managed without a fully integrated purpose-built software tool.

Many years ago, before we had a comprehensive integrated tool, we used MS Word, Excel and PowerPoint. These products enabled us to produce good-looking reports for maps, matrices and some of the other required outputs like business cases. However, the lack of integration meant that a change to data in any one of the products had to be manually applied to the other products. This was not only unproductive but often, through error, led to a set of inconsistent documents. Also this combination of software products did not support any of the following:

- analysis;

- scenario modelling;

- consolidation of duplicate entities;

- portfolio management;

- resource planning;

- benefit tracking and reporting.

Although the value of a comprehensive and integrated software tool is enormous, it should always be remembered that it is purely an enabler. It will not change the culture of an organisation or motivate stakeholders to behave differently.

7.10   The Strategy for BRM

The scope and sophistication of BRM is scalable and should be adjusted to meet the needs of each particular programme, taking account of size, complexity and impact. Unfortunately the most common distinguishing criterion is cost and, while it is true that a programme intended to deliver £40m worth of benefits would normally involve more in-depth analysis, greater stakeholder engagement, and more detailed benefit planning than a programme expected to deliver £40,000 worth of benefits, cost is not the best determinant for scalability and certainly should not be the only one.

I recall a situation in a large pharmaceutical company, with whom we had worked for several years, where one of the directors mandated that BRM was to be applied to all projects costing more than £100,000. At one level I was encouraged by this directive; but I did not understand why it could not be applied to all projects, but just scaled appropriately. Furthermore, if there was to be a cut-off, then why was this not based on benefits rather than costs? It would be far more important to apply BRM to a project costing £75,000 with expected benefits of £500,000 than to a project costing £120,000 expecting benefits of £200,000.

Whatever granularity you feel is appropriate, taking account of any directives of your particular organisation, the intended approach to BRM should be documented at the outset. This should include:

- the overall process, including gateways and review points;

- the tools and techniques to be used;

- how and when stakeholders will be engaged, including perhaps a schedule of workshops;

- how the benefits will be valued and benchmarked;

- the proposed benefit reporting regime;

- roles and responsibilities related to benefit realisation;

- the skills and resources required;

- the budget agreed for the BRM activities.

Once defined and agreed, this information should be documented. The document containing this information is referred to in MSP as the Benefits Management Strategy for the Programme. I prefer the title 'Strategy for BRM' in order to reduce confusion with the Benefit Realisation Plan (BRP).

The Strategy for BRM outlines the way in which BRM is to be applied to the programme while the BRP describes how, when and under what circumstances specific programme benefits will be achieved. The BRP is likely to include benefit trajectories and a set of Benefit Profiles.

The Strategy for BRM should cover the specific deployment of the components introduced in Section 7.4, namely:

- reference to the documented customised methodology, with any necessary details or qualification (for example, if only a particular sub-set is being applied);

- reference to senior management endorsement of the approach;

- source of intended BRM support and expertise (for example, Benefit Facilitator);

- nature of the change delivery mechanisms most likely to be employed;

- roles, responsibilities and organisational structures to support BRM, perhaps with named individuals;

- governance plans, including review and decision points;

- intended use of any BRM software.

This Strategy for BRM is often produced, as recommended, before any benefits have been identified and therefore cannot and should not make reference to specific benefits.

Lay foundations for success, by creating an environment in which BRM will thrive. Whilst acquiring and developing BRM expertise, focus existing BRM expertise where it will count most. Document these preparations and intentions in a clear 'Strategy for BRM'.

PART II
The Application of BRM to Programmes and Projects

Part I has given an overview of BRM, providing context and introducing some of the tools and techniques.

Part II returns to the beginning and describes the whole process again, focusing application on programmes. In this way it:

- amplifies the detail contained in Part I;

- introduces new tools and techniques;

- provides more information on the 'how?';

- includes more examples;

- considers more complex situations.

This application considers BRM in the context of Programme and Project Management and therefore includes topics which some would feel are broader than BRM. These topics are included for completeness, but coverage may be brief (for example, with whole life costs, procurement and supplier relationships), if they are adequately covered in other literature.

Part III considers the application of BRM to Portfolio Management.

Part IV considers some of the longer-term issues around creating a supportive environment, and concludes with a summary of success factors, including some tips for getting started.

8

Vision and Objectives

'Without a vision the people perish.'

(Proverbs 29.18)

'I have a dream that my four little children will one day live in a nation where they will not be judged by the colour of their skin but by the content of their character.'

(Martin Luther King – August 1963)

8.1   What is a Vision and Why Do We Need One?

The *Oxford Dictionary* defines vision as 'imaginative insight', or 'statesmanlike foresight'.

In the context of change, I think of a *vision* as 'a picture or description of some desired future state'. Some, including Martin Luther King, refer to this as a 'dream'.

In a religious or spiritual context, vision carries the sense of revelation from on high and usually relates to future situations, rarely to the immediate. In a business context, I believe vision will also generally come from the top; it may relate to either short or long-term opportunities, (more often the latter). If we are in a burning building we don't need to establish a vision and agree supporting objectives in order to get out. However, if we need to motivate a large number of people to move in the same direction over a long period of time, then a clear vision is essential.

This may be why the approach described in this book has been particularly enthusiastically received by organisations whose change life-cycles often run into years rather than weeks or months – the pharmaceuticals industry, oil and gas exploration, the public sector, especially where large national change is required.

Irrespective of its source, vision describes a future state, without necessarily giving any indication of how it will be achieved. The mechanism for realising the vision is described in terms of a strategy or a suitable change delivery mechanism, such as a programme. A vision should be clear and non-ambiguous, easy to understand and communicate, and its realisation should be easy to determine or measure. Examples are:

- America's 1960s' vision of putting a man on the moon and bringing him safely back again by the end of the decade.

- Microsoft's vision of a computer in every home.

Often a vision is not so specific and measurable (for example, a safer world) and the picture is open to a variety of interpretations. Where this is the case it is important to have a set of more specific objectives supporting the vision – see Section 8.6 below.

A vision will normally relate to, and be valued by, some organisational entity or stakeholder group – a nation, a company, a division, a department. The stakeholder group which values and looks forward to the fulfilment of the vision is not necessarily the stakeholder group responsible for realising the vision.

I propose the following definition of a '**vision**', in the context of change and benefit realisation: 'A concise description/picture of the desired future state of an organisation or organisational unit, resulting from planned change.'

8.2   Related Terminology

Several related terms are frequently used, often loosely and with varied meanings, in business and other organisations. These include objective, strategy, mission, driver, goal, target and blueprint. Below are some recommended definitions for these terms, with indications as to how they relate to one another.

Objective – 'something sought or aimed at' (Oxford Dictionary). Although this seems very similar to a vision it carries clear intent – a sense of active seeking. Without supporting objectives, a vision may be little more than a dream. I might have a vision of winning at Wimbledon and may even imagine receiving the cup, but as I lack the youth, ability and intention to try, this vision is no more than a pipe dream or fantasy.

An **objective** then is 'a statement of purpose, which is specific and carries clear intent'. An **objective** should answer the question 'why?'. Sometimes so called objectives in business cases answer the question 'how?'. An understanding of purpose is important for stakeholders, who want to know why change is necessary. I recommend therefore that all objectives should indicate the purpose of the change and begin with the word 'to'.

The vision of a safer world is unlikely to be fulfilled without supporting objectives and strategies.

Strategy – this originally had a military connotation but is now widely used in business. The Oxford Dictionary describes strategy as – 'the management of an army in a campaign, a plan of action in business or politics'. In a business context, a suitable definition is: 'The plan of action or management mechanism needed to achieve an objective or vision.'

Mission – according to the Oxford Dictionary, combines the ideas of purpose or vision and end goal with the mechanism for reaching it. Two relevant definitions are – 'a particular task or goal assigned to a person or group' and 'a military or scientific operation or expedition for a particular purpose'. A mission statement is 'a declamation made by a company of its general principles of operation'. So, in the context of a business or organisation embarking on change, Mission is 'the purpose for which the organisation exists'.

Driver – 'some internal or external event or situation which is stimulating or driving the need for change.' This could be new legislation, competitor activity, staff unrest, customer dissatisfaction or an anticipated or current problem or an opportunity.

Drivers may occasionally lead to the creation of a vision, though more often the vision sits over and above the drivers and may exist before the drivers appear on the radar screen. If drivers are used to determine a vision, it is important that opportunity drivers are given equal importance to problem drivers. There may be occasions (for example, when a ship is sinking) when it is vital to focus on fixing problems in order to survive, but an organisation that is preoccupied with fixing problems will probably struggle to grow and could easily be overtaken by competitors.

Although a vision may seldom be formed from a set of drivers, drivers may well influence it. Consider the vision of a safer world, which might have the following supporting objectives:

- to reduce the risk of terrorism;

- to reduce gun-related crime;

- to reduce domestic crime.

The tragedy of 9/11 became a significant driver. The vision existed pre-9/11, so 9/11 did not create or change the vision but it did increase the focus on the first of the three supporting objectives.

Goal – 'a general term for the purpose of change which may be any combination of vision, objectives and benefits'.

Target, target value – 'a defined end point or improvement, normally expressed as a numeric value'.

Targets are generally applied to objectives and benefits.

Blueprint – 'a model of the future business, organisation, people, processes, information and technology required to achieve the vision'.

Whatever form this takes, its importance lies in describing how the business changes integrate with the implementation of enablers (capabilities), to create a cohesive solution or new environment, capable of delivering the vision.

Once set, a vision is unlikely to change (at least for a considerable time) whereas the supporting objectives – the blueprint and the strategies to achieve the vision – may all change, particularly in response to significant events or changes in the external environment, such as a 9/11.

8.3   Receiving, Determining and Owning the Vision

A vision will generally come from the top – from a government minister or permanent secretary in the public sector, from a Chief Executive or Board in the private sector. It should involve pushing barriers, breaking new ground, creating a step-change, rarely simply responding to change drivers such as legislation or fixing current problems.

Unless a vision comes from a genius or the insight of an entrepreneur, it is often helpful to employ a brainstorming process to create and refine it, although in some cases it may evolve over a longer period. Although regular reviews should check whether external changes undermine its value or change its focus, a vision should ideally stand until it is fulfilled.

Irrespective of the source of a vision, its fulfilment will require strong commitment which may sometimes be very costly. When large numbers of people are required to move or change, strong leadership will also be necessary and this will, in most organisations, demand the support and commitment of the top team. They should provide the required leadership and direction and encourage colleagues to share the vision, participate in any refinement and commit to its fulfilment.

If a clear overall sponsor is directing the Phase 1 activities to communicate the vision and to scope the pathway to its achievement, it may be helpful to recognise him/her formally in this role – in MSP terms to establish them immediately as Senior Responsible Owner (SRO) – instead of doing this in Phase 2 or at the start of Phase 3.

Although top-level sponsorship and commitment is almost always necessary, it is rarely sufficient. A large programme in a pharmaceutical company was, according to the top management consultancy who had put together the Business Case, expected to generate massive benefits. The Chief Executive and top management team were committed to the vision, but the middle layers of management had not 'bought in'; after about nine months the whole programme fell apart. At this stage **sigma** was asked to help and had to start virtually from scratch, working with senior and middle managers to create a more realistic vision owned by all levels of management. Although not easy, this was nevertheless successful, though a year had been lost in the process.

This vital, securing ownership of the vision is often extremely challenging; once achieved this endorsement of the vision should be formally documented, perhaps in the recommended Case for Change. When thinking of the challenge of securing this endorsement, I am reminded of the following story:

The minister of a Baptist church decides that God is calling the church to a new vision of what it is to be and to do. So at the elders' meeting, he presents the new vision with as much energy, conviction and passion as he can muster. When he has finished and sat down, the chair of the meeting calls for a vote. All 14 elders vote against the new vision, with only the minister voting for it.

'Well, pastor, it looks like you will have to think again,' says the chairman. 'Would you like to close the meeting in prayer?' So the minister stands up, raises his hand to heaven, and prays, 'LORD, will you not show these people that this is not MY vision but it is YOUR vision!' At that moment, the clouds darken, thunder rolls, and a streak of lightning bursts through the window and severs in two the table at which they are sitting, throwing the minister and all the elders to the ground.

After a moment's silence, as they all get up and dust themselves off, the chairman speaks again. 'Well, that's fourteen votes to two then.'

8.4   Documenting and Communicating the Vision

Any vision needs to be documented and communicated. In particular it should be shared with all those who will be affected – the stakeholders. The vision itself might be described in a single concise statement; it is usually helpful to share also the related objectives and the associated Blueprint. This fuller understanding is particularly important when the vision is broad or vague.

One representation of a vision is an Objectives Map, now also called a Strategy Map, which has been given prominence through Kaplan and Norton's book entitled Strategy Maps,[1] and is briefly described in Section 8.7 below. This visual representation can help in the communication of the vision, communication which is often neglected, and frequently at considerable cost. A recent survey found that only 2 per cent of communication within organisations relates to vision.

A cleaner at NASA's Mission Control Center in Houston was one of a number of people briefly interviewed by a reporter during the 1960s. When asked what his job was, he replied, 'helping to put a man on the moon' – doubtless a response to the clearly communicated vision of President Kennedy, who in 1961, said: 'I believe that this nation should commit itself to achieving the goal, before this decade is out, of landing a man on the moon and returning him safely to earth.' He elaborated with the words: 'In a very real sense, it will not be one man going to the moon; if we make this judgment affirmatively, it will be an entire nation. For all of us must work to put him there.'

---

1   *Strategy Maps*, Kaplan and Norton (Harvard Business School Publishing Corporation – 2004).

8.5   Mechanism for Achieving the Vision

To achieve a vision some kind of change delivery mechanism will be required. I will assume that for a vision, this will be a programme – a Vision Programme (see Section 5.5). However, there is merit in leaving the formal establishment of this programme until after its direction, scope, key stakeholders and related benefits are more clearly defined.

For example, the key programme role of Sponsor or SRO, should be filled from the stakeholder group who will receive the greater proportion of benefits (see Section 6.7). This requires a more detailed understanding of the potential benefits, including how they will be experienced by key stakeholders – information which is provided in the recommended Benefit Distribution Matrix – see Section 9.4a. Although the formal appointment of an SRO, and the establishment of a Programme Board may be left until Phase 2 or even Phase 3, it is vital that there is some form of definite sponsorship at a senior level, even at this stage.

Assuming, that a programme is envisaged, which will be formally established in Phase 3, who should undertake the scoping and more detailed definition work described in the following four chapters? My recommendation is that this work be undertaken by a Benefit Facilitator (see Section 6.13).

Even when a Programme is already in place by this stage, in which case the Programme Manager may be available to undertake this work, I strongly recommend that this is still done by the Benefit Facilitator, who probably has greater benefits experience and will be more objective.

For convenience I assume in the following sections up to the end of Chapter 10, that the delivery mechanism is a programme and that facilitation of the various activities and workshops described is undertaken by a Benefit Facilitator.

8.6   Objectives and Strategy Maps

In **sigma**'s experience of working on large change initiatives with management teams from different industries, there is frequently a considerable diversity of views as to why a particular change is being introduced – and this diversity may exist even when there is already an established programme and a documented Business Case. This is usually indicative of one or more of the following:

- managers have varying backgrounds and aspirations;

- business cases are not taken seriously;

- there are too many objectives to assimilate easily;

- some documented objectives are answering the question 'how?' and not the question 'why?';

- objectives, even if understood, are not owned by the whole management team.

In response, **sigma** has evolved a workshop process for determining, refining and agreeing a set of genuine objectives. Provided all members participate in the workshop, the engagement process usually ensures that outputs are owned by the whole management team.

The process starts with an open question, relating to the broad scope or vision if already defined, for example, why do we want to improve document handling? It is important that this question does not imply a solution (for example, 'why do we want a new document management system?'). Workshop participants are asked to write three or four answers, in about five words each, to this question on separate cards.

Under the guidance of the participants, these cards are then clustered on a large display board and a summary card is written for each group. Summary cards are written as improvement objectives.

The objective cards are then placed on a new board in a 'cause and effect' relationship diagram. This diagram, linking the objectives together and possibly to the vision is referred to as a Strategy Map. An example of such a Strategy Map is shown in Figure 8.1.

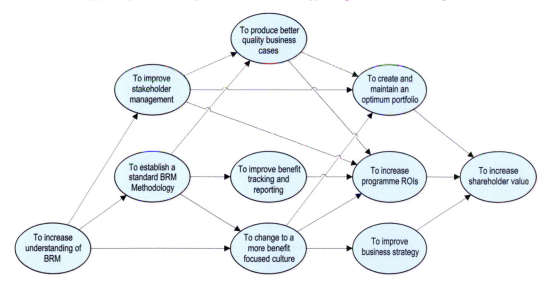

Figure 8.1   Strategy Map for embedding BRM within an organisation

This particular map was developed with a senior management team from one of the high street banks, and relates to a proposed change initiative: to embed Benefit Realisation Management (BRM) throughout the bank. The change initiative was to be managed as a programme.

The diagram, based only on the cards written by the participants, reveals a diversity of aspirations, culminating in a set of ten fairly wide-ranging objectives. In order to communicate the purpose of the change to the full set of stakeholders, it is best to reduce the number of objectives to between two and four, ensuring that this reduced set of objectives is an appropriate end set for the particular programme or change initiative.

Considering the far right objective, 'To increase shareholder value', it is clear that it would be inappropriate to hold the Programme Manager accountable for achieving this, so it sits beyond the scope of the programme. Similarly if we take the far left objective, 'To increase awareness and understanding of benefit realisation issues', the sponsor would consider this totally inadequate as an end objective and would not sanction the funding.

If we now continue the assessment, working from right to left, applying the same kind of considerations, we fairly quickly arrive at the following three objectives as both bounding the scope and summarising the purpose of the programme:

- to create and maintain an optimum portfolio;

- to increase programme ROIs;

- to move towards a more benefit focused culture.

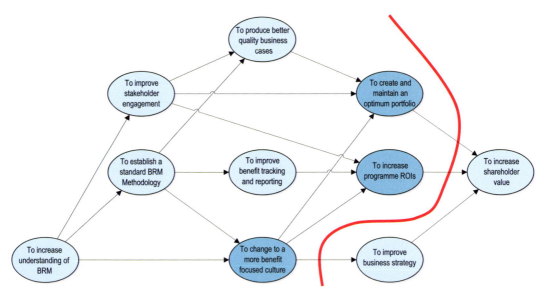

Figure 8.2   Strategy Map with primary objectives and programme boundary marked

Ideally these objectives are mutually independent and therefore appear below one another in the diagram, but often, as in the above case example, this is not possible. Since these objectives define the boundary of the programme they are often referred to as *bounding objectives*.

The whole process should be facilitated, working with the management team, so that they have fully bought in at each stage and to the final outcome – the bounding objectives for the particular change initiative. The Strategy Map, whose creation is a key part of the process, need not be discarded once the bounding objectives have been determined; it continues to describe a valid path to their achievement and the consequential impact to which they are likely to contribute. So the map is valuable to the Programme Team and can form a useful attachment to a Business Case and should also be of interest to the Portfolio Board with their responsibility to manage actively the whole portfolio.

There is usually little difference between a vision and a single end objective, except perhaps in the form of words; there should, however, be a considerable difference between the vision and supporting objectives. For example, to stay alive and healthy may be a good personal objective, but it is a limited vision for a whole life. If a person's vision was to see the world, climb Everest or have a positive impact on society, then to stay alive and healthy would be a very important supporting objective.

8.7   Bounding the Change

The scope of any programme must be bounded in particular by an appropriate set of bounding objectives. To be appropriate these objectives must be owned by the sponsor, the funding source and the Programme Manager. There is often a constructive tension between sponsor and Programme Manager, the sponsor favouring objectives as far as possible to the right-hand end of the Strategy Map and the Programme Manager those towards the left of the Strategy Map. The determination will have to be a compromise between these two extremes.

Ideally these bounding objectives should be clearly aligned to business strategy and stretch the organisation. They should be under the control of the programme although the objective(s) to which they contribute are likely not to be (for example, increased shareholder value).

I was involved in a very large programme for a pharmaceutical company, whose scope covered the creation, assembly and submission of a dossier of documents to be sent to the regulatory authorities to support an application for approval of a new drug. Such a dossier typically comprised five to ten million pages, including diagrams and tables, and took many months to assemble and submit.

The programme was intended to speed up the whole process and so I said that I presumed that the vision or end objective for the programme was to achieve faster approval of new drugs. I immediately met with strong resistance believed to emanate from senior management. My suggestion was unacceptable because neither the programme nor the company controlled the decision-making processes of the regulatory authority and so neither could be responsible for faster drug approval. The acceptable alternative objective was to achieve faster submission of the dossier, since this was under the control of the company and the influence of the programme

Though very uncomfortable with this objective, I agreed to work with it but soon observed that two of the benefits which they had already identified were:

- fewer significant queries from the regulatory authority;

- faster response to regulatory queries.

The stakeholders considered these to be important benefits and were surprised when I suggested that they were not valid, since they were outside the scope of the programme as they had now defined it – for once the faster submission had been achieved the programme was complete. After we had developed together the Strategy Map for the programme (see Figure 8.3) they began to understand the relationship between the three bounding objectives, for which the programme would be accountable, and the ultimate purpose of the programme which was to achieve faster approval of new drugs. Gradually they began to see how the single objective – *to achieve faster submission of the dossier* – was on its own an inappropriate end objective for the programme, though it was fine as one of three complementary bounding objectives.

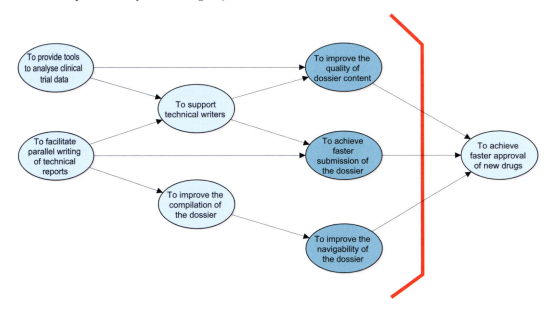

Figure 8.3   Strategy Map for a pharmaceutical document management programme

It is extremely important to identify and agree appropriate end objectives – getting them wrong can undermine the true purpose of the initiative, increasing the likelihood of failure. In the above example with the end objective – to achieve faster submission of the dossier – there is a real risk that the quality of the dossier might be compromised, in order to achieve the faster submission, which could lead in turn to more queries and a greater likelihood that the drug is not approved. The more appropriate end objective – to achieve faster approval of new drugs – would not engender these problems.

A useful test for bounding objectives is as follows: if the achievement of all the proposed bounding objectives constitutes success for the programme even when consequential objectives are not achieved then they are genuine bounding objectives. This test works for the previous two Strategy Maps and the one in the following diagram (Figure 8.4). This map comes from an investigation into home-working by a company which wanted to grow its business on its current site, where there were limiting constraints on accommodation and parking.

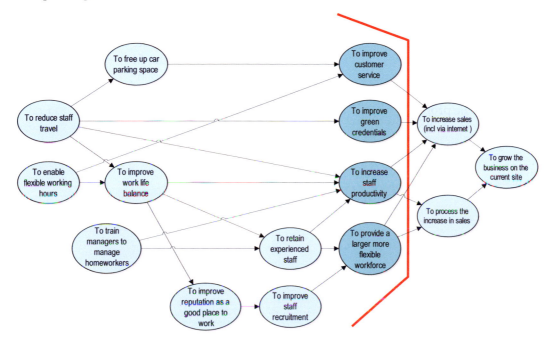

Figure 8.4   **Strategy Map for a company exploring home-working to grow its business**

8.8   Foundations for Success

I have described here a fundamental foundation for success. This process, for establishing a clear vision, determining the supporting objectives and then selecting an appropriate subset to summarise but also bound the investment, provides a clear picture of the end in view. It addresses that top hindrance to success mentioned in Chapter 1 – *vision/objectives are unclear.*

To complete the foundation laying, there are three other checks which should be undertaken, namely:

- that the bounding objectives are strategically aligned with the organisation's mission;

- that the senior representatives of the key stakeholders are committed to this way forward;

- that the proposed investment in change complements existing change initiatives, providing a balanced portfolio of change.

Chapter 23 describes how this fits into the overall change process.

Provided a clear vision is established and a set of bounding objectives are determined and documented, which:

- **support the vision;**
- **appropriately bound the change;**
- **are aligned to the organisation's mission;**
- **are owned by key stakeholders;**
- **complement the existing portfolio of changes;**

the change initiative will be launched on a potential voyage to success.

9

Benefits

'The main thing is to keep the main thing the main thing.'

(German Proverb)

'Great things are not done by impulse but by a series of small things brought together.'

(Vincent Van Gogh)

9.1   Why Consider Benefits?

Prior to 1990, in the UK and probably throughout the world, the primary purpose of benefits was to justify a proposed investment. Someone had an idea for change, which would cost money, so benefits were identified to offset or justify the expenditure. Once the proposal had been approved and the expenditure sanctioned, a project team worked to deliver the change – often the implementation of a new computer system – but there was rarely a further thought about the intended benefits.

In 1990, I observed the beginnings of a significant change. A director of a major multinational asked what benefits the company had achieved from its enormous investment in IT throughout the 1980s. No one could satisfactorily answer his question. Senior Managers from other large multinationals started to ask similar questions and received equally embarrassing responses. A shift towards benefit measurement began, intended to ensure that any benefits put forward in an expenditure justification were actually achieved.

Although this was a significant improvement on the pre-1990 situation, measurement alone will not deliver benefits; without a structured approach to benefit realisation the measurement process could easily become simply the herald of bad tidings. This was confirmed by a recent survey indicating that only 25 per cent of the projects which measure benefits actually see results in line with expectations. It may also account for the fact that 20 years on from 1990 only one-third of UK organisations are actively measuring and reporting the benefits of change.

The primary reason for considering benefits should be that organisations want to achieve them. Benefits should be the start, the middle and the end – the main thing – and as the proverb says, 'The main thing is to keep the main thing the main thing.' Benefits need to be the reason for change, the drivers for determining and managing the individual components of change and the prize at the conclusion of the change.

Unfortunately a mindset still exists which thinks the primary purpose of benefits is expenditure justification. I remember some years ago working on a project which used some sophisticated technology to improve virtual team working. Following a very successful pilot it was offered to a much wider group of internal clients with the proviso that the client also bought some coaching and some BRM.

A senior manager, responsible for some North Sea oilfields, expressed interest but made it clear that he didn't want any of this 'benefits stuff', as a result of which I was dispatched to Aberdeen to talk to him. Early in our conversation he said, 'I don't need any of this benefits stuff. I don't need to justify this expenditure to anyone.' I responded that I did not understand the connection between the 'benefits stuff' and justification. He looked blank, so I repeated myself. He continued to look surprised, so I explained that the 'benefits stuff' was to enable his team to get the maximum value from the investment which he had already decided to make. I saw the penny drop as he said, 'Oh, I'll have some of that then.'

9.2   What is a Benefit?

Since this book is about benefits, it is important that we have a shared understanding of the term. As mentioned in Section 3.4, the definition of a benefit, which **sigma** has used successfully for over 20 years, is 'an outcome of change which is perceived as positive by a stakeholder'.

This definition is short and easy to remember but contains all the key elements. It distinguishes the benefit – the positive outcome – from the change, which gives rise to the benefit. The change consumes resource, costs money and needs managing. Benefits are the positive outcomes (for example, more sales, increased customer satisfaction, improved staff morale). Although they cannot be directly made to happen, and therefore do not have a direct cost, it is important to measure to check that they have been achieved.

For an outcome to be a benefit for a particular stakeholder, the stakeholder must perceive it as positive. If their perception is negative, the outcome is called a **disbenefit**. So a benefit is not an absolute, it always relates to a stakeholder, which may be the whole organisation. This relativity is recognised in the *New Oxford Dictionary* definition of a benefit: 'an advantage on behalf of'.

Usually benefits are of value to the organisation and measurable, but because these attributes do not always apply, I prefer to leave them outside the definition. The structure used in the glossary, namely – definition, elaboration and quality gate – does capture these dimensions. Applying this to 'benefit', we have:

DEFINITION

A benefit is an outcome of change which is perceived as positive by a stakeholder.

ELABORATION

Typically benefits are outcomes which are valuable to the organisation and measurable.

QUALITY GATE

- Does the wording start with an adjective indicating the direction of improvement – for example, reduced, increased, greater, fewer, better, improved, less, more?

- Would we expect the value to change gradually?

- Does it link to a programme objective?

- Could we identify one or more measures for the benefit?

Some people define benefits more narrowly. I have come across the following rather limited views about benefits:

- if is not in the Business Case then it is not a benefit;

- if it is not the end point of the change initiative then it is not a benefit;

- it is not a benefit unless it can directly be related to a cost reduction or an increase in revenue.

These views usually stem from the belief that the primary purpose of benefits is to justify some proposed expenditure. By recognising that the primary reason for considering benefits is to realise them, enabling stakeholders to experience the beneficial outcomes from the planned change, organisations are likely to take a much broader view of the nature of benefits.

One manager, who felt that if something was not the end point of a change initiative then it was probably not a benefit, considered that 'fewer steps in a process' was not a benefit. She argued that the benefit is the value resulting from 'fewer steps in a process'.

On the basis that 'fewer steps in a process' satisfies the criteria proposed for a benefit, namely:

- there is at least one stakeholder who perceives it as valuable;

- it was valuable to the organisation;

- it is expressed starting with 'fewer', an adjective indicating the direction of improvement;

- the value is likely to change gradually;

- we can find a measure for it;

- for the measure we can determine a baseline;

it is in fact a benefit, perhaps an enabler-benefit rather than an end benefit.

MSP 2007 contains in its glossary the following definition of a *benefit*:

> 'The measurable improvement resulting from an outcome which is perceived as an advantage by one or more stakeholders.'

This appears to be based on the **sigma** definition, with the addition of measurement; however, there is an important difference. In the **sigma** definition the benefit is the outcome of change, whereas in the MSP definition the benefit results from the outcome, suggesting three steps instead of two:

$$\text{change} \rightarrow \text{benefit } (\textbf{sigma})$$

$$\text{change} \rightarrow \text{outcome} \rightarrow \text{benefit (MSP)}$$

I believe that in most situations this extra step introduces an unnecessary level of complexity; one that several organisations have struggled with when attempting to implement MSP.

If we consider the simple cause and effect map in Figure 9.1 showing how a combination of enablers (new system and simplified process), combine with the training of staff in the new ways of working (business change) to give rise to three consequential effects. The complete change is clear (in yellow and white) but what is the outcome? In a sense 'fewer errors' is the direct outcome but this has all the characteristics of a benefit (beneficiary, baseline, target, improvement timescale) so why not call it one? In fact I would call all three of the green boxes 'benefits' and would expect for each: baselines, targets and improvement timescales. My 25 years of experience in the field tells me that this approach works well.

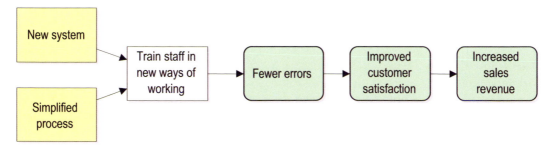

Figure 9.1   Simple cause and effect map showing enablers and changes giving rise to benefits

9.3   Benefit Identification

Benefit identification is clearly a critical process. It should engage a broad and appropriate cross-section of stakeholders in an interactive forum, such as a workshop. For further information on stakeholder workshops see Section 2.6.

The process is iterative and works best when a variety of different techniques are used, in a sequence, carefully planned to fit the particular business environment and the type of investment. There are two primary starting points for all benefit identification:

- the purpose – vision and objectives – of the change initiative;

- the stakeholders who are seeking the benefits or who are likely to be affected by the change.

A suggested solution – an enabler or capability – should not be the starting point for benefit identification.

Within a workshop we always begin with *purpose* (normally working back from the bounding objectives) and invariably consider *stakeholders*. In addition to these two considerations we frequently use other frameworks. The application of three different approaches, which complement each other, usually leads to the identification of a comprehensive set of benefits. A single approach, however good, is usually inadequate.

Recommended frameworks and techniques are described in the next two sections on Benefit Classification and Benefits Maps. These frameworks are more than tools for benefit identification – they also support the management and analysis of benefits, aid communication and lay foundations for valuing and tracking benefits.

9.4   Benefit Classification

Classification of benefits according to a variety of different criteria increases understanding of the nature of the benefits, aids analysis and improves communication. Frequently, organisations have defined their own specific categorisation of benefits to be used in business cases and other documents intended to support decision making.

I will describe five classifications, frequently used by **sigma,** adopted by various client organisations and now recommended in MSP 2007, explaining their use and value. These are introduced as benefit classifications but can equally usefully be applied to measures (see Section 10.4)

A)   BY STAKEHOLDER

One widely used approach is the classification of benefits and disbenefits according to the stakeholder, who will feel or experience their impact. The result of this classification is often expressed in matrix format and is generally referred to as a Benefit Distribution Matrix. An example of such a matrix, for an oil refinery project, is given below:

Production	Logistics	Traders	Technical	Global
• Reduced clerical effort • Improved blending • Faster supply production modelling • Faster response to operations • Better valuations	• Improved scheduling • Reduced incidents • Improved and faster training of operators		• Reduced software maintenance costs • Improved performance monitoring	• Improved problem anticipation • Reduced losses • Improved quality control • Better loss understanding

Figure 9.2   Benefit Distribution Matrix for an oil refinery project

This matrix is easily created, often during a workshop, and shows the distribution of benefits across the various stakeholder groups. It not only helps stakeholders to understand what they should expect, but also raises awareness of impacts on other stakeholders. And it enables those responsible for the change to identify potential problem areas and to plan mitigating action.

In this example the Project Manager quickly saw that the Traders were not expecting to receive any benefits (using a visual representation such as a matrix this is difficult to miss). He then spent time with them to understand what was important for them, namely: improved control, reduced stocks and optimised product densities. Because this was done early in the change life-cycle, he was able to make a small adjustment to the proposed project scope in order to provide the Traders with the benefits they were seeking.

An alternative form of Benefit Distribution Matrix, this time including disbenefits, is given in Figure 9.3 – it relates to a programme for embedding BRM within the culture and practices of an organisation.

In this instance, the Programme Manager should seek ways to mitigate the impact of perceived disbenefits and give particular attention to stakeholders whose disbenefits equal or outweigh their benefits.

Key Benefits and Disbenefits by Stakeholder	Board	Sponsor (e.g. SRO) & Programme Board	Programme Director/Manager	Business Change Manager	Programme Team	Enabler Project Teams	Business Manager	Business User
Benefit								
More optimum programme portfolio	B	B					B	
Earlier recognition of ineffective programmes	B	B						
Improved stakeholder engagement			B		B		B	B
Clearer sense of direction			B		B		B	B
More effective programme management			B		B			
Better use of resources			B		B			
Improved management of risk			B		B			
Reduced Enabler costs				B		B		
More financial benefits realised	B	B		B				
More non-financial benefits realised							B	B
Greater visibility of realised benefits			B					
Improved Programme image			B		B			
Disbenefit								
Extra effort by the business							D	D
Slower start to the programme					D	D	D	D
Enabler project targets threatened						D		

Benefit	(green)
Disbenefit	(red)

Figure 9.3   Benefit Distribution Matrix for embedding BRM within an organisation

B)   BY CATEGORY

Categorising benefits into groups, which are relatively independent of one another, can be useful for:

- aiding benefit identification;

- facilitating the analysis of a large number of benefits;

- benefit consolidation across a portfolio of changes.

Although a basic group of categories is sometimes mandated by an organisation, to achieve the above aims a purpose-built set may be required. Two sets which have proved useful are:

General benefit category

- cost reduction

- revenue generation

- risk reduction

- productivity

- workforce satisfaction

- customer service

- company image.

Category related to a particular type of activity – for example, team working

- commitment

- skill acquisition and sharing

- monitoring and control

- problem resolution

- decision making

- risk

- empowerment

- productivity

- costs.

In one very large programme for a pharmaceutical company, 13 workshops were run with different groups of stakeholders, through which almost 500 benefits were identified. Many duplicates were identified and consolidated. Scanning a list of 500 looking for duplicates, is tedious, time consuming and prone to error, so initially the benefits were sorted into the general categories using a list similar to the first list. This took less than 30 minutes and resulted in nine groups, each containing between 25 and 75 benefits. These groups were much easier to scan, enabling a more efficient search for duplicates.

Once potential duplicates had been identified, further tests were used to ascertain whether they were indeed the same. Even benefits with identical descriptions might have been different, especially if different stakeholder groups had identified them.

MSP 2007 lists the following categorisation – based on business area

- policy or legal requirement (mandatory)

- quality of service

- internal improvement

- process improvement (productivity or efficiency)

- Personnel or HR management

- risk reduction

- flexibility

- economy

- revenue enhancement or acceleration

- strategic fit.

Categorisation can also aid consolidation across a portfolio of changes. Many organisations look to a portfolio of changes to contribute to achieving a corporate goal. This is sometimes expressed as a single measure such as a Key Performance Indicator (KPI) or a 'Benefits Bucket'. Where a single indicator is insufficient, the use of benefit or measure category may be more appropriate. For example, a corporate goal may be to reduce costs, so a corporate benefit category would be 'cost reduction' into which the following three benefits, delivered by different programmes, fit: lower sales costs, less marketing spend and reduced logistical costs.

C)   BY BUSINESS IMPACT

Classifying benefits by business impact is helpful when checking strategy alignment and balance and when comparing the relative significance of benefits. Two forms of business impact have proved useful. The first classifies benefits according to three strategic improvement areas namely:

- productivity or internal improvement;

- risk minimisation or survival;

- growth.

The second classification, known as the Sigma Grid, is based on the Boston Matrix. The Boston Matrix, and its variant the Cranfield Grid, are normally used and are very useful in analysing and balancing the impacts of a portfolio of investments (see Section 24.4). The **sigma** Grid, which uses four similar quadrants, considers the impacts of a set of benefits for a single programme or project.

The benefit classification is as shown in Figure 9.4.

Strategic	Speculative
Benefits which primarily support **future business opportunities** – business development, growth	Benefits with a **high achievement risk,** but often high reward – e.g. arising from experimenting with the way we do things
Benefits which will deliver **critical improvements to today's operations** – e.g. increased efficiency and effectiveness	**"Nice to have"** benefits, in the sense that the organisation's growth or survival will not depend on them. Usually related to improvements to non-critical activities. **Often quick wins.**
Key operational	**Support**

Figure 9.4   The sigma Grid showing benefits by business impact

This grid is useful in a variety of ways for:

- comparing the relative significance of benefits;

- ensuring that the balance of benefits, between the quadrants, matches expectations;

- as an initial framework for benefit identification;

- checking alignment with the investment classification and strategy.

Of these two business impact classifications, we have found the **sigma** Grid to be the most useful. It has been particularly popular with the public sector for examining the relative significance of benefits. Further consideration of its value can be found in Section 13.3.

D)   BY SIGMA VALUE TYPE

When first involved in BRM in 1986, I became concerned about the following, frequently used classifications of benefits:

- tangible and intangible;

- quantifiable and qualitative;

- hard and soft.

First, there were no clear and consistent definitions of these terms; some definitions included measurability, some included financial values, and some neither. Second, in each instance there were only two types and, in each case, benefits of one type (for example, tangible) were taken seriously while the other (for example, intangible) were invariably ignored.

So we introduced new terms which addressed both of these issues, initially opting for five value types, namely:

- *Definite financial* – the benefit has an accurately predictable financial value – for example, reduced computer costs from replacing an obsolete system with a modern package – this benefit is unlikely to be affected by external changes such as competitive activity and currency exchange rates.

- *Expected financial* – the benefit has a financial value which can be predicted, based on trends or experience elsewhere – the degree of confidence is less as this benefit could be affected by external changes (for example, oil price or exchange rate) – sometimes a probability rating may be attached to the value.

- *Logical financial* – logically, the financial value of the benefit should improve but there is no data or experience on which to base a realistic prediction – it should be measured to monitor the improvement.

- *Qualitative* – a measurable, non-financial benefit.

- *Intangible* – a benefit that would be difficult or impossible to measure, usually non-financial.

The biggest advantage of using these value types proved to be that many more benefits came into the frame for serious consideration. Prior to introducing this classification, we found that many organisations limited tangible benefits to those which were definite and expected financial benefits (or occasionally just the definite financial ones) and ignored the rest. Whereas organisations which adopted the new framework tended to treat seriously all benefits from any of the first four value types. Although they still tended to ignore the intangible benefits, using this framework meant that very few were so classified, so it was a far less serious problem.

A few years on, we realised that the framework gave insufficient recognition to non-financial benefits, which invariably comprised the largest group. By the early 1990s, we were finding that for most change initiatives, about 90[1] per cent of the benefits were non-financial. Today the division is similar and applies in both public and private sectors.

This 90:10 split may come as a surprise to many, so I should explain what I mean by a non-financial benefit. A financial benefit must be directly expressed and measured in cashable monetary terms. All other benefits are non-financial. We strongly discourage the giving

---

1   Based on the eight different Benefits Maps illustrated in this book the figure is 93 per cent.

of pseudo-financial values to non-financial benefits. For a fuller treatment of this topic see Section 9.6, and Chapters 15 and 27.

As a result we revised the value type framework to give equal prominence to both financial and non-financial benefits. This revised classification, known as the **sigma** Value Types, is defined and illustrated below, and includes examples of each type of benefit.

Value type		Definition	Example	
			Financial/ Cashable	Non-financial/ Non-cashable
T a n g i b l e	**Definite**	Value may be predicted with confidence or certainty – not affected by external factors	Reduced costs	Fewer steps in a process
	Expected	Value may be predicted on the basis of someone else's experience or based on historic trends	Increased sales	Quicker performance of tasks
	Logical	Logically a benefit may be anticipated whose value may be measured but not predicted	Improved management of insurance risk	Greater customer satisfaction
Intangible		May be anticipated but difficult to substantiate	Improved image	

(Measurable — indicated along the right side spanning the Tangible rows)

Figure 9.5   sigma Value Types

We have deliberately included the terms tangible and intangible in the hope that greater consistency of definition will eventually be established, which also classifies the majority, rather than the minority, of benefits as tangible. In fact Douglas Hubbard[2] in his book *How to Measure Anything* states that intangibles are a myth.

Using this framework, we would expect to:

- measure all benefits, except any which are exceptionally difficult to measure (usually the intangibles);

- set realistic target values for the definite and expected benefits, financial and non-financial;

- use the target values for the definite and expected financial benefits in any financial justification, including the calculation of Net Present Values (NPVs).

Many organisations use this framework within their Business Case process. It now also forms part of the MSP guidance, as established good practice – MSP 2007 page 71.

---

2   'How to Measure Anything– Finding the Value of Intangibles in Business' by Douglas Hubbard.

Many feel that 'improved image', my example of an intangible, can be base-lined and measured and that in fact most benefits can be measured. This and other considerations have led me to prefer the modified set of **sigma** Value Types (Figure 9.6), where intangible is defined as 'reduced risk of a potentially disastrous consequence' where the consequence is something that has never or only rarely occurred. So, with this definition, it would be meaningless to try to base-line an intangible benefit. Examples would include: 'reduced risk of corporate collapse' or 'reduced risk of another 9/11'. Though they cannot be base-lined, for certain investments they could represent significant benefits.

Value type		Definition	Example	
			Financial/ Cashable	Non-financial/ Non-cashable
T a n g i b l e	Definite	Value may be predicted with confidence or certainty – not affected by external factors	Reduced costs	Fewer steps in a process
	Expected	Value may be predicted on the basis of someone else's experience or based on historic trends	Increased sales	Quicker performance of tasks
	Logical	Logically a benefit may be anticipated whose value may be measured but not predicted	Improved management of insurance risk	Greater customer satisfaction
Intangible		Avoidance of potentially serious or disastrous consequences	Reduced risk of corporate collapse	Reduced risk of major accident, fatalities, another 9/11

(Measurable — for the Tangible group; Cannot baseline — for the Intangible group)

Figure 9.6   Modified sigma Value Types

E)   BY CHANGE TYPE

In assessing the balance and alignment of the whole investment (see Section 13.3), it is useful to know whether the benefit will be achieved by:

- doing new things;

- stopping doing existing things;

- doing existing things a bit better.

We refer to these as 'change types'.

9.5   Benefits Maps

A number of objectives will support a vision, each of which is likely to lead to the creation of a number of benefits. These benefits will probably be related to one another – those likely to be achieved early paving the way for later benefits, and eventually the latest benefits are achieved. The latest benefits, which are usually a decomposition of the objective, are called 'end benefits'. To show these relationships, I recommend the use of Benefits Maps.

A Benefits Map is a diagram showing a set of benefits and how they relate to one another – the left to right flow describes a series of cause and effect relationships. Figure 9.7 shows part of a Benefits Map for increasing the sales contribution for a consultancy business. The end benefits are shown in the brighter green.

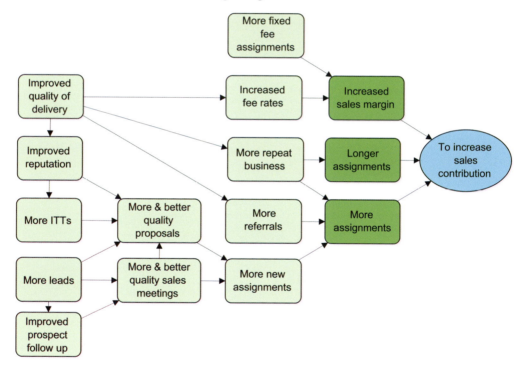

Figure 9.7   Benefits Map for objective: 'To increase sales contribution'

The initial Benefits Map, as generated in Phase 2 of the change process (see Section 7.8), is aspirational, effectively representing a 'wish list'. Once the changes and enablers, needed to deliver the benefits, have been identified and added, the map (now a Benefit Dependency Map or BDM) represents a set of feasible options, so it is possible, by weighting the paths and scoring the benefits, to select the higher value routes – the 'super highways' – ignoring or postponing the rest. In Phase 4 the BDM (perhaps with some routes removed) represents a plan; in Phases 5 and 6 it becomes a report of actual progress towards the achievement of the vision.

A Benefits Map is usually created starting with the objective (at right-hand end) and then working right to left. The first step is to work out a set of end benefits which fully represent the objective; they should be necessary and sufficient. Sufficiency is established if, with all benefits achieved, everyone (especially stakeholders) would agree that the objective had been fulfilled. Necessity is established by removing each benefit in turn and testing whether the objective would still be fulfilled – if yes, the removed benefit is not an end benefit but is likely to be an intermediate benefit, which will sit further to the left in the Benefits Map.

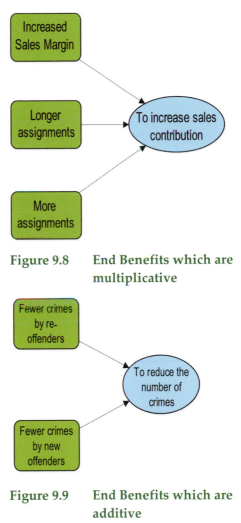

This decomposition of objective into end benefits is essentially the same as subsequent decompositions of benefits into contributing benefits; it may take one of several forms. The relationship may be arithmetic, relate to process, or neither.

Considering the end benefits from the adjacent Benefits Map, the relationship is arithmetic – multiplicative (see Figure 9.8).

In this example, if the average sales margin increases by 20 per cent, the average length of assignment by 50 per cent and the number of assignments by 50 per cent, then sales contribution increases by 170 per cent (since 1.2 x 1.5 x 1.5 = 2.7).

Figure 9.8   **End Benefits which are multiplicative**

In the adjacent diagram the relationship between the end benefits and the objective is arithmetic – additive (see Figure 9.9)

Here, the sum of fewer crimes by reoffenders and fewer crimes by new offenders gives the total reduction in the number of crimes.

In the next example (Figure 9.10), which comes from a workshop with a large government department, there is no arithmetic relationship between the end benefits and the objective, though there is a process relationship; the set of end benefits was nevertheless deemed to be necessary and sufficient.

Figure 9.9   **End Benefits which are additive**

Working with senior managers both from HR and the business community, it took about 75 minutes to identify and agree the five end benefits displayed in the following diagram. Some benefits suggested at the outset were later dropped and Benefit 5 was added late in the process. This might seem a long time to identify and agree five end benefits; in fact they are the foundation of the investment so it would have been worthwhile spending twice as long.

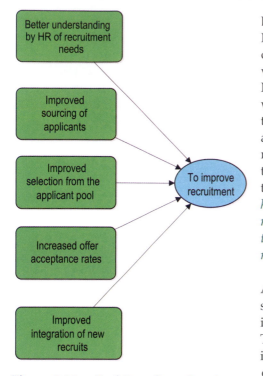

Figure 9.10   End Benefits related to process

Despite their similar appearance, Benefits Maps and process diagrams should not be confused. In this example the process flow runs vertically down from Benefit 1 to Benefit 5. Not all Benefits Maps have a close relationship with process (for example, in the previous two examples, where the relationships are arithmetic, the end benefits are not directly related to steps in a process); when they do, the process is likely to run vertically, as in this instance, rather than horizontally. *We have found that sometimes workshop participants mistakenly link benefits according to process rather than cause and effect. If this remains uncorrected many problems may result.*

As in the above three examples, end benefits should be independent of one another (that is, there should be no link between them). This means that each benefit can be achieved independently of the others. To achieve the objective fully all end benefits must of course be realised.

There is no unique mathematically correct Benefits Map for a particular objective. Although at any stage a set of contributing benefits should be necessary and sufficient, there may be options on the set type. For example, in considering the contributing benefits for the objective 'to reduce crime', there are at least three different set types, namely:

- type of offender;

- type of crime;

- inclination to commit crime.

These have different merits. The first two result in benefits which are fairly easy to measure, but the third is more valuable in determining the required changes. In Figure 9.9 we used 'type of offender', but

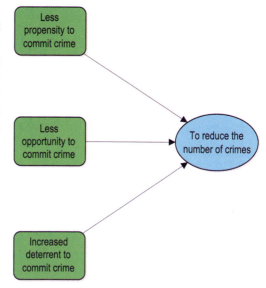

Figure 9.11   Alternative End Benefits for objective: 'To reduce the number of crimes'

inclination is important for determining the required changes, when the necessary and sufficient set of end benefits could be as in Figure 9.11.

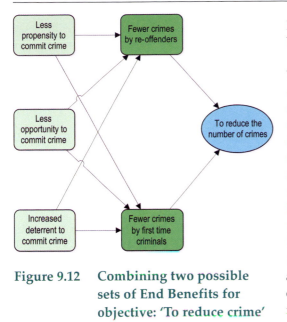

In such situations it may be possible to use both (Figure 9.12).

This combination allows us to measure the change in the type of offender, to weight more heavily the 'fewer reoffenders' and then to use different proportions, for the inclination-offender relationships. Since the Benefits Maps to the left of each of the 'inclination' benefits turn out to be mutually independent (Figure 9.13), it is better to have the 'inclination' benefit set to the left of the 'offender type' benefit set. Unfortunately, at the stage these decisions are being made, this information is not available which is where experience will count. I know of no simple 'rule of thumb' for making these judgements.

Figure 9.12   Combining two possible sets of End Benefits for objective: 'To reduce crime'

Having taken care to produce a high quality right-hand end to our map, we are now ready to work steadily leftwards adding and/or identifying feeder benefits. Benefits may be added from a pool of benefits, previously identified using another process (see Section 9.4), or identified using the map logic alone.

The result of continuing this right to left process might be as described in the diagram below:

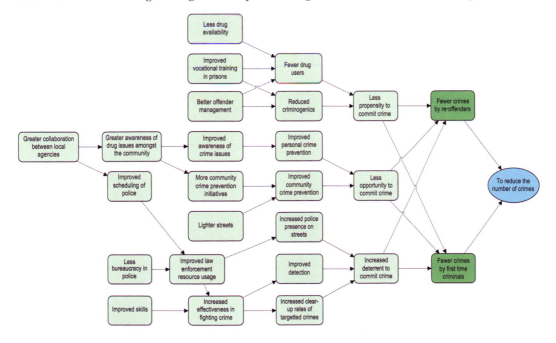

Figure 9.13   Benefits Map for the objective: 'To reduce the number of crimes'

If the Benefits Map is determined after a programme has been established or at least envisaged, certain potential benefits may be deemed to be outside scope. It is better to include initially all benefits determined by applying systematic logic within the context of the particular business environment, and later to mark some as outside the scope of the currently proposed change initiative. Using the above diagram as an example, the top benefit 'less drug availability' is an important benefit but it was considered to be well outside the scope of the proposed change initiative.

A Benefits Map is an extremely valuable tool. The set of Benefit Maps derived from the agreed bounding objectives should become the backbone of the change initiative – the central core which gives everything purpose and holds everything together.

A senior committee of a large organisation undertaking an extensive programme was resistant to the message conveyed by a Benefits Map. Because the map was built around a bounding objective which they had agreed, they could not challenge or dismiss it. The map was a graphic representation of view held almost universally by a cross-section of those who made the business work on a day-to-day basis. So it was almost impossible for the committee, especially any individual member of it, to dodge the issues.

This example illustrates the valuable political advantage available to Programme Managers and perhaps SROs from the use of Benefits Maps.

One company enlarged a critical Benefits Map many times and then placed it on the wall of a coffee lounge. As well as being given the opportunity to study it, staff were encouraged to amend or comment on it.

Once the Benefits Map has been created and agreed it is necessary to work left to right, to determine the enablers and the business changes needed for delivery of the benefits. As these are determined, they can be added to the diagram so creating a BDM, which should then be a key tool of project or programme planning. This process is described more fully in Section 11.2.

A Benefits Map can be likened to a military campaign plan – the benefits are equivalent to the positions to be taken on the way to achieving the end goal. It is also a powerful vehicle for non-ambiguous communication and a valuable template for benefit tracking and reporting.

9.6   Valuing Benefits

Valuing benefits may be difficult for a variety of reasons, not least because the concept of value is complex and prompts several questions:

- Does value have to be financial?

- Does value vary depending on the stakeholder who will receive the benefit?

- Is value the same as a target improvement?

- Does value depend on the purpose for which we are valuing it?

Certainly value need not be financial – in the world at large it generally is not. The *New Oxford Dictionary* I consulted offered 13 separate definitions of value, of which only one was financial, namely – 'the amount of money or goods for which a thing can be exchanged in the open market'. We talk about 'value for money' which implies we spend money to acquire value, which must then be different from money. On the other hand, when we talk about investing money, we are usually looking for a monetary return.

Values vary depending on the views of the stakeholders experiencing them and on the purpose for which valuation is being undertaken. That value does vary depending on the stakeholder receiving the benefit can be illustrated by the fact that some people purchase most of their garments in sales because they do not consider them good value at full price whereas others buy at full prices, presumably perceiving their value differently.

Of my 13 dictionary definitions of value, the most relevant is 'the numerical measure of a quantity or a number denoting magnitude on some conventional scale'.

This links value to a numerical measure, which leads me to suggest that a suitable definition for the *value of a benefit* is 'the magnitude of the improvement associated with the benefit'. The value can be a forecast or predicted value, a target value or an actual value. Setting realistic target values, and subsequently tracking actual values, are often best done at measure level. So the value of the benefit *fewer complaints* might be *a 10 per cent reduction in complaints*.

A house is a good example of something that has several values, depending on the purpose of the valuation. These include:

- value for insurance purposes, which probably equates to the replacement cost assuming it was completely destroyed;

- rateable value, used for determining Council Tax;

- value to the family living in the house which would be non-financial;

- market value, assessed by estate agents, and used by mortgage lenders;

- sales value which is the value someone is prepared to pay for it.

So if value depends on the purpose of the valuation, what is the purpose for valuing benefits? I believe that there are three main purposes:

- to use in an investment justification (for example, a Business Case);

- to compare and rank benefits, probably in order to focus on the higher value benefits;

- to provide targets at which to aim and by which to confirm subsequent success.

The fact that these are clearer when the benefits are financial could lead to the giving of an artificial financial value to a non-financial benefit. The value should always relate to the benefit as described, not to some possible consequential effect.

In most organisations there is a powerful drive to value benefits financially irrespective of whether their achievement will actually generate or save cash. The reasons are:

- it is the simplest, most obvious common currency for comparing and ranking benefits;

- since most costs are expressed financially, financial benefits are the most useful for providing a justification – for example, a net value trajectory.

Unfortunately it is misleading and dangerous to give financial values to benefits whose achievement will not directly generate cash – see Chapter 27.

Consider as an example of a definite non-financial benefit, 'fewer steps in a process'. Suppose there are currently 65 steps in the process and that as a result of the proposed change, we confidently expect this to reduce to 40. We have a baseline of 65 and a target of 40. Its direct measure is the number of steps in the process, which is not a monetary benefit, and since we are confident of achieving the target the benefit is 'Definite Non-financial'.

Some would say that fewer steps should lead to 'improved productivity' on which we can put a financial value – but does it, and can we? Let's take a closer look by considering the options outlined in Figure 9.14.

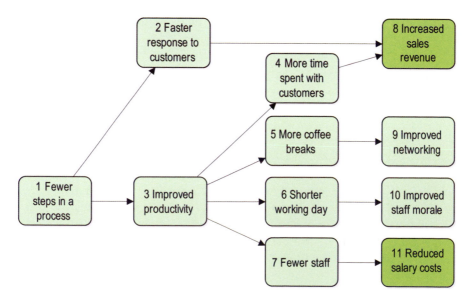

Figure 9.14   Why 'fewer steps in a process' should not be assigned a financial value

The diagram shows part of a possible Benefits Map, describing a set of possible paths, of which not all may become part of the change plan.

Fewer steps might lead to 'improved productivity', 'faster response to customers' or both. 'Improved productivity' is not a financial benefit (it is directly measured in the number of applications processed per person per hour). In fact the only financial benefits are 8 and 11, the two in brighter green.

Based on this Benefits Map, some would put a financial value on 'improved productivity' because they anticipate it leading to reduced salary costs or increased sales revenue. This anticipation is based on several implicit assumptions, which are rarely made explicit (in a Benefits Map for example). Such lack of transparency makes it difficult to spot double counting of benefits and whether or why benefits are not being achieved. 'Increased sales revenue' and 'reduced salary costs' clearly carry financial values, and if 'improved productivity' is also given a financial value then there is double counting.

I am convinced that the only practical and accurate approach to these issues is to separate the benefits, but link them in a Benefits Map, for the following reasons:

- It clearly communicates intentions – for example, is it intended that improved productivity should lead to fewer staff or a shorter working day or is it some of each? – if both the percentage split can be indicated on the links.

- It avoids any possible double counting of financial benefits – if any path passes through two financial benefits then double counting will occur.

- It allows for the time factor – for example, even if 1 to 3 to 7 to 11 is an intended path, the trigger benefit 'fewer steps in a process' is likely to be achieved many months before 'reduced salary costs'. We will want to know when fewer steps has been achieved, but allocating it a monetary value distorts the accuracy of the cash flow.

Between some of the benefits in the map, further change must be managed to allow the flow through. For instance, moving from 'fewer steps' to 'improved productivity' may require the introduction of new procedures, accompanied by staff training. To move from 'improved productivity' to 'fewer staff', some staff may have to be made redundant.

In this case example, the value of the benefit 'fewer steps in a process' is 25 fewer steps. This is not financial and I see no need to try artificially to give this a financial value; to do so would be misleading for the reasons given above. Often a major change in mindset is required at senior levels, to recognise that putting monetary values on non-financial benefits is extremely unhelpful. Senior managers and committees, who require investments to comply with an artificial conversion to money, frequently lose credibility; the investments are then less likely to succeed.

One reason why managers may be reluctant to drop pseudo-financial valuation is that they believe without it, benefits will be vague and ambiguous. In fact non-financial benefits can have equally definite target values and can be tracked in the same way as financial benefits. **sigma** Value Types (see Section 9.4D) help to convey this message; where clients have used them in business cases, they have generally been well received by senior managers and review bodies.

The director responsible for drug development in another pharmaceutical company, with whom we had worked for several years, stated that he did not want us to put a financial value on the benefit 'earlier approval of new drugs'. The programme on which we had been working was expected to shave one month off the time taken to obtain approval for a new drug. He was not only happy, but preferred to see the value of this benefit expressed as one month off the normal approval time. Later, if he needed to consider the financial implications of this benefit, he could determine a value based on the particular product, the country of distribution and the year.

Some people will go to great lengths to give everything a financial value, including human life, yet even when this is done it is often not consistently applied. The UK spends on average seven times as much investigating a murder as it does investigating a road traffic fatality. This difference is not because the worth of a life varies depending on the cause of death. It is also not related to any consequential reduction in the occurrence of similar deaths; if it were, the investment ratio should probably be reversed (1:7 instead of 7:1) since it is easier to prevent traffic deaths than to prevent murders. Clearly other considerations apply, highlighting the incongruity of putting financial values on life or death.

In countless instances artificial monetary conversion of benefits has put projects and programmes at great risk. For case examples see Chapter 27.

9.7   Ranking Benefits

We generally use two different methods, with different merits, for ranking benefits, both of which avoid giving them artificial financial values. One method of ranking benefits is the **sigma** Grid, described in Section 9.4C.

The other method involves the generation of a score for each benefit. This score can be based on a single map (a Map Score) or on the complete set of maps relating to a vision or programme (a Strategy Score). To do this we work from the far right of each Benefits Map (for Map Scores), or the Strategy Map (for Strategy Scores). To compute individual objective or benefit scores we must start with a single end point against which we can assign a budget or total score.

So in considering the Strategy Map for the programme to embed BRM within an organisation (Figure 8.1), we need a single end point summarising the programme to which we can assign a budget. Since the single end objective 'to increase shareholder value' is well beyond the scope of the programme, it is helpful to create a more appropriate end objective which summarises the three bounding objectives, for example, 'to maximise business value from all investments in change' (see Figure 9.15).

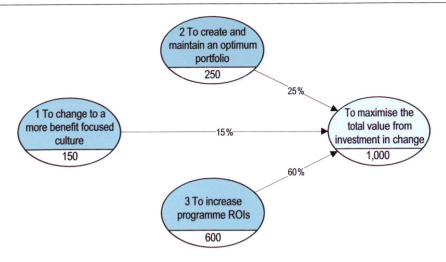

Figure 9.15   Ranking/weighting objectives

If we now consider how we would want to apportion the total budget, say 1000 units of funding, between the three brimary objectives, we may choose to invest 15 per cent on objective 1, 25 per cent on 2 and 60 per cent on 3, giving respective objective scores of 150, 250 and 600. These percentage weightings are best determined in a workshop environment with stakeholders of appropriate seniority who understand the issues. It should take account of both the fundamental importance of the contributing objective and the current degree of 'brokenness' for the particular organisation.

This process can now be applied to the three Benefits Maps, whose end objectives are each of the above. At the end of the process we will have a weighted set of Benefits Maps, where the links into each benefit are weighted with percentage contributions; a set of scores is then calculated for each benefit. This highlights the relative importance of different paths through the maps and the significance or ranking of the benefits, as illustrated in Figure 9.16 – the Benefits Map for Objective 3 from the above Strategy Map.

An earlier, slightly simpler, example of a Benefits Map with weighted paths and benefit scores is given in Figure 4.12 in Section 4.7.

Maps of this type are created in three stages:

1. An unweighted Benefits Map is first created working systematically right to left from the objective, where for each benefit, a necessary and sufficient set of contributing benefits of a consistent type, are identified (see Section 9.5).

2. Starting with the objective and working right to left, the proportion of investment to be allocated to each of the contributing benefits is determined. This proportion is not based on cost (that comes later) but on the relative contribution, anticipated value or improvement opportunity. This may be a subjective view based on the experience of those involved in the debate. If it is considered that the realisation of a benefit requires more than the achievement

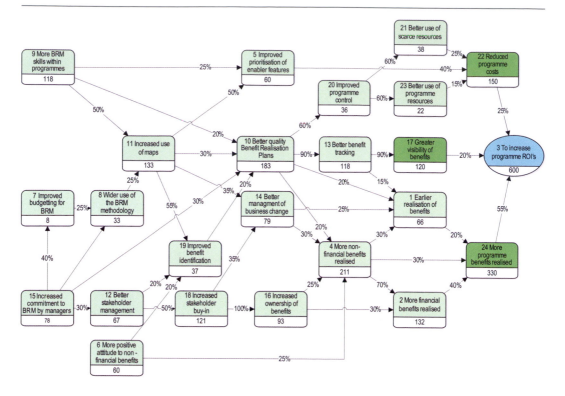

Figure 9.16   Benefits Map with weighted paths and scores

of the contributing benefits, then the sum of the percentage contributions (weightings) will be less than 100.

3.   Once weightings have been agreed for all paths, a score can be given to the right most entity, or this can be picked up automatically from the Strategy Map (Figure 9.15), and scores then calculated for each of the benefits. The starting score could be a financial value (for example, the total budget for the programme) or just a number (say 1000). A number is sufficient to see the relative importance of different paths and benefits, and avoids a possible confusion between the notional value or score and the cost of achieving the benefits (see Chapter 11). The calculation process works right to left and each benefit score will be the sum of the component scores from each of the benefits to which it contributes. In the Benefits Map (Figure 9.16) the bounding objective 3 picks up its score of 600 from the Strategy Map (Figure 9.15); Benefit 17 only contributes to Objective 3 and so its score will be 120 (20 per cent of 600). Benefit 13 contributes to both Benefit 17 and Benefit 1 and so its score is 118 (90 per cent of 120 + 15 per cent of 66).

Note that some left-hand benefits finish up with high scores, indicating their relative importance; these should not be taken in isolation as it is vital that the paths through the Benefits Map are not ignored. However it would generally be prudent to start the change identification process (see Chapter 11) by focusing on the left-hand benefits with high scores and determining what needs to be done differently – which enablers and business changes are required – in order to deliver the high-scoring benefit.

As mentioned in (2) above, it is **not** essential that the weights on paths into a single benefit add up to 100 per cent, since there may be other influences, not specified, which will also contribute to the specified benefit.

An alternative form of scoring highlights those benefits where the sum of the input weightings is not 100 per cent. In this model each score is the difference between the Strategy or Map Score for the benefit and the sum of Strategy/Map Scores for contributing benefits. The difference, or residue, must be provided by means other than the contributing benefits (for example, by enablers and changes). This is illustrated in Figure 9.17.

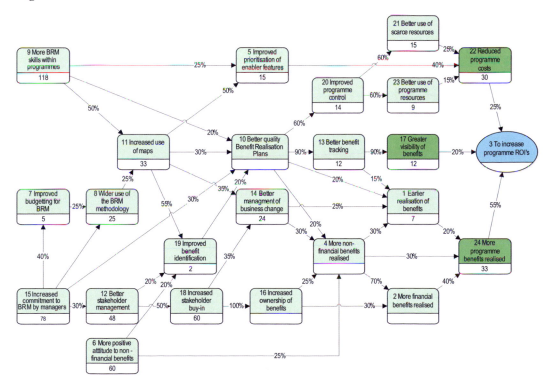

Figure 9.17   Benefits Map with weighted paths and residual scores

Entities with non-zero scores mean that their achievement is dependent on more than the supporting benefits. For example Benefit 5, 'improved prioritisation of enabler features' is dependent on 'more BRM skills within programmes' and 'increased use of maps', but also 25 per cent on other factors not specified in the diagram – these other factors could be enablers and changes, to be identified in the next step, but may be deliverables from other programmes.

9.8   Validating Benefits

Although benefits are likely to have been identified through a workshop process involving representatives from the key stakeholder groups, they will usually also require validation outside the workshop by both those who are deemed to be recipients of the benefits and those who will be accountable for their realisation.

Validation commonly covers three aspects:

- that the benefit is realistic and achievable as a result of the planned changes – here Benefits Maps and BDMs are useful;

- that both the stakeholders, who are scheduled to receive the benefit, and those accountable for its realisation, are appropriate and have 'bought in';

- that target values for the benefits are achievable and owned. For this the views from stakeholders close to the action are important.

If no one is prepared to own the benefit then is it real? A useful exercise involves checking that the total benefits expected to be received by the different stakeholders equates to the total benefits for which stakeholders are accountable.

9.9   Repository for Benefit-related Information

Effective BRM involves gathering, processing, analysing and communicating a large quantity of benefit-related information. It is difficult to see how, in large or complex programmes or portfolios, BRM can be handled effectively without a comprehensive and cohesive software product that brings together all the facets of benefit realisation and facilitates analysis and communication. This is discussed more fully in Chapter 29. The core of this repository can simply be viewed as a template which holds all the information related to a single benefit. A set of completed templates, one for each benefit, is the equivalent of a database of benefit-related information, which can be used for analysis and from which other documents (for example, Benefit Realisation Plans (BRPs), Business Cases) can be generated. This template is called a Benefit Profile.

THE BENEFIT PROFILE

We recommend that, as a document or template, this should occupy no more than a single page. It would normally contain:

Details about the benefit:

- number;

- description;

- programme or organisational objectives supported;

- other benefits to which this benefit contributes;

- impact of the benefit (for example, **sigma** Grid);

- other classifications (for example, **sigma** Value Type, Balanced Scorecard Category).

Dependencies:

- the enablers or enabler features on which the benefit depends, perhaps subdivided into: Information, Technology and Other;

- the business changes on which the benefit depends, perhaps subdivided into: Process, People and Other;

- earlier benefits on which the benefit depends;

- risks of non-achievement of benefit.

Benefit tracking information:

- the person(s)/roles accountable for the benefit;

- the person(s)/roles who will receive the benefit;

- one or more measures, with the following information for each measure:
    - description
    - how the measure is to be tracked
    - baseline value
    - target value
    - time when improvement is expected to start
    - time when target value is expected to be reached
    - to whom the measure is to be reported
    - frequency of reporting.

This information for an individual benefit would be of particular use to the person responsible for realising it (for example, the Benefit Owner).

A complete set of Benefit Profiles covering all benefits for the Programme could be regarded as the database of information relating to benefit realisation. From this core repository other information can be generated including:

- most of the information required for a Business Case (project cost and resource information may need to come from elsewhere);

- the information required for Investment Assessment Matrices (IAMs) described in Section 13.3;

- the information required for the BRP.

9.10 Avoidance of Double Counting and Double Claims

I have heard managers from large organisations say that if all their projects which had claimed headcount reductions had succeeded then there would be no staff remaining in the organisation. That there are still staff in these organisations is because either the claims are unreal or the benefits have not been realised.

A typical example of pseudo benefits is a change intended to improve productivity by 5 per cent, saving about two hours per week per person. For 2000 staff likely to be affected by the change, a full-time equivalent (FTE) saving of 100 staff can be calculated, and is probably claimed in the justification for the change. To realise this benefit, then, 100 staff must be made redundant. This is very unlikely to happen because:

- it is unlikely the removal of 100 was actually intended;

- it is impractical since the 100 staff are made up from parts (twentieths) of 2000 people.

Many double-counting problems occur because the cart is put before the horse – people with ideas for enablers such as computer systems look for benefits to justify their ideas.

When organisations start with the end in mind, then work back from this end goal, double counting of benefits (for example, headcount reduction) is much less likely to occur. Suppose the CEO of an organisation with 1000 staff believes it is possible to slim the workforce by 5 per cent (50 staff), no more and no less. He then considers a set of project proposals each of which is claiming to reduce staff numbers and selects and authorises three, which together will reduce staff numbers by 50. Once he has sanctioned these three, any subsequent proposal claiming to reduce headcount will automatically be invalid and should be rejected.

Double counting of benefits rarely applies to non-financial values as they are seldom additive, but usually occurs as a consequence of either the giving of financial values to non-financial benefits or as a result of claims never being realised.

Another extremely valuable tool, in addition to the Benefits Map, to reduce the probability of double counting or overclaiming is the Measures Dictionary (see Section 10.10)

9.11 Disbenefits

The importance of considering potential disbenefits should never be underestimated. Ignoring them can seriously damage benefit realisation. However, you should not confuse disbenefits with:

- current problems, which are intended to be fixed by the proposed change;

- costs such as increased running costs; and

- risks.

Accepting the definition of a disbenefit, given in 3.4, namely: 'an outcome of change which is perceived as negative by a stakeholder' makes it clear that the costs of change are quite different from any disbenefits which might arise as a result of the change.

In general, disbenefits are the potential negative outcomes likely to affect stakeholders, especially those who will experience a large amount of change. Disbenefits include such outcomes as: loss of status, loss of power and influence, and slower start to the enabler delivery process. Extra resource during the transition or in the subsequent Business-as-Usual (BAU) environment are sometimes treated as disbenefits (see DVLA case example in Chapter 30); however I prefer to see these recognised as costs of the programme.

Frequently, disbenefits are perceived by stakeholders as more detrimental than they actually are; their concerns can often be mitigated by spending time with them, understanding their concerns and communicating some of the positives. Spending time with stakeholders whose disbenefits outweigh their benefits, (as highlighted in a Benefit Distribution Matrix – see Section 9.4A) is vital. Overlooking their disbenefits may cause key stakeholders to become uncommitted, resisting the required changes and even refusing to cooperate. In these circumstances, risk will arise: not to the delivery of the enabler, but much more importantly, to the achievement of real benefits. A fuller consideration of risks including the relationship between disbenefits and risks is given in Chapter 16.

In practice, working back from the end goal or vision, we are identifying a sequence or route map of potential outcomes. Whether or not these outcomes are actually realised will depend on the changes that are identified and implemented. So we should look for changes that are likely to lead to the realisation of the identified benefits, and changes that will lead to the non-realisation (or minimisation) of the identified disbenefits. Section 11.2 examines some techniques for identifying changes which fulfill these conditions.

The purpose of change should always be the realisation of benefits. It is therefore worth investing time and energy in:

- **identifying a comprehensive set of benefits;**
- **classifying and validating them;**
- **creating high-quality, robust Benefits Maps;**
- **determining high priority paths;**
- **securing ownership;**
- **assessing impact on stakeholders (including disbenefits).**

Don't be deflected from keeping the main thing the main thing.

Measures

'Any man who selects a goal in life which can be fully achieved has already defined his own limitations.'

(Cavett Robert)

'The best way to predict the future is to invent it.'

(Alan Kay)

10.1   Why Measure?

We have often been asked to help organisations with benefit measurement. Responses to our asking them why they want to measure have usually been illuminating and have often influenced our response.

I have learned that many organisations want to measure in order to:

- satisfy management;

- justify a previous decision;

- tick the achievement box;

- sometimes lay blame.

To do this they focus on the measurement of financials, which may be helpful in learning lessons for future investments, but is predominantly backward looking.

I believe that most people, when they go to work, want to do a good job, they want to feel they are contributing, that they are meeting their targets and deadlines and that they are part of a team moving successfully towards the achievement of a shared vision or goal. So measurement should be helpful to everyone, especially those stakeholders who are beneficiaries of the benefits.

Satisfying this wider group of stakeholders requires the monitoring of a much broader range of metrics, including many which are non-financial – quality, service, satisfaction, speed and productivity. Monitoring is not intended to wield a big stick when targets are not met, rather it should help people to understand why, and to get back on track. This type of monitoring is much more forward looking and more clearly contributes to improving future performance – 'what you measure is what you get'.

As far as possible measurement should encourage the desired behaviours and this should be an important consideration when determining measures – see Section 10.5. Measurements should always influence decisions and lead to action (other than the wielding of the big stick); if this were more widely understood, I believe more organisations would be prepared to invest in measurement.

Earlier I likened the Benefits Map to a military campaign plan, the benefits being equivalent to positions to be captured. Continuing this analogy, measurement is the intelligence cycle. If then a particular benefit is not achieved (that is, a position is not captured) in the target timescale, this important intelligence should be passed to those responsible for later targets, and adjustments to the Change Management Strategy (campaign plan) may need to be made.

In both situations intelligence is received not only from the programme (the battlefield) but also from many other sources. Ideally all relevant intelligence should be combined and its implication assessed using the Benefits Map (campaign plan).

In summary, the overall purpose of measurement is to drive action which may include:

- determining and implementing mitigating strategies when targets have not been achieved or the environment has changed;

- encouraging the desired behaviours;

- rewarding achievement.

10.2   What are Measures and Metrics?

From any set of raw data, information can be derived from different analyses and computations of the data. In the context of monitoring and tracking benefits I will use the term 'metric' to refer to the raw data and 'measure' to refer to the computed information. So a **metric** is a recorded piece of data, often captured by a computer system – for example, details of sales made, details of calls made by phone enquirers. A **measure** is a meaningful computation derived from an analysis of the metrics, where 'meaningful' means that it is worth reporting to check progress towards the realisation of a benefit and so inform some decision making.

The simplest computation is where the measure equals the metric. Most measures will be more sophisticated than this; for example, if the metric is the recorded detail of calls to a call centre, many meaningful measures are possible from the same set of metrics including: the average response time, the median response time and the longest response time.

So the measure is the entity whose value is to be reported (for example, 'total monthly sales value') – it is not the value itself (for example, £300,000), nor the target improvement (for example, +30 per cent), nor the means of measurement or reporting (for example, quarterly financial review), nor the benefit (for example, more sales). This measure will be computed from the set of metrics – the values of the individual sales. Other measures can be computed from this same set of metrics, such as the percentage of sales which are less than £20,000 or the average sales value for a specific product. By combining with other metrics we can create combination measures such as the average annual sales per employee.

10.3   Relationship Between Benefits and Measures and Changes

In relation to a change, a benefit has been defined as 'an outcome of change perceived as positive by a stakeholder'. In relation to a measure, a benefit could be defined as 'the improvement in a measure arising from a particular programme/project'. Measures are therefore different from benefits, but there is a clear relationship between them. This can be many-to-many, one-to-many, a many-to-one or one-to-one. Unfortunately, inconveniently, this relationship is seldom the one-to-one case, as is illustrated in the following two examples.

The measure for 'increased sales of Product X', an expected benefit from Programme A, will be 'sales of Product X', which appears to be a one-to-one relationship; but Programme B also expects 'increased sales of Product X'. The measure 'sales of Product X' is the same in both cases but the benefit improvements are distinct, even though they look the same. They are distinct because they arise from different programmes and their target values may also be different. For Programme A the improvement target may be 10 per cent whereas for Programme B the improvement target may be 15 per cent. Together they should generate a 25 per cent improvement in the measure value and we have an instance of two benefits related to a single measure – a many-to-one relationship.

In a different situation, a certain change initiative was expected to 'improve staff morale'. There is probably no single measure which can adequately track such an expected improvement. So the following four measures were identified:

- a staff satisfaction rating (from a quarterly survey);

- average number of days of sickness per staff member;

- the staff attrition rate;

- the management view of staff morale.

This then is an instance of one benefit with four measures. Because these measures are not directly aligned to the wording of the benefit, some people would understandably prefer to call them 'indicators' rather than 'measures'. But since indicators will have the same attributes as measures (see Section 10.4), I cannot see any great value in making this distinction, and I shall continue to refer to them all as measures.

Now any one of the above measures might also be linked to benefits from other change initiatives or even to other benefits from the same change initiative – for example, the staff attrition rate may also be a measure for the benefit 'reduced staff turnover'. Generally I would discourage duplicate use of the same measure within the same change initiative, since it easily leads to double counting.

If we include relationships between measures and changes the situation can become more complex. For example, within a single programme we might have the same benefit being generated by two changes. The options are:

- the benefit is achieved only when both changes have occurred;

- each change separately generates an improvement in the benefit/measure value.

These situations would be represented by different map structures (see Figure 10.1) but with a single benefit in each case.

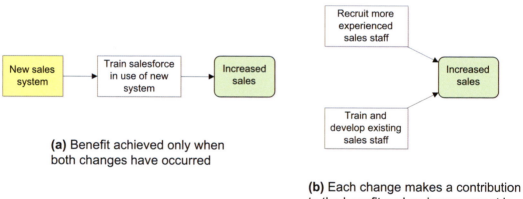

(a) Benefit achieved only when both changes have occurred

(b) Each change makes a contribution to the benefit and an improvement in the measure

Figure 10.1   Change to benefit relationships

10.4   Measure Attributes and Categories

Measures have many important attributes or related characteristics. Some relate only to the measure, irrespective of the related benefit. These include:

- unit of measure;

- the combination of metrics which define the measure (the formula);

- frequency of measurement and reporting;

- method of measurement;

- baseline value, if available;

- measure category (for example, **sigma** Value Type);

- target or predicted value, where appropriate (for example, for **sigma** Value Type *Definite and Expected* – see Section 9.4D), as indicated by predicted values in the diagram (Figure 10.2);

- improvement timescale – T1 to T3 for M1 and T2 to T4 for M2;

- Measure Monitor – person responsible for monitoring the measure;

- beneficiary of the expected improvement.

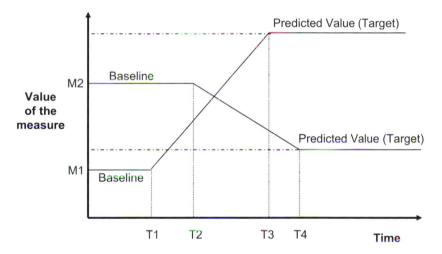

Figure 10.2   Measure predictions

Others relate to the specific benefit-measure relationship and these include:

- Benefit–measure contribution – this is the contribution to the measure target expected from the particular benefit – MV1 to MV2 for Benefit 1 and MV2 to MV3 for Benefit 2 in the diagram below (Figure 10. 3);

- Improvement timescale – T1 to T2 for Benefit 1, T2 to T3 for Benefit 2 (Figure 10.3);

- Owner or accountable person – the person accountable for the improvement in the measure related to the particular benefit, usually the Benefit Owner.

In this situation Benefit 1 may be expected from Programme A and Benefit 2 from Programme B and the measure may relate to a corporate goal and so may be a KPI, a Balanced Scorecard

Category or a Benefits Bucket. Attributing improvements in the measure to a particular programme is difficult, though it becomes easier if we can separate the improvement times (see Figure 10.3) and/or we are monitoring the achievement of all the feeder benefits.

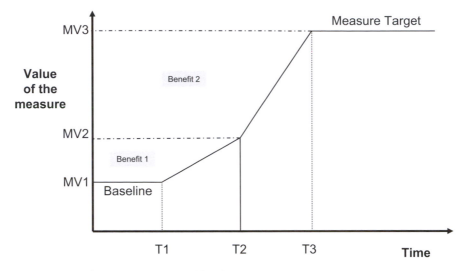

Figure 10.3   Benefit–measure contributions

10.5   Good and Bad Measures – Characteristics of a Good Measure

A good measure achieves the following:

- motivates behaviours which will contribute to success;

- meets the needs of relevant stakeholders;

- supports, or at least does not undermine, the vision or end goal.

In autumn 2004, the UK national press reported two situations where a young patient urgently needed an ambulance and suffered trauma because none was available. In each instance there was a queue of ambulances containing patients outside the local hospital's Accident & Emergency (A&E) department because the department was not ready to accept the patients.

The ambulance service had no doubt transported their patients to the hospital fast enough to achieve their targets for getting patients to hospital quickly. A&E was achieving its targets for dealing with patients within a certain time by getting the ambulance crews to hang on to their patients until they were ready to deal with them. Both the ambulance service and A&E were meeting their targets, but was this benefiting the primary stakeholder, the patient?

This is a classic case of targets which do not relate to measures which are for the benefit of the primary stakeholder, in this case the patient; the measure should have been the time taken between the 999 call and commencement of appropriate treatment. Had this more relevant measure been used, the outcomes in the above cases would have been quite different. The current drive for joined-up government may hopefully engender the necessary support and commitment, in situations such as the two described, where the most appropriate measures cross organisational boundaries.

Often, as in the above cases, the most appropriate measure is not chosen because:

- the measure would be more difficult to monitor;

- targets would be more difficult to achieve;

- political considerations come to the fore, especially where the measure would span more than one organisation;

- no one in the organisation has the vision to realise that the proposed combination of individual targets will not achieve the overall target.

A serious danger is that those metrics which are easy to monitor will be chosen. Because it is so important that measurement encourages the desired behaviour, it is worth spending time, in consultation with the stakeholders, to determine suitable measures, even though they may prove difficult to monitor. This is especially important when national targets are being set with penalties for failure to achieve.

Within the NHS one metric which was being monitored was the number of cancellations of surgical operations. This metric did not distinguish between the reasons for the cancellation or whether the rescheduled surgery was brought forward or put back. One NHS surgeon frequently brought forward his patients' operations, to their delight. Each time this happened, it registered as a cancellation of the originally scheduled time, and he was eventually penalised for the rise in cancellations – which was a result of his commitment and dedication.

In addition to the three criteria listed at the start of this section, measures should also be:

Relevant	Would change in value matter to stakeholders or predict change in subsequent measures?
In appropriate format	Would a ratio or percentage be more appropriate than an absolute value? Would a median be more appropriate than an average?
Predictable	Will it be reasonably easy for the appropriate stakeholders to determine a predicted (target) value?
Inexpensive to track	Is the measure or are the underlying metrics already tracked by the organisation or can their value be generated by a computer system?
Incorruptible	Could individuals take inappropriate action to massage the values?
Timely	Will reporting frequency be sufficient to observe trends without being onerous?
Unambiguous	Can results be displayed graphically in such a way that all stakeholders can understand them?
Consistent	Will data be collected in the same way using the same criteria over the foreseeable future?

Figure 10.4   Characteristics of good measures

10.6   Identifying Measures

The starting point for identifying measures is the Benefits Map. A change initiative may have more than one map, for example, one for each of the two or three bounding objectives. Between them, they should contain the full set of benefits, related in cause and effect chains, starting with quick wins on the left through to end benefits on the right. The complete set of end benefits, perhaps from several maps, should support the fulfilment of the vision.

I recommend, when identifying measures, working from right to left through each map, but first, two challenging but related questions must be addressed, namely:

- How many benefits should we measure?

- How many measures per benefit?

In response to the first question, many organisations consider it impractical to measure more than three to six benefits per map, or even per change initiative. This is very short-sighted – it might be better not to measure anything, saving the cost of measurement, than to measure too few benefits, which produce meaningless results and no useful action. For a fuller exploration of these issues see the analysis of a banking case example in Chapter 15.

People often say that they will just measure the key benefits; many would then select some or all of the end benefits as key; I would argue that the key benefits are those at the left-hand end, because if they are not achieved, none of the others will be. Of course once these left-hand benefits have been realised, the key benefits, by the same argument, become the next benefits to the right. Thus it can be easily seen that all benefits are key benefits.

One senior manager recently said she felt the left-hand benefits were actually more important since, in some situations, it could take several years to reach the end benefits and by then the world may have changed; meanwhile much value may have been achieved from the early (left-hand) benefits.

The number of measures per benefit is likely to vary and will depend on the wording of the benefit. Although it would be convenient if there were a single measure for each benefit, several aspects of improvement are often implied within the wording. For example, the benefit 'increased sales' suggests both an increased volume and an increased value of sales, so at least two measures are needed – the volume of sales and the value of sales. It would also be possible to split the original benefit into two benefits – increased sales volume and increased sales value and give each a single measure. Sometimes this will be the best option, but if both benefits are dependent on the same changes and prior benefits, it is neater, and will keep the maps less cluttered, if the single benefit 'increased sales' is used with the two measures – sales volume and average sales value.

In this instance another alternative would be to reword the benefit as 'increased sales revenue' which could then have a single measure 'sales revenue'. Sometimes this might be an appropriate option, but it could lose valuable information, for if both sales volume and average sales value are tracked it is easy to combine them to produce sales revenue whereas the reverse is not possible. Generally the metrics, which are likely to be recorded for each sale, would cover sufficient detail to enable the simple compilation of both average sales value and sales volume.

There are often other reasons why more than one measure may be required, including:

- meeting the needs of different stakeholders; and

- balancing the measures so that they are complementary or opposing.

Consider the benefit 'improved response to telephone enquirers seeking an insurance quotation'. There is a large number of possible measures. These include:

a)   number of rings before any response;

b)   total time before enquirer speaks to a person;

c)   time to a satisfactory conclusion of call;

d)   time taken for an enquirer to receive a quotation;

e)   quality of the dialogue;

f)   friendliness of the telephonist;

g)   length of queue;

h)   number of quotations provided per telephonist per day;

i)   number of accepted quotations per telephonist per day.

If we consider the primary stakeholder for this particular benefit, the enquirer, then the first six measures, a) to f), are of greatest interest, g) is not directly apparent to the caller though of indirect interest, since it affects a) to d), and h) and i) are of interest only to the insurance company. Although details of all calls may be monitored providing a basic set of metrics, random assessments are probably used to report e) and f) and measures derived from the metrics are used for reporting the remainder. Generally the derived measure is the average, though this is not always the best statistic, as in this situation. For example, if the average for b) drops from 5 seconds to 4.5 seconds while the maximum rises from 3 minutes to 8 minutes, is this an overall improvement for enquirers? Probably not, since the change in the average for the majority will be hardly discernable, whereas the slower response would not be missed by those experiencing it. So for b), and probably for each of a) to d), reporting maxima rather than averages is probably the most useful.

Other worthwhile statistics include the median – the middle value, when all the data is arranged in order of magnitude, and the mode – the most frequently experienced value.

Sometimes, including complementary or opposing measures can avoid distorted or unbalanced emphasis. In this example, the quality of the dialogue or the friendliness of the telephonist may be in tension with the time it takes to receive a quotation, so to balance d) either e) or f) should also be monitored.

In the above example we have considered nine possible metrics and some related measures. It is not necessary to track all nine to check that an appropriate balanced improvement has been achieved. I suggest selecting a maximum of four different measures for a single benefit, taking into consideration:

- the interests of different stakeholders, including how well the measure will generate the required behaviours;

- any need to balance opposing measures;

- ease and/or cost of measurement.

As already mentioned, the measure identification process is best undertaken using the Benefits Map, since some of the suggested measures may more appropriately be attached to different benefits. For instance, in the above example h) might more appropriately be attached to an improved productivity benefit, if such exists in the Benefits Map.

Recently **sigma** worked with a large government department; several workshops were run – one for each objective – each one creating a relevant Benefits Maps. Measures were not selected for all benefits; instead a few key benefits (mostly end benefits) were selected, the maps were put aside, and measures – often as many as six – were determined for each of these key benefits.

On taking a closer look at these measures I realised that only a few related directly to the selected key benefits – the others were measures of what would be necessary to achieve these key benefits – that is, measures of earlier benefits. Having effectively discarded the Benefits Maps, the participants were creating in their minds a virtual Benefits Map. If they had retained their Benefits Maps and identified a single measure for each benefit, the total number of measures would have been similar and the whole picture would have been far more transparent.

Measures are best identified through carefully structured and well-facilitated workshops, whose participants include the key stakeholders. Participants must be familiar with Benefits Maps and appreciate what constitutes a good measure. Measure identification is intellectually demanding and time consuming; we find three to four hours a suitable length for a workshop.

We use the Benefits Map as the framework for the workshops, working systematically from right to left seeking one or two measures for each benefit. Occasionally we end up with more than two measures, sometimes with none. It is reasonable to accept the occasional benefit with no measures, providing the benefits on either side have measures.

If a three- to four-hour workshop proves insufficient to identify suitable measures for all the benefits, it is useful to focus initially on those benefits with a high Strategy or Map Score – see Section 9.7. It is more important to check that these benefits are being achieved since they have a greater impact on subsequent benefits. They are also likely to link to a wider range of consequential benefits and so are of interest to a larger group of stakeholders. These should therefore be tackled while there is broad stakeholder representation. Low-scored benefits can be tackled later with smaller groups of stakeholders.

It may well be appropriate during this process to revise the Benefits Maps – this should be acceptable and even encouraged since the whole BRM process is iterative. Most revisions will occur in the wording of the benefits. While drilling down to more precise definitions of measures, people often realise that the wording of the benefit is vague or ambiguous and want to make it more accurate. Or a single benefit may require splitting into two benefits, or sometimes linkages require revision.

If a software tool, similar to that suggested in Chapter 29, has been used for the mapping, this tool can also be used to record the measures as they are identified and to relate them to a Measures Dictionary if one exists. A good alternative is to capture the measures in a mind-map such as the one in Figure 10.5.

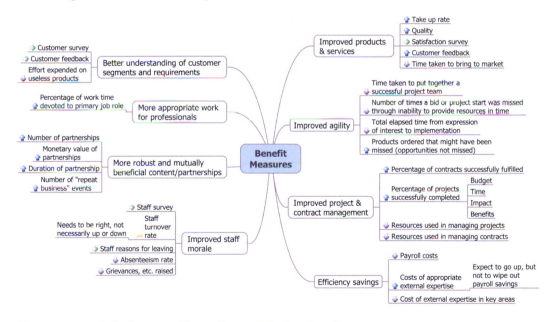

Figure 10.5   Mind-map of benefits and their related measures

10.7   Setting Targets

After measures have been identified for each benefit, baselines must be determined and improvement targets and timescales set. Essentially the information in the earlier diagram (Figure 10.2), which for convenience is repeated below (Figure 10.6), is required.

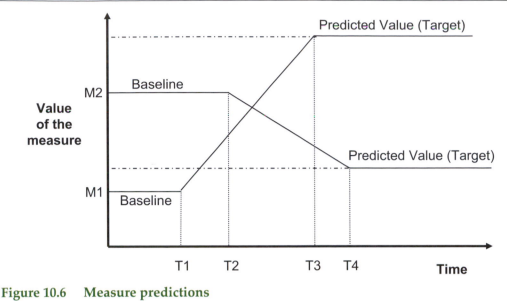

Figure 10.6   Measure predictions

If there are no baselines (which can be simply determined from the Measures Dictionary if it exists – see Section 10.10) they must be generated from measuring (see Section 10.8).

Like measures, targets should encourage desired behaviours, so it is vital to engage in participative evaluation with the relevant stakeholders, especially those who will be affected by any dependent changes, in exploring the likely consequences of proposed targets. The more widespread the application of the target, the more care is necessary in selecting and checking it, particularly in the case of national targets set by the government. Without due care and stakeholder involvement we arrive at ludicrous situations such as those outlined earlier relating to primary healthcare.

The accuracy to which targets can be set will vary depending on the measure. This variation can be categorised using the **sigma** Value Types (see Section 9.4d), where for 'definite' measures we would expect an accurate target, for 'expected' measures we would expect a target, but realise it may not be achieved fully and/or may need to be updated over time, especially if there are significant external factors which could impact the target. For 'logical' measures it is probably not possible to determine realistic targets, so it may be better not to set targets. It would still be important to track the measure, creating learning for future target setting, while avoiding the frustration of failing to achieve an unrealistic target.

If no baseline exists when targets are set (this is often the case if they are set in workshops), a percentage improvement will usually suffice. This can easily be translated into an absolute value as and when baselines are established.

With respect to timing, improvement is likely to start at some time in the future, T1 for measure M1 and then to improve steadily until the target is reached at time T3. In practice this improvement may not be steady or linear, as suggested by the diagram, but for prediction purposes this is usually the best which can be offered. Generally I suggest using a three-monthly time interval, though monthly or annually may sometimes be more appropriate.

Because of poor target setting in the past, especially by central government, there is sometimes sensitivity about the term 'target' and some organisations have chosen to replace 'target' with 'estimate' or 'predicted value'.

10.8   Measuring

When I ask groups of managers when they should start measuring, their responses invariably equate to 'as soon as you know what it is you need to measure'. I then ask whether this is what happens in their organisations and their response is always 'No!'

Measurement should start as soon as the measures have been determined, in order to:

- generate some baseline data for measures, where none exist;

- ensure that any early achievement of benefits – quick wins – is recognised and reported;

- increase the chance of it happening – if the start of measuring is delayed, it is more likely not to happen at all.

What then is the problem? I suggest the following possibilities:

- The importance of measurement has not been understood.

- People think measurement is difficult and time consuming.

- There is uncertainty as to whether improvements in the measure values can be attributed to the programme.

- Some stakeholders may not want to see the benefit realised.

- There is a common misconception that measurement should start after everything else has been done.

- No one has been appointed to undertake the measurement.

It is important to consider each of these potential hindrances to measuring.

A)   THE IMPORTANCE OF MEASUREMENT HAS NOT BEEN UNDERSTOOD

As indicated in Section 10.2, measurement of benefits is equivalent to the gathering of intelligence during a military campaign; it is unthinkable that any military commander would contemplate any military campaign without continuous intelligence gathering both from the field and from elsewhere. Strategy, tactics and the whole deployment of resources are dependent on this information. Sadly, it is still fairly common for project and programme managers to exercise their responsibilities, overseeing the acquisition and implementation of enablers and the management of business change, without any intelligence on progress towards the achievement of benefits.

The primary purpose of measurement is to influence decisions, driving and shaping future action. Delivering enablers and implementing business change without tracking and reporting benefits is comparable to shooting in the dark.

B)   PEOPLE THINK MEASUREMENT IS DIFFICULT AND TIME CONSUMING

Generally the most difficult part of measurement is the identification of suitable measures and this has been addressed in Section 10.6. Once they have been identified we first need to check whether they are actually being tracked elsewhere in the organisation. This is easily done if the organisation operates a Measures Dictionary (Section 10.10). If the required metrics are not already being tracked then it will be important to set up a measurement mechanism, including tracking frequency and a person to be responsible for measuring. This information should then be added to the Measures Dictionary if it exists.

C)   THERE IS UNCERTAINTY AS TO WHETHER IMPROVEMENTS IN THE MEASURE VALUES CAN BE ATTRIBUTED TO THE PROGRAMME

It is far more important to know that a target has been achieved than to be able to apportion precisely contributions to each of a set of projects or programmes. So measurement is vital even when attribution is difficult or impossible.

One of the best ways to attribute benefits to a programme is through the use of the Benefits Map. Usually benefits at the left-hand side of the map are more clearly a direct consequence of an integrated set of specific enablers and business changes and so for these benefits attribution is straightforward. Benefits on the far right – end benefits – are more difficult since they are susceptible to far more external influences over a much longer time period. So if only end benefits are measured there is little hope that improvements in measure values can honestly be clearly attributed to the programme. If on the other hand all benefits on the map are measured, then the knock-on effects can be seen as targets are progressively achieved.

D)   SOME STAKEHOLDERS MAY NOT WANT TO SEE THE BENEFIT REALISED

Certain stakeholders may be resistant to measuring, because they do not want the benefit to be realised – one such instance could be when the benefit is 'reduced headcount'. Situations like this are rare, but when they do occur sensitive management is needed; members of staff whose jobs are at risk should not be asked to track the benefits.

Apart from situations similar to the above, most instances arise for one or more of the following reasons:

- The stakeholders have not been involved throughout the process – in benefit identification, the construction of a Benefits Map and the determination of suitable measures and targets.

- The programme is a 'cart before the horse' programme – that is, the benefit has been created to justify a preconceived solution rather than as a step on the path to achieving of a vision.

- Measurement may expose vulnerable people, for example, those who might be held accountable for a benefit, especially if they are unconvinced that it is realisable.

In one workshop situation a sales team was reluctant to acknowledge that increased sales was a valid benefit from a programme whose main purpose was to increase sales! When I expressed surprise, they explained their concern that acknowledging the benefit would lead to them being given tougher sales targets. They had not bought in to the programme and become confident that it could enable them to sell more, without having to work twice as hard to reach the anticipated tougher targets. Once they had seen the completed Benefits Map, which they had helped to construct, they began to understand that 'increased sales' was a realistic benefit, which didn't require them to be super-human. At this point their attitude towards the programme became significantly more positive.

E) THERE IS A COMMON MISCONCEPTION THAT MEASUREMENT SHOULD START AFTER EVERYTHING ELSE HAS BEEN DONE

Although the situation is improving, organisations may even today not start to think about measurement until late in the programme life-cycle, often after the enablers have been implemented. When measurement starts so late in the life-cycle, early benefits will be missed, gaps in baseline data will not be filled and the measurement regime will not provide the early intelligence to shape and steer early changes.

In all other respects this hindrance to effective measurement is similar to my first hindrance – that is, the importance of measurement has not been understood.

F) NO ONE HAS BEEN APPOINTED TO UNDERTAKE THE MEASUREMENT

Measurement is undertaken more regularly and accurately if those undertaking it also benefit from it. So it is best to work with stakeholders who are likely to benefit from the improvement, engaging them in the benefit identification process, measure and target setting and subsequently in the ongoing monitoring and reporting. Probably a large number of people will be involved in capturing the raw metric data; so in addition to these people it is important to have a defined role for gathering and consolidating this information and calculating the values of the related measures. I shall refer to this role, which could also include responsibility for reporting the results to the various interested parties, as **Measure Monitor**.

This role could be part of our recommended Benefit Facilitation Role – see Section 6.13 – and could include responsibility for the Measures Dictionary – see Section 10.10.

10.9   Measures Dashboard – Reporting Measures

For measurement to lead to action, measures must be reported to the people who will ensure that the necessary action is taken. In one organisation I met a woman who spent all her time generating reports relating to different types of measurement. These reports were then meticulously indexed and filed; sadly no one ever saw them unless they chose to request them, which they rarely did.

Visual reporting – charts, dials, graphs and tables – is generally helpful. A set of meters of this kind, gathered on a single screen or sheet of paper, is often called a dashboard. As different models of car require different dashboards, so do different stakeholders.

Another option, which avoids overwhelming people with data, is to report by exception. If there is a good plan, action will be required only when there is a deviation from expectation. So exception reporting, which presents only those metrics which have fallen outside a specified tolerance of the relevant target, is an effective mechanism.

Sometimes the above two reporting approaches are combined. The complete set of relevant data is reported with deviations from plan highlighted using a colour code – usually green to indicate a measure is within a narrow tolerance of target, amber for values within a wider deviation from target and red for values that are way off the mark. This is often referred to as a RAG status. Some organisations use a BRAG status, where a fourth colour (blue) is used to indicate that the target has been achieved and monitoring of this measure is now complete. Applying the BRAG status to the Benefits Map gives a powerful form of dashboard reporting. In this situation blue is used for benefits which are not due to have reached their target. A set of four dashboard reports using this approach is given in Chapter 15, Figures 15.4 to 15.7.

10.10 Measures Dictionary

An organisation measures many things as part of its regular monitoring of business performance. With continuing investment in change, the number of metrics being monitored will continue to increase. This monitoring will generate baseline data for future investments likely to impact these particular metrics.

Much effort is often wasted recording and tracking metrics which are also being tracked elsewhere. This happens when person A has no knowledge of person B and what that person might be measuring.

The most practical solution is for the organisation to establish a Measures Dictionary, containing all the metrics which the organisation is measuring, each with an expanding history of actual values. If the success of a new investment is to be tracked using metrics not in the dictionary, these must be added; as metrics are recorded, baseline values for these new metrics will be determined.

So as measures are identified for a particular investment, they must be checked against the Measures Dictionary to see if they can be computed from existing metrics.

The Measures Dictionary should hold, in addition to an historic set of actual values for each measure, the predicted values or target contributions for each change initiative. So a predicted increase of 30 per cent in the measure 'monthly sales value' may be made up from the following target improvements – 5 per cent from Programme A, 15 per cent from Programme B and 10 per cent from Programme C. This central recording of targets makes it relatively easy to spot when several programmes collectively are claiming more benefits than can realistically exist.

Each measure may also be subdivided into a set of dimensions. For example, sales may have both a product and a region dimension, so we could monitor sales of product P in country C. The dictionary might also hold the names of the individuals (the Measure Monitors) responsible for the monitoring of each measure and/or the mechanisms by which the measures are computed and the underlying metrics are being tracked.

As benefits are realised and improvements are attributed to particular programmes, this information might also be held in the dictionary against the corresponding prediction or claim.

10.11 Measure Owner

A Measure Owner is the person with the overall responsibility for a measure, in particular for the planned total improvement in the measure. So the Chief Executive or Managing Director is likely to be the owner of the measure 'profit', while the Sales Director would be the owner of the measure 'sales revenue'.

The owner is not necessarily the Measure Monitor and Measure Owners are usually different from Benefit Owners. A Benefit Owner is responsible for the improvements in one or more measures relating to a specific benefit from a particular change initiative.

> **While much of the BRM process will add value when it is only partially applied, an incomplete or inappropriate set of measures could yield no value or worse, encourage inappropriate or undesirable behaviour.**

Identifying and Assessing Benefit Dependencies – Changes

'I have six honest serving men. They taught me all I know. Their names are what and why and when and how and where and who.'

(Rudyard Kipling)

'It is not necessary to change. Survival is not mandatory.'

(W Edwards Deming)

11.1 Fundamental Dependencies

Most benefits depend on some combination of earlier benefits, as indicated in the Benefits Map, and on changes. These changes are of two basic types:

- enablers

- business changes.

Where an *enabler* is defined as: 'something that can be developed/built/acquired, normally from outside the environment in which it will be embedded and where the benefits will be realised'. An enabler may be any of the PPIT types – People, Process, Information and Technology – including: information, IT systems, buildings, policies, processes and skills. An enabler is normally costed, budgeted and formally planned, usually within a project or programme.

In contrast a *business change* is: 'a change which occurs within the business/operational environment, often a new way of working or a new business state, which may utilise a new enabler'. An example of a new business state could be five depots rationalised into three. A business change, as distinct from an improvement in BAU, should be costed and managed as part of a project or programme, more often the latter.

Both types of change require activities to bring them into being, where an *activity* is 'a task or piece of work with a defined timescale and resource requirements'. For clarity when naming these activities, it is helpful to begin the name with the imperative form of a verb. For enabler activities these might be – design, create, acquire, develop, build, implement. And for business change activities these might be – investigate, develop, implement, train, appoint, establish.

We distinguish between these two types of change activity, because they are frequently funded separately and managed differently. Only too often, the business change is not adequately funded or suitably managed, and as a result many planned benefits are never realised. Although this distinction is important I will often use the more general term 'change' to cover either or both in combination.

11.2   Identifying Required Enablers and Changes

The challenge is to identify the optimum set of changes to deliver the benefits in support of the vision or end goal. We have determined why, we now need to determine the what, when, how, where and who.

These changes and related change activities might be identified through any of the following processes:

- directly from the Benefits Map, which is in effect a structured requirements process;

- a matrix-based brainstorming; or

- an alternative structured requirements process.

Choice of appropriate process will depend on the type of business environment and the nature of the likely change; however, the process which we most frequently use is the Benefits Map.

Working from the Benefits Map, we start this time from the left-hand end, identifying and adding to the diagram the enablers and changes needed in order to achieve the left-hand benefits. On the assumption that these benefits will then be achieved at some future time, we move to the right of these benefits and consider each path in turn, identifying and adding further changes and enablers, as required.

The process should be continued, working left to right, until the process is complete. In doing this you should not expect to identify enablers and changes on every path. For example, if a benefit, 'fewer errors' is linked to a benefit 'fewer complaints', no enabler or change may be required between them, though there could be three months difference between achievement of their respective targets.

An example of a completed map is given in Figure 11.1.

This map is called a **Benefit Dependency Map (BDM)**, since it contains not only the map of expected benefits, but it also shows the enablers and changes on which the benefits

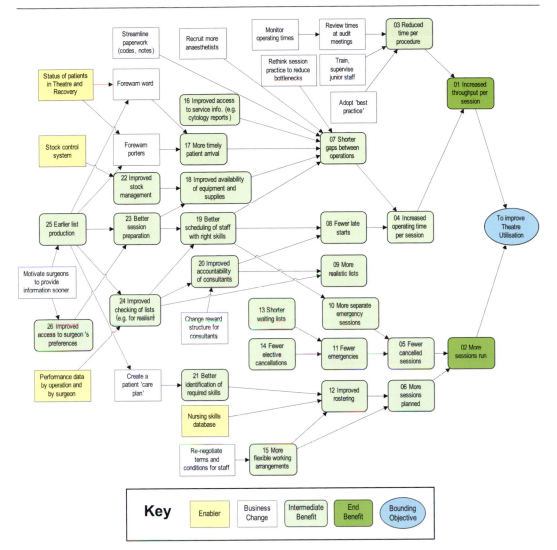

Figure 11.1   BDM for objective: 'To improve theatre utilisation'

depend. Figure 4.13 in Section 4.7 is an earlier example of a BDM for the objective 'to reduce carbon footprint'. A BDM is a good initial component of the Blueprint – the document which defines the future business state and the transition path to it.

You will note that many paths contain no enablers or changes. This may mean that the enabler or change has not yet been identified; it is more likely that no intermediate action is needed, for example, moving from 'shorter waiting lists' to 'fewer emergencies' (lower middle part of map), may not require any additional change, though there may be a time lag. If, in such a situation, there was no significant timing difference and no other links into Benefit 11, it would probably be worth combining benefits 13 and 11 into a single benefit.

Note that some changes are dependent on the realisation of an earlier benefit (for example, the change 'forewarn porters' is dependent on benefit 25) while most are not. Benefit 12 ('improved rostering') is dependent on the enabler ('nursing skills database') and on benefits 21 ('better identification of required skills') and 15 ('more flexible working arrangements'). If residual scores had been calculated for all the benefits, the 'nursing skills database' would represent the extra input required related to the non-zero residual score for benefit 12.

An alternative method for identifying required changes is to list the identified benefits and disbenefits down the left-hand side of a matrix. Then by considering a row at a time, brainstorm the changes required to achieve each benefit or to mitigate the impact of each disbenefit. Then add these changes along the top of the matrix and mark the relevant cells. In a workshop environment we usually distinguish between enablers and business changes by the colours of the cards we use; yellow and white respectively (from the fried egg analogy). An example of such a matrix, relating to a document management programme for a pharmaceutical company, is given below in Figure 11.2. In this instance all but one of the changes are business changes rather than enablers.

	Understand RA requirments	Develop good project managers	Share understanding of dossier processes	Secure sufficient resources	Promote understanding of 'big picture'	Reward willingness to work as a team	Establish a mentoring function	Motivate staff to capture required information	Recruit and develop the right people	User-friendly documentation of processes
Improved (Dossier) project planning	▨	▨						▨		
Improved Doc.Mgt. processes & responsibilities			▥	▨		▨				
Reduced personal input						▨				
Improved cross department communication		▨			▨	▨				
Improved quality of first draft study report	▨					▨				
Better sharing of regulatory Q&As						▨				
Better project repping					▨	▨				
Reduced document review cycle time						▨				▥
Fewer review cycles										▥
Better regulatory repsonse team working	▨					▨			▨	
Improved navigation and format quality			▥							

Figure 11.2   Benefits and the changes on which they depend

The marked cells can subsequently be annotated or colour coded, as in the diagram, to indicate who has responsibility for the particular change. Note that this set of benefits is dependent on a higher proportion of business changes than enablers (nine compared to one) which is not at all uncharacteristic.

Although the two processes are mechanistically different, the results should be similar or at least consistent. Ideally the set of changes should be the same and cell marking should cover at least all the direct map relationships between changes and benefits. A column in the matrix with a large number of marked cells should relate to a change towards the left-hand end of the Benefits Map, since left-hand end changes are likely ultimately to contribute to most of the changes to their right.

Of the two processes, I prefer the BDM, since relationships are easy to see and there is a clear distinction between direct and indirect relationships. But the BDM can become very busy; the matrix approach gives a tidier representation and gives equal consideration to both benefits and disbenefits, something which is not so easy to do within the Benefits Map.

Workshops are recommended for applying either or both of the above techniques.

Sometimes the enabler is a given, as illustrated in the example from a pharmaceutical company (Figure 11.3). Even in this situation a map is still vital in order to show how the enabler will ultimately deliver the end goal and in the course of creating this route map the required business changes and any additional enablers will be determined.

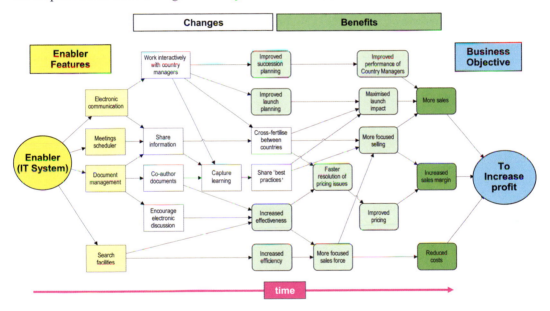

Figure 11.3   A BDM for a pharmaceutical company where the enabler was a given

Sometimes feedback loops are identified creating circular paths (dotted path in Figure 11.4) or the equivalent – the same benefit appears at both ends of the map.

'Improved staff morale' is one benefit which frequently appears at both ends of a map – it is important to realise this benefit in order for other benefits to be achieved, and once most benefits are achieved staff morale will improve. In these situations I recommend the benefit is included only once in a Benefits Map, where it is first needed (that is, towards the left-hand end), and that feedback loops are not included.

It is not possible to score benefits from weighted paths if circular paths exist.

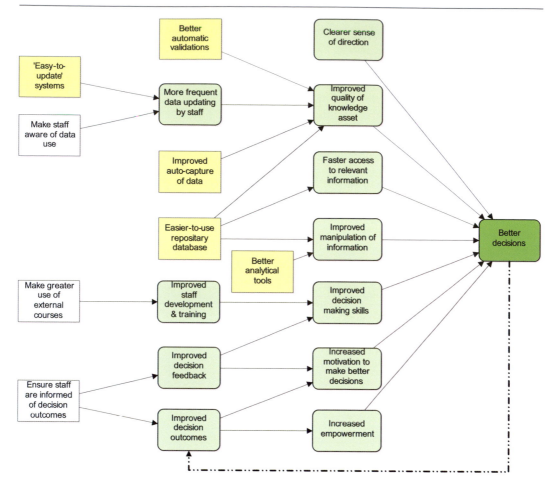

Figure 11.4   BDM with circular loop

11.3   Importance of the Benefit Dependency Map

A programme is likely to have two to four bounding objectives (Sections 8.6 and 8.7), and for each bounding objective there is likely to be a BDM, though in some circumstances a BDM may cover more than one objective. The resulting set of BDMs represents a fundamental description of the programme. These maps sit at the centre of the programme and feed many of the other required documents, such as:

- Blueprint – in fact the maps are themselves a form of Blueprint, though more detail will be required.

- Benefit Profiles – about 80 per cent of their content can generally be acquired from the workshop process that also generates the BDMs.

- Risk Register – particularly for the risks of not realising the benefits.

- Stakeholder Profiles – summarising all the impacts for each individual stakeholder or stakeholder group.

- Change Action Plan – including the owners, timescales and costs for each of the required changes. This will help formulate the required projects.

- Benefit Realisation Plan (BRP).

- Business Case.

This relationship is illustrated in Figure 11.5.

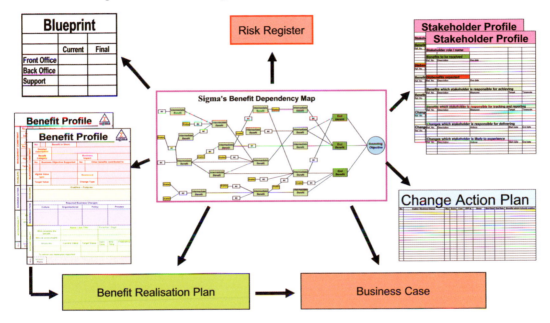

Figure 11.5   The centrality of the BDM

The direct value of a BDM is that it:

- provides the framework for identifying the required enablers and changes;

- identifies the sequence in which they should be implemented;

- facilitates choosing between solution options by weighting the paths of the BDM and scoring the benefits and if necessary the potential enablers and business changes;

- helps in grouping the prioritised enablers and changes into meaningful chunks of work such as projects;

- informs the Stakeholder Profile for each significant stakeholder group – for template see Figure 24.4;

- provides a framework for monitoring all intermediate milestones – for enablers, changes and benefits.

11.4   Processing the Identified Changes

Using either of the workshop processes described in Section 11.2, a large number of changes may have been identified; they may be fairly high level and the distinction between enablers and business changes may be inaccurate. Before deciding which are to be undertaken and including them in plans, several checks and refinements are required. The process is likely to be iterative to make best use of resources. For instance, there is little point in specifying a change down to the smallest detail if it might later be dropped.

The basic steps for this further analysis are listed below, in a suggested chronological sequence:

- categorise the changes;

- identify and consolidate duplicates;

- determine a score for each change, based on map weightings;

- decide which changes are actionable – that is, have significant scores and are not already being delivered by another change initiative;

- specify actionable changes in greater details, using maps and experienced focus groups;

- group actionable changes where there is some synergy;

- determine the stakeholders responsible (owners) for each change;

- determine the resource requirements and likely costs for each change.

The first step is to identify and consolidate any duplicates within the scope of the investment being considered. If a large number (for example, 100+) of changes have been identified for the programme or proposed investment, group them first in suitable change categories, such as those listed below; you can then scan much shorter lists looking for likely duplicates. Once candidate duplicates are identified, consider the benefits which they are enabling (possibly from more than one map) in order to ensure that it makes sense to consolidate them into a single change.

Once duplicates have been consolidated, score the changes before attempting to cost them. Obtain the scores by weighting each of the paths for all the BDMs of the programme, and then assigning a score (usually 1000) to the vision or end objective. It is possible to compute a score for each of the entities, benefits and changes by working right to left as described in Section 9.7. This score, based on the integrated set of maps for the programme, is called the Strategy Score, as distinct from the Map Score, which is calculated in a similar way but based on a single map. Using this scoring system, you can identify high-scoring entities and high-scoring paths, so that, with limited resources, you can give priority to those with high scores.

Changes should be specified in sufficient detail to enable the determination of resource and timing requirements and costs, while considering all the benefits, from all the programme maps, which the change supports.

Suppose the enabler, a new car, appears on three Benefits Maps. On one map it contributes to 'fewer serious accidents', on another to 'lower running costs' and on another to 'improved image'. When determining solution options for this enabler, all three benefits must be considered.

Once the changes are specified in greater detail, check them against existing change initiatives to see whether they already exist in someone else's plan. If they are new and of sufficient importance, based on their score, they become 'actionable' and need to be assigned to groups with similar characteristics, taking into consideration the earlier grouping by change category.

The steps of specification and grouping require, in addition to the maps, the expertise of both those who will experience the change and of those who will receive its consequent benefits. This brainstorming activity is therefore best undertaken in small workshops or focus groups.

Small changes, which impact only stakeholders from within a single business unit, might best be addressed as part of good management practice, improving the BAU situation. But if such work packages are required to fulfil the vision, they should also remain under the oversight of the Programme Manager.

The consolidated changes which are to be actioned can be listed in a Change Action Plan – a suggested template is given in Figure 11.6.

For these actionable changes, high-level cost estimates will be needed and should be determined in conjunction with the stakeholders who will be responsible for the changes. To support this activity and to improve the balance between stakeholder impacts and workloads, a change-stakeholder matrix could be constructed. For examples see Figure 24.4 in Section 24.3. This information should also appear in the Stakeholder Profile for the relevant stakeholder group – see Figure 24.3.

Template for actioning and costing Enablers and Business Changes

No.	Enabler / Business Change	Map	Score	Cost	PPPId.	Owner	Start Date	End Date	Benefits which it directly enables

Figure 11.6   Template for Change-Action Plan

11.5   Categorising and Consolidating the Changes

Before packaging changes into cohesive groups and then assigning them to specific delivery mechanisms, it is helpful to categorise the changes. The two main reasons for doing this are:

- It can simplify the identification of duplicate changes – this works in a similar way to that suggested for identifying benefit duplicates (see Section 9.4B).

- It can help to determine whether changes fall within the scope of a particular delivery mechanism.

Categorisation may cover several objectives and so possibly several Benefits Maps.

A useful categorisation for enablers is:

- people

- process

- information

- technology.

You could sub-divide each of these, especially when looking for duplicates, among several hundred enablers.

A useful categorisation for business changes is:

- culture

- strategies/policies

- processes

- practices/procedures.

You could sub-divide each of these, especially when looking for duplicates, among several hundred changes. A particular change may extend over several objectives and therefore several Benefits Maps.

Once the changes and enablers have been categorised, examine each group in turn to look for consolidation opportunities. Exact duplicates should obviously be consolidated into a single entity; it may also be sensible to consolidate two different but similar entities. For example, the two enablers:

- a database containing the training courses staff have attended, the skills they possess and a summary of career history; and

- a database containing job grade, skills summary, current job and likely release date for each member of staff;

have considerable overlap and so could be merged into a single enabler.

The two business changes:

- train staff to become much more customer focused; and

- train staff to exploit the potential of the new customer database

affect the same stakeholder group and share similar end goals, and so might be combined into a single training course.

11.6   Prioritising the Changes

It is worth prioritising or scoring the changes before spending significant time and effort in specifying them in greater detail and costing them. Both change identification processes described above can assist with prioritisation.

You could use the Benefit-Change Matrix to prioritise changes by giving highest priority to the changes whose columns contain the most marked cells – because the change whose columns contain a large number of marked cells is likely to equate to a change from the left-hand side of the Benefits Map, which would normally be implemented earlier than changes to the right of the map. The matrix also highlights changes which support benefits which contribute to a large number of other benefits. Its value ends here because it assumes that all links have equal importance when in fact they do not.

I prefer to approach prioritisation by creating the BDM from a weighted and scored Benefits Map, as described in Section 4.6 Figure 4.13 and in Section 9.7 Figure 9.16. Another example is given in Figure 11.7.

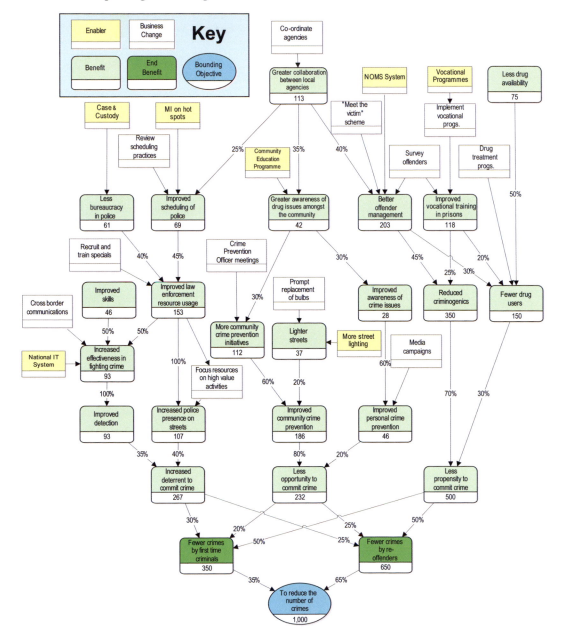

Figure 11.7   A BDM for objective: 'To reduce crime' with weighted paths and benefit scores

It can sometimes be helpful to continue weighting the paths back to the enablers and changes and then to compute scores for these entities as well as for the benefits, as illustrated in the generic map in Figure 11.8.

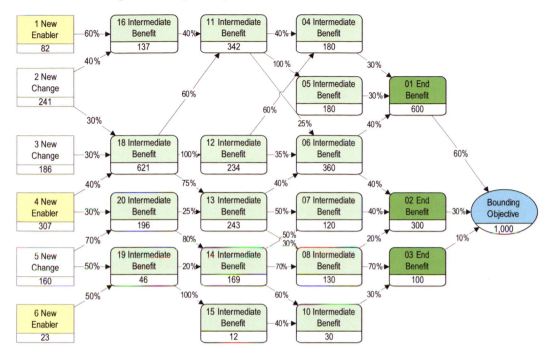

Figure 11.8   A generic BDM showing the impact of weighted paths and scored entities

If the right-most score represents the budget for this bounding objective (normally computed by entering the programme budget into the weighted Strategy Map), then the computed enabler and change scores would be the notional budgets for implementing these changes. So in Figure 11.8 if the unit is £1000 this would give a notional budget of £23,000 for new enabler 6. So if this enabler only costs £6000 its implementation becomes a 'no brainer' whereas if it cost £150,000 there should be serious questions as to whether it is worth implementing, relative to other investment options.

11.7   Specifying the Changes

Once you have a set of unique changes, which have been correctly tagged as enabler or business change and appropriately categorised, you will need to specify them in much greater detail. For enablers the detail must be sufficient to create an Invitation to Tender (ITT), irrespective of whether the intention is to acquire internally or externally. For business changes the detail should enable relevant stakeholders to check feasibility and identify any associated risks, including potential resistance.

Update the Blueprint with this detail, showing how the enablers integrate with the business changes. Then check this new working model with stakeholders to consider practicalities and especially to ascertain whether the expected direct benefits are still realistic.

When generating a detailed specification of a change, always work from the BDM, since this provides context and understanding of what may be a high-level view of the requirements. Without this context, the change specification may be insufficient to generate the benefits or the requirements may be over-specified, resulting in unnecessary extra cost. If as a result of consolidation the change appears in more than one BDM then the specification must be determined and checked against each map.

One very large programme invested a huge amount of effort in constructing a dozen detailed BDMs. Each one subsequently underwent an independent review process. In all, several hundred required changes were identified.

The desire to realise benefits, and the time and energy devoted to the mapping process, were impressive. Then in view of a perceived critical deadline and the large number of changes to be considered, the changes were copied from the BDMs, listed and grouped. The subsequent more detailed specification and related costing were then largely undertaken with little or no further reference to the BDMs.

Undertaking this further analysis without using the BDMs brings into question the quality of the change specifications; checking that the expected benefits are still realistic becomes difficult and one of the most valuable mechanisms for prioritising the changes is lost.

11.8   Matching and Costing the Required New Changes

The next step is to match requirements against existing or planned change initiatives, an activity which often proves difficult. Organisations rarely hold a register of changes in progress at any level of detail, let alone the level required for this matching.

It would be interesting to know how much time and effort is wasted by organisations in duplication or reinvention of the wheel. In addition to the immediate waste of money there may be knock-on negative financial effects for years to come. For example, I have encountered organisations which run over a dozen payroll systems and an even greater number of different accounting systems. A change register, along similar lines to the recommended Measures Dictionary, would pay handsome dividends in most companies.

If a change, necessary to a particular programme, has already been built into the plans of another project or programme, it is important to check the details, including planned completion dates. This dependency should, if possible, be registered with both programmes.

Finally the changes must be costed provisionally, prior to a formal tender process. In situations where costing is likely to be expensive, it may be better to consider prioritisation first (Section 11.6), and then concentrate only on the high-priority paths and the 'no brainer' enablers and changes.

11.9   Procuring Enablers and Services

Procuring enablers and related services requires:

- precise definition of requirements – these should be 'fit for purpose' without frills which are unnecessary for the realisation of the benefits;

- the issuing of ITTs or Request for Proposals (RFPs) based on these requirements, for external (or possibly internal) procurement;

- use of benefits when comparing tenders, especially when assessing any features offered over and above the requirements;

- consideration of benefits when introducing any penalty clauses in the contracts for procurement.

To reinforce the focus on benefit realisation, it is helpful to link payments to suppliers with the realisation of benefits; however, this is not straightforward as the realisation of most benefits is dependent on business changes which are rarely under the control of the supplier.

Identify benefit dependencies by using BDMs to:

- **determine the required changes and so ensure they are benefit driven;**
- **prioritise the changes and so optimise the use of limited resources;**
- **check proposed changes are 'fit for purpose' (necessary and sufficient);**
- **sequence the implementation of the changes;**
- **engage those responsible for change.**

In so doing, you will know – what, why, when, how, where and who – and be on a reliable pathway to success.

Structuring Change Delivery

'We shrink from change; yet is there anything that can come into being without it?'

(Marcus Aurelius)

'There is nothing wrong with change, if it is in the right direction.'
(Sir Winston Churchill)

12.1 Why and When do We Need a Formal Change Mechanism?

The mechanism for managing change will depend on the characteristics of the change, on the sourcing of resources and funding, and the range of stakeholders impacted. A collection of change delivery mechanisms with their respective attributes was described and discussed in Chapter 5.

If a change and its consequential benefits lie completely within a business unit and the unit is prepared to fund the change, it is probably best addressed internally, as part of good management practice. If however the complete set of changes is characterised by one or more of the following:

- is significant or even radical;

- affects multiple stakeholders, in terms of benefits, disbenefits and or change;

- requires major internal resources;

- requires substantial investment in procurement;

- is likely to be spread over several years;

then it is almost certainly best managed using a formal structure such as a project or a programme.

Change delivery mechanisms depend on the characteristics of the required changes, so establishing and resourcing a delivery mechanism is best undertaken at the start of Phase 3, after the vision and objectives are agreed, some benefits have been identified, and the nature and size of the required changes is understood. I prefer this starting point, which is later than that adopted by many organisations, for several reasons:

- Potential change initiatives are most often thrown out at either the first or second review; early establishment of a programme structure which may not be required is wasteful and may be difficult to disband.

- The calibre of the programme manager should depend on the characteristics of the programme (for example, a strategic programme demands a high calibre entrepreneurial style of management, a support programme requires a more caretaking style).

- The organisational structure should depend on the objectives and scope of the programme, including the breadth and complexity of the required changes.

In one programme the organisational structure had been established, and roles filled, before the objectives were clearly understood and owned. On examination it became clear that the programme should have been structured differently, but changing at that stage was politically difficult. Better to work through some of the fundamentals of the change before putting in place a structure which is difficult to alter.

Projects or programmes are often set up at an earlier stage, to ensure the provision of a resource to undertake the work of Phases 1 and 2. This resource is already available in an organisation which has established the recommended Benefit Facilitator role. Postholders can facilitate the necessary workshops and analysis of the first two phases. If the role has been properly set up, the occupants are less likely to have preconceived ideas about a solution than project or programme managers, and they will not have vested interests in the idea progressing into a fully fledged programme.

12.2　Projects and Programmes

Since a benefit is an outcome of change which is perceived as positive by a stakeholder, it is dependent on the 'change'.

Changes fall into two main categories:

- the implementation of new capabilities – frequently information and technology capabilities but also new buildings or a new organisational structure – generally called enablers;

- business changes – generally these are process related and/or people related, including changes in behaviour and attitude which impact working practices, communication and decision making.

So each benefit is dependent on some combination of enablers (Es), business changes (BCs) and earlier benefits (Bs) as illustrated in Figure 12.1.

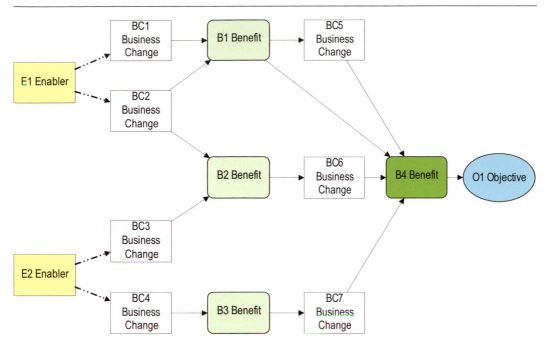

Figure 12.1   A simple BDM for a programme

There is a left to right flow over time. Dotted lines imply sequence and the unbroken lines indicate both sequence and cause and effect. B4 is the ultimate end benefit, which is the equivalent in benefit speak of the objective O1, and B1, B2 and B3 are other essential intermediate benefits, which will be realised sooner and on which B4 depends.

This BDM is a critical tool for benefit realisation as it maps the route to the achievement of the end benefit B4. The diagram illustrates why it is difficult and perhaps inappropriate to separate accountability for benefits from accountability for enablers and changes. Certainly the investment sponsor or SRO should be accountable for the whole.

The challenge is to find an effective way to share or devolve this overall accountability. It is possible to create individual accountability for a single benefit or a group of benefits. In the illustration the person accountable for B1 would need to direct/manage/oversee those responsible for managing the acquisition of enabler E1, the implementation of business changes BC1 and BC2, and for tracking benefit B1. Once B1 is achieved the person responsible for B4 would need to ensure that BC5 was properly managed.

Continuing with the illustration, the acquisition/development and subsequent implementation of E1 and E2 could be managed as separate projects – P1 and P2 say (see Figure 12.2). This leaves open the question as to how and where the change is managed and whether the benefits can be related to the individual projects P1 and P2.

BC1, BC2 and BC5 could all be managed as part of P1 and BC3, BC4 and BC7 as part of P2. B1 is a consequence of P1 so could be claimed as a benefit of P1. Similarly B3 could

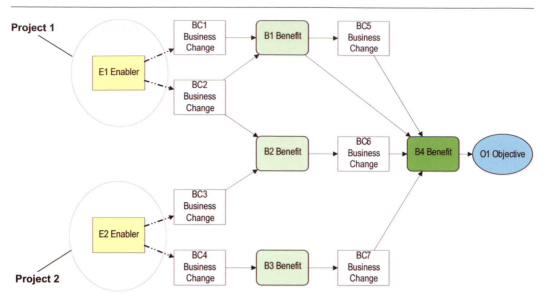

Figure 12.2   Programme structure with two enabler projects

be claimed as a benefit of P2. B2, B4 and BC6 are not exclusively within P1 or P2 which demonstrates the need for a programme which will embrace projects P1 and P2. B2 and B4 become programme benefits and BC6 a programme change.

This diagram also points up one of the tensions inherent in programme management. The owner of B1 needs influence over the managers of BC1 and BC2, the owner of B1 needs influence over the managers of BC2 and BC3: success for the whole will depend on effective resolution of any competition arising from such multiple dependencies. The implications for programme management hierarchies/structures can be highly significant, though openly acknowledging the tensions, for example in a diagram, goes a long way towards making them manageable rather than role threatening.

In this situation the Programme Director/Manager would share the sponsor's overall accountability for all the enablers, changes and benefits. Furthermore, in order to create the most effective focus, the programme should be regarded as aiming to deliver the objective O1 and end benefit B4. Ideally its name should reflect this – for example, PIST (Programme to Increase Sales by Ten per cent), rather than SAD (Sales Activity Database) which puts the focus on the enabler.

With the programme defined in this way it is possible for projects P1 and P2 to deliver simply the enablers E1 and E2 and for all the business changes to be managed at programme level. This distribution of responsibilities usually gives optimum utilisation of available skills.

An alternative programme structure where there are two broader-based projects is illustrated in Figure 12.3.

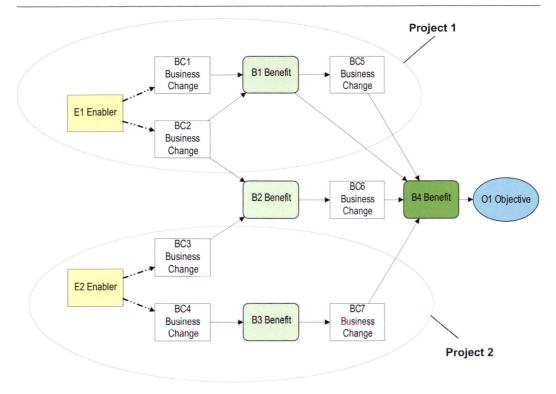

Figure 12.3   Programme structure with two broader-based projects

The potential disadvantages of this structure are: the programme could require three business change managers which is a poor use of a scarce resource, and the affected stakeholders may find themselves dealing with three people rather than one.

12.3   Establishing a Programme

Although several delivery mechanisms were described in Chapter 5, the mechanism which best exploits the potential of BRM is the Vision Programme, closely followed by the Business Project. Our focus will therefore be on the Vision Programme,[1] from here on referred to as the programme, which will be considered in the context of large or major change.

Senior-level commitment is vital in establishing the programme, so the overall sponsor and the Sponsoring Group (who set or embrace the vision, and own the outputs from Phases 1 and 2) should be formally established, as SRO and Programme Board respectively. The SRO is likely to have been involved, perhaps informally, in Phases 1 and 2, and may have set the vision or at least supported and promoted the idea.

---

1   In a similar way MSP delivers greatest value when applied to a Vision-led Programme (MSP 2007 pages 6–7).

Several of the roles described in Chapter 6 now need to be established. The SRO will champion the vision and have ultimate accountability and personal responsibility for its successful achievement, in particular the realisation of the benefits. They should have the required authority and experience, credibility with senior colleagues, and preferably come from the stakeholder group who will receive the highest proportion of benefits. This extremely important role requires serious time commitment; we do not recommend that anyone should be SRO for more than one or two significant programmes at once.

The Programme Board, chaired by the SRO, should include senior representatives of the primary stakeholders, who should own the vision for the programme, ensure provision of the necessary resources (especially the contribution from their own business areas), and provide leadership and direction particularly in the area of business change.

In addition to the SRO and Programme Board, a Programme Director/Manager must be appointed. The purpose of this role is to manage actively, on behalf of the SRO, the integration of capability delivery and business change in such a way as to ensure the achievement of the planned benefits. Very large programmes will benefit from appointing both a Programme Manager and a Programme Director.

The Programme Director reports to the SRO and Programme Board and should normally be an ex officio member. Those responsible for implementing capabilities (generally Project Managers) and those responsible for leading and coordinating change (the Business Change Manager) would normally report to the Programme Director/Manager.

The Programme Director will direct the programme within the strategy, plan and budget set by the sanctioning body under guidelines agreed by the Programme Board. The Programme Manager will manage the Programme Team and (directly or indirectly) all suppliers of enablers/capabilities, and will coordinate and monitor the business changes required in the affected business units. The Programme Manager, on behalf of the SRO, should be ultimately accountable for the realisation of benefits.

Experienced programme managers and directors who also understand the business and have credibility and influence with top management do not 'grow on trees'. Some organisations hire experienced programme managers, hoping they will quickly acquire credibility and an understanding of the business; other organisations take experienced business managers and train them in programme management. Whichever route is taken, candidates need an understanding of BRM which goes beyond simply knowing it is important. To address this need, some organisations set up one-day master classes in BRM for SROs and longer events for Programme and Project Managers. Appointing these people no earlier than the start of Phase 3 optimises the use of this scarce resource.

12.4   Programme Structure

A programme's structure and organisation will vary, depending on its size, complexity, likely duration and the nature of the business change; there are some important principles common to all programmes:

- A programme normally involves the creation or acquisition of enablers which, through business change, must be embedded within the culture and practices of the organisation, in order to generate benefits, in support of the vision or end goal.

- Creation or acquisition of the enablers are often managed as separate projects.

- Business change is a critical activity which needs careful management; as it usually spans several projects it is more appropriately handled at programme rather than project level.

- Designing the new business model, the Blueprint, integrating enablers and business changes, is also a critical activity.

- Benefit realisation is closely linked to business change and is generally dependent on more than one project, and so it should be managed at programme level.

- Stakeholders must be involved in identifying and owning benefits and in shaping and implementing the Blueprint, so stakeholder engagement is a key programme activity.

Based on these principles the diagram in Figure 12.4 illustrates a useful generic model.

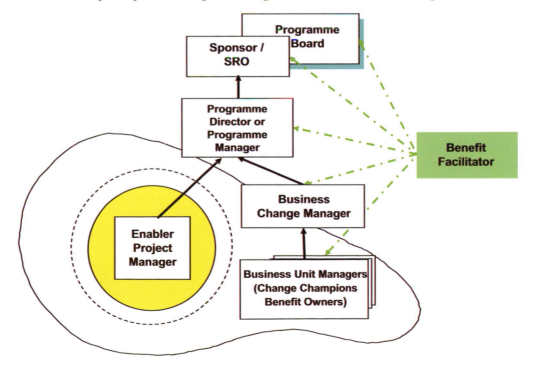

Figure 12.4   A generic programme structure

Many Benefit Owners will reside within, and may be managers of, the business units; these managers are crucial to the success of the programme. In addition to owning the local responsibility for benefits, they are likely also to be responsible for the dependent business change, thus representing an important part of the programme structure (this is the reason why they are included in the above diagram). If, as in many instances, business change is a large part of the programme, it will require coordination. This is the role of the Business Change Manager (also known as BCM), who will also ensure that the change happens.

Some programme structures place the Business Change Manager at the same level as the Programme Manager, reporting directly to the Programme Director if there is one, or directly to the Sponsor or SRO. Sharing the major responsibility for programme success between two people makes it too easy to 'pass the buck'. It also doubles the number of people who report to the SRO, who often (contrary to good practice) has SRO accountability for five or six programmes, in addition to their day job. The only situation in which I see advantage in having the Business Change Manager report directly to the SRO is one in which significant business change is required outside the control and sphere of influence of the Programme Manager. In this case the SRO must influence his or her peers and sometimes his or her superiors on behalf of the Business Change Manager.

In line with the above model (Figure 12.4), I have seen effective structures (see Figure 12.5), employed in some very large programmes, based around the following four workstreams:

- a programme management workstream which coordinates the other three streams, but has specific responsibility for stakeholder engagement and benefit realisation;

- an architecture workstream which creates and maintains the Blueprint;

- an enabler workstream which oversees the projects responsible for procuring the enablers and any related services, and for implementing them;

- a business change workstream which ensures that the required business changes are implemented in the various operational units, sometimes well outside the control of the programme.

The roles of Portfolio Office and Benefit Facilitator should sit outside the programme so that they can be more objective and may be shared by several programmes., In very large programmes, where sometimes there is a Programme Office within the programme, it is important that there is good communication between Programme and Portfolio Offices. Appointing a Programme Director in addition to a Programme Manager is probably relevant only for exceptionally large programmes.

There may be important related activities outside the scope of the above, but on which the above depend – new policies, or even new legislation. These might be managed in a separate workstream or be included in the programme management workstream.

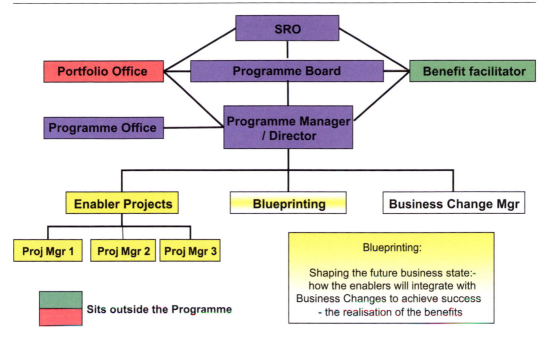

Figure 12.5   Generic programme structure for a large programme

12.5 Programme Support

Most programmes (and large projects) are likely to need administrative and process support. This is normally provided by a Programme/Project Support Office (PSO), a Programme Management Office (PMO) or a Portfolio Management Office. The new generic term for this office is a P3O.[2] For an organisation this might be a single office, though it could be a hierarchy of offices – portfolio, programme, project.

If the office is exclusive to a single programme, its responsibilities are likely to cover much of the programme administration, including:

- scheduling of meetings;

- preparations for Programme Boards and any other review meetings;

- maintaining the Issues Log and Risk Register;

- administering any BRM software (see Chapter 29);

- maintaining the programme plan and monitoring performance against it;

- benefit tracking and reporting prior to programme closure;

2   See P3O Portfolio, Programme and Project Offices published by TSO.

and is best referred to as a Programme Support Office (PSO) If, however, the office is a permanent corporate unit supporting all programmes, the services it provides could include:

- guidance on programme and project processes and standards;

- custodianship of the Measures Dictionary;

- administration of any BRM software (see Chapter 29);

- consolidation of the (initial and ongoing) results from benefit tracking;

and it is then best referred to as a Programme Management Office (PMO) In this scenario, the Benefit Facilitator role could sit within the PMO. If this office is also supporting the Portfolio Board a better title might be the Portfolio Office.

12.6   Initiating Projects

Although the majority of programme projects are likely to be initiated fairly early in the programme life-cycle, they can be added at any stage. Projects are usually the delivery mechanisms for creating or acquiring enablers; the related business changes will be managed centrally at programme level. However, for projects initiated late in the life-cycle (sometimes as a result of poor initial planning), it may be sensible to include the business change within the project.

My work for one organisation required frequent use of meeting rooms of varying sizes. As the organisation had recently completed a programme to create a modern, cohesive and efficient working environment for staff, in a new purpose-built building, this should not have been a problem. The building included a large complex of meeting rooms of varying sizes, and dates for my meetings were known six weeks in advance. However, no rooms were available for most of these meetings; so rooms were frequently hired elsewhere and some two-day events had to be split between two different buildings.

Had the programme underestimated the demand and had the new offices built with insufficient meeting facilities? Not at all. Investigation uncovered the fact that the majority of meeting rooms were empty on most days, including on those days when external facilities were hired for my meetings. Staff were block-booking rooms well into the future, in case they were required, but were either not using them or were using large rooms for small meetings.

The programme had failed to provide policies and guidance on the use of rooms, and to put in place the necessary procedures and systems. Addressing the problem at this late stage in the programme life-cycle probably required the initiation of a new small project, incorporating enablers, such as policies and systems, and business change to embed them in the working practices of the organisation.

12.7   Programme Closure

One organisation with which **sigma** worked had several large programmes which simply existed, each with no clear beginning and no planned end. It is important not only to commission and establish a programme, but also to close it formally; yet deciding when to close a programme is not trivial.

The realisation of programme benefits is likely to continue beyond the point when most programme activity is complete. Closure of the programme at this point and before significant benefits have been realised is perhaps premature, even though benefit tracking and reporting may continue after closure. It is certainly essential that all planned business change has been implemented, and a benefit tracking and reporting regime established and tested before closure.

In the programme involving a new office block, described in the previous section, the programme was initially regarded as complete once all the staff were in the new building. Shortly afterwards benefit reporting ceased. At that stage, not only were the new facilities not being used appropriately, but vacated old buildings had not been sold or re-let. We wondered where accountability for benefits resided.

Don't shrink from change but rather adopt a programme/project structure which will move change in the right direction – towards the achievement of the vision. Don't close the programme too soon – remember it is not the end; benefit tracking must continue.

'What the caterpillar calls the end, the rest of the world calls a butterfly.'
(Lao Tsu)

13

Valuing, Assessing and Optimising the Whole Investment

'People hear what they see.'

(Bobby Darin)

'A ruffled mind make a restless pillow.'

(Charlotte Brontë)

13.1 The Power of the Visual

Quality communication is a Critical Success Factor (CSF) for benefit realisation. Transparency, assumptions made explicit, minimal risk of ambiguity – all are vital. Because language alone is open to a wider range of interpretation, and important messages can often be missed in pages of text, we recommend extensive use of the visual. Pictures, diagrams, maps, tables and consistent use of colour facilitate the presentation of key messages more powerfully, providing contexts for words, reducing misinterpretation and clarifying relationships between entities.

In earlier chapters, pictures, maps, tables and colour have been liberally used to aid communication and increase clarity. This chapter uses a variety of matrices to consider the value of a change initiative from a range of perspectives, by analysing and assessing the complete set of benefits.

13.2 Representations of Investment Value

If a programme is expected to generate 60 different benefits, the 60 Benefit Profiles together define the worth of the programme. This will seem to many stakeholders a cumbersome description of programme worth. Sponsors and other senior stakeholders, once they recognise that financial benefits alone cannot give the full picture, will want a summary of the programme benefits.

If worth were fully defined by financial benefits then a simple summary would be the total of the financial benefits. If these benefits are to be realised in different time periods, they can be accounted for in a simple spreadsheet, and the NPV of the time sequence of financial contributions can be calculated.

Desirable as it may be to represent the worth of an investment with a single value in this manner, it is rarely or never possible, since the worth of the non-financial benefits cannot be included. Although in most change initiatives, the majority (typically about 90 per cent) of benefits are non-financial, they are treated in most business cases as the poor relation, receiving hardly a mention. Even when they are listed, little is said about them. Since they are normally the majority of benefits, and financial benefits usually depend on them, they deserve and should receive far greater prominence.

One useful way to represent and communicate the full set of benefits for a programme is the Benefits Map (see Section 3.5); an alternative approach with different merits is described in the next section.

13.3   Investment Assessment

Different from the Benefits Map, but equally useful, are matrices, which contain all the planned benefits (financial and non-financial), and where the horizontal and vertical dimensions of the matrix are benefit attributes taken from the Benefit Profile. These matrices not only hold all the benefits, in an added-value format, but are useful for assessing the investment from a variety of perspectives, and are therefore generally referred to as **Investment Assessment Matrices (IAMs)**.

An IAM is another very useful visual tool which:

- aids analysis;

- checks alignment – for example, with business strategy, stakeholder expectations;

- checks for balance;

- checks consistency;

- facilitates communication.

These are of particular value to the Programme Director/Manager and the Benefit Facilitator, and useful to the Programme Sponsor and Programme Board.

If there are 20 attributes of a benefit listed in the Benefit Profile then 190 different IAMs,[1] can be generated, many of which may be of little value; others, however, will be useful for analysis, optimisation and communication. Below are a few examples of commonly used IAMs.

---

1   Two can be chosen from 20 in $20 \times 19/2$ (= 190) different ways.

A)   BY BUSINESS IMPACT AND VALUE TYPE

The cells contain the benefits expected from an insurance company project, showing both their **sigma** Value Types and their business impact based on the **sigma** Grid. These could have been presented in a simple list but presenting them in this format serves two purposes:

- as a consistency check – with this matrix all benefits should lie on the shaded diagonal line;

- for communicating added value – from the vertical dimension: the degree of confidence in any targets set and the nature of the value; from the horizontal dimension: which benefits will develop and take the organisation forward, which are solving some of today's critical problems, which are of high potential but also high risk, and which are just support or 'nice to have' (see Sections 9.4C and 9.4D).

Value type	Business Impact	Speculative	Strategic	Key-operational	Support
Definite	Financial			Reduced salary costs	Reduced telephone bill
	Non-financial			Greater administrative productivity	
Expected	Financial		Increased sales revenue from other products		
	Non-financial		Improved responsiveness to clients		
Logical	Financial		Improved management of insurance risk		
	Non-financial	Improved image	Greater client satisfaction		
Intangible		Increased client confidence			

Figure 13.1   IAM – by business impact and value type

B)   BY BENEFICIARY AND BUSINESS IMPACT

This gives the complete set of benefits for a public sector project, showing which stakeholders will feel their value, and their business impact, based on the **sigma** Grid. This classification is useful for considering the relative significance of benefits without trying to value them artificially in a pseudo-common currency, such as money. In this case we can hold within the same framework, in a meaningful way, the trivial but useful benefit 'reduced postage and fax costs' and the strategic benefit 'fewer dangerous drivers on the road'.

Beneficiary / Business Impact	Public	Magistrates Courts	DVLA	Police	Govt.
Speculative	• Improved public perception				• Less call on legal aid
Strategic	• Fewer dangerous drivers on the road • Improved sentencing	• Fewer adjournments • More up-to-date information		• More remands • Improved sentencing	
Key Operational		• Reduced duplication • Fewer interruptions for staff • Improved staff productivity • Reduced court costs	• Quicker turnaround • Reduced duplication	• Faster access to DVLA inf. • Reduced duplication	
Support		• Less document handling • Reduced postage/fax costs	• Less document handling		

Figure 13.2   Investment assessment – benefits by beneficiary and business impact

C)   CHECKING THE DEGREE OF TRANSFORMATION

A primary purpose of this matrix is to check the balance between the columns. If all the benefits were in the middle column – that is, were the result of doing things a little bit better, this suggests that the organisation may be automating what they have always done and are not taking the opportunity to transform the way they do things.

Such a matrix should not automatically lead to the assumption that what is being done is wrong – it merely provides a challenge. It is like holding up a mirror, and if management are comfortable with what they see, they can simply move on.

Value type	Change type	Doing new things	Doing things better	Stop doing things
Definite	Financial			Reduced telephone bill Reduced salary costs
Definite	Non-financial		Greater administrative productivity (e.g. fewer errors)	
Expected	Financial		Increased sales of other products	
Expected	Non-financial		Improved responsiveness to clients	
Logical	Financial	Improved management of risk		
Logical	Non-financial	Increased client confidence		
Intangible		Improved image		

Figure 13.3   Investment Assessment – checking the degree of transformation

D)   USING BENEFITS TO DRIVE THE SELECTION OF ENABLER OPTIONS

Mapping system features – planned and potential – against the benefits which they will enable, facilitates choice between options.

Based on the above example, why do we need feature F3? The response might be that F1 to F5 come as a standard package with no option but to purchase the F3 module. Even when this is true, other unnecessary and perhaps costly action should be avoided – implementation of F3 and training staff in the use of F3. It is easy to imagine that no sensible organisation would train staff in the use of a feature which yields no benefits; unfortunately this is a misconception, organisations often contract out their training, either to the software supplier or to an external agency whom they 'leave to get on with it' with a copy of the system user manual.

The diagram should also prompt the question – can we take and implement the potential feature PF1 instead of F3?

Benefits / System Features	B1	B2	B3	B4	B5	B6
Planned F1	✓					
F2		✓	✓			✓
F3						
F4		✓			✓	
F5	✓				✓	✓
Potential PF1		✓	✓			
PF2						
PF3	✓					✓

Figure 13.4   Using benefits to select enabler options

Use IAMs throughout the life cycle to visualise and optimise the overall worth of the programme and to spot any need to readjust.

The Time for Action – Change Management

'Vision without action is a daydream. Action without vision is a nightmare.'
(Japanese proverb)

'Take time to deliberate, but when time for action has arrived, stop thinking and go in.'
(Napoleon Bonaparte)

14.1   Attitudes to Change

Most of this book is about assessing, analysing and planning, all of which are important, but without the related actions they are all futile. When I was at school and college, I found it much easier and more enjoyable to make revision schedules than actually to revise, yet without the revision, the schedule was a complete waste of time.

This reluctance to act and make things happen is probably widespread in society – hence the saying 'Procrastination is the thief of time', but especially among those who enjoy analysing and planning. In workshops, when people are identifying the changes needed to deliver the benefits, they are often reluctant to express these as actions and to be specific. They tend to suggest such vague changes as 'marketing' or 'training', rather than 'market the new product' or 'train the sales force in the use of the new contact management system'.

Benefits arise as people do things differently, as they change the way they work, communicate and make decisions. Reluctance to change therefore requires prompt and careful handling. Reminders of the vision, end goal, and benefits, with potential value to those who are being asked to change, are especially helpful. If stakeholders have been engaged and involved throughout the life of the programme, this reluctance should be slight and may easily be overcome through the enthusiasm of early adopters who become local champions.

In Chapter 8 we began with change drivers, to confirm the vision and to identify the objectives, then went on to identify, assess and structure the benefits, then to create plans for their realisation through the implementation of the required solution or Blueprint. Now is the time to change, to make the Blueprint a reality.

14.2   The Blueprint – Basis for Change

The purpose and motivation for change should be the achievement of the vision; the target should be the Blueprint. It describes the planned future state of the organisation with the transition path, and shows how the various enablers such as information, systems, policies and working facilities integrate with changes in the operational environment such as:

- work patterns;

- procedures, processes and organisation;

- relationships between stakeholders;

- roles and responsibilities;

- attitudes and behaviours;

- culture – empowerment, attitude to risk and failure.

High-quality BDMs should provide the core of the Blueprint, which must be steadily developed and refined through the programme life cycle. Stakeholder engagement, issue resolution, risk management and the early results of benefit tracking all contribute to this refinement.

The behavioural change essential to effective delivery of benefits is often identified but then not specifically planned for or measured. Political complications sometimes arise when major behavioural changes are required from the top of the management structure.

14.3   Responsibility for Change

Responsibility for change ultimately lies with the operational units where the change is to occur; the more these people are motivated to change, the more successful the programme is likely to be. Because the benefits are dependent on the change, the Sponsor or SRO and the programme leadership who are accountable for benefits, have a vested interest in the effectiveness with which change is implemented. The programme leadership should therefore ensure that the programme includes clear responsibilities for change (see template for Change Action Plan in Figure 14.1), adequately supported by the programme structure (see Section 12.4).

Changes ➜ Actions ➜ Projects

No.	Enabler / Business Change	Map	Score	Cost	PPPId.	Owner	Start Date	End Date	Benefits which it directly enables

Figure 14.1   Template for Change Action Plan

14.4   Strategy for Implementing Change

Achieving or managing the required change is a large topic on which many books have been written. So I do not intend to cover it in this book. In this chapter I am highlighting a few important considerations which are pertinent to the BRM process.

Whatever approach or strategy is adopted it should be based on the Blueprint and be documented in what I refer to as the Change Strategy.

14.5   Sequencing Change to Maximise Benefit Realisation

There are many instances when simultaneous implementation across all or a large number of sites is impractical or high risk. In such situations roll-out must be sequenced. Unfortunately this sequencing is frequently driven by whims, politics or a desire to impress, rather than by an intention to maximise the realisation of benefits.

In a project which was automating a company's procurement processes, roll-out involved loading information on all the company's suppliers, and persuading staff to change the way they procure by adopting the required new processes. The greatest benefits were to come from automating the high volume of low-value purchases, so it would seem natural for these to be implemented first. Not so – the suppliers from whom they purchased large, high-value, complex items were set up on the system first. It was then possible to report to management on how well the project was progressing – in a short time they had implemented the system for a high percentage, by value, of their total procurement spend. Sadly, benefits were not used to drive their roll-out strategy.

To maximise benefit realisation it is important to balance potential benefits against risks. Suppose it is intended to roll out a new Blueprint to four manufacturing sites. For practical reasons this must be done sequentially and it is likely to take three months at each site. In order of magnitude of potential benefits, I shall refer to the sites as A, B, C and D. So the best roll-out sequence looks like A, B, C, D, but unfortunately significant resistance is expected from A and it is important to ensure that the first implementation is a great success. The compromise sequence might then be B, C, A, D.

Implementation plans should always seek to maximise benefit realisation; creating such benefit-driven plans is a crucial element of the change process which should normally occur early in Phase 5.

14.6   Overcoming Stakeholder Resistance

Sometimes the general resistance to change may intensify, especially when a particular stakeholder sees only disbenefits. This situation calls for focused attention and creative responses. A structured and focused response is illustrated in the case of a computer company experiencing a downturn in profits.

This computer company had grown rapidly to become a significant international player but having recently fallen out of favour, it was rapidly losing market share, with consequent falling profits. Its growth had been achieved largely by setting tough targets linked to attractive bonuses, and then making these targets tougher year on year. The salespeople were committed to achieving their bonuses – it was not uncommon for expensive family holidays to be planned in anticipation of the additional remuneration. As the targets grew tougher, corners were cut and customers were often sold equipment which poorly matched their needs – sometimes the initial installation did not even work without replacing solution components.

Naturally, management were concerned and the IT Director proposed a project which involved building a knowledge-based system to help the sales force to model client requirements, using checklists to ensure the workability of any proposed solution. As part of the project, the sales force would be provided with laptops and trained in the new system, and in the new ways of working. The sales force could see only difficulties and resisted the change. They recognised they would have to take training time out from selling, change their whole approach (that is, instead of striking deals over fancy lunches, they would have to sit down with the client in front of a laptop), and they would be constrained in the range of options offered. In consequence they did not believe they could achieve their targets.

The table in Figure 14.2 helped to assess the situation, focus effort and determine some actions:

Considering the benefits expected from the project by the primary stakeholders, it is easy to see that the sales force, with their short-term focus, saw no benefits. This did not go unnoticed by the senior managers, who then recognised the need to change the reward

Stakeholder Group	Perceived Benefits	Changes Needed	Anticipated Resistance	Level of Commitment C = Current R = Required				
				Anti	None	Let it happen	Help it happen	Make it happen
Customers	More customer needs met	None	None					
Senior Business Management	Improved Company reputation for quality products	Provide incentives to sales for error-free system configuration	Reluctance to change reward structures		C	Actions?		R
Sales Reps.	None	Use new system when quoting	Extra time and effort when quoting	C		Actions?	R	
Technical support	Less & easier configuration checking	None	None					
IT Developers	More interesting development work	Develop and implement new system	None					

Figure 14.2   Overcoming stakeholder resistance

structure for the sales people, rewarding sales only when they led to error-free system configurations.

This process may appear rather bureaucratic, so it is worth noting that the generation of the content of at least the first three columns of this table required little new effort, since it should already exist in the Benefit Profiles, or in the BRM database if software is used. The anticipated resistance is easily identified and recognises the fact that although senior managers saw the need for a new incentive model, some felt the proposal was complicated and uncertain, whereas the existing system was tried and tested.

The Programme Manager, realising that only two of the five stakeholders were showing resistance, could focus her energies on these two stakeholders, so making best use of limited resources. With this focus, she examined the current and required levels of commitment of these stakeholders and determined actions to motivate the change.

> **Once the planning is complete and the maps are reliable, use the vision to inspire action and the benefits to optimise results.**

15

Benefit Tracking and Reporting

'Be like a postage stamp. Stick to one thing until you get there.'

(Josh Billings)

'Just because something doesn't do what you planned it to do doesn't mean it's useless.'

(Thomas Edison)

15.1   Fundamentals of Benefit Tracking and Reporting

Benefit tracking and reporting has a dual purpose:

- to monitor performance;

- to improve performance.

In athletics, it is only through monitoring that records are set and future performance is improved. Business is similar – measurement helps people to know how well they are doing and, so long as measures are appropriate and targets realistic, should provide the motivation to improve.

Basic steps are:

1. build a Benefits Map for each objective, or a consolidated Benefits Map, ensuring they are of high quality and owned by the key stakeholders;

2. choose which benefits to track;

3. identify a suitable set of measures for each benefit to be tracked, utilising existing metrics whenever possible;

4. determine improvement targets for each measure;

5. for each benefit with multiple measures, set the criteria to decide when the benefit has been achieved;

6.   decide to whom each measure should be reported;

7.   begin tracking all the measures which have been identified and reporting the results to the relevant stakeholders;

8.   investigate missed targets.

This process is critical (see Chapters 1, 9 and 10), yet there are many potential pitfalls, which include:

- not tracking sufficient benefits;

- inappropriate measures;

- unrealistic targets;

- targets that motivate inappropriate behaviour.

A case example illustrating the application of this process follows:

15.2   Case Example – Preparing For Benefit Tracking and Reporting

A high street bank asked us to help them to track the benefits of a particular programme, one of three commissioned by the Sales Director to increase sales revenue. It involved implementing a customer database and sales system across their retail network, at a cost of £28m.

1.   BUILDING THE BENEFITS MAP

Upon examining the expected benefits, we immediately saw that they were not mutually independent, so we agreed to work with the management team to understand the causal relationships based on management expectations; the Benefits Map in Figure 15.1 below was the result:

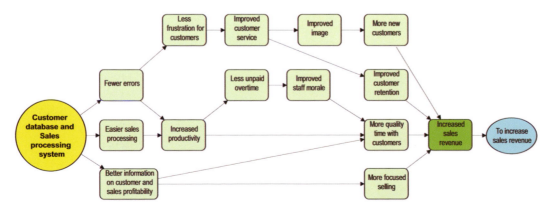

Figure 15.1   Benefits Map for objective: 'To increase sales revenue'

The Benefits Map is a key tool in tracking and attributing benefits. It operates like a signalling map of train movements – as time passes, steady movement along the paths or tracks can be seen, with benefits lit up as targets are achieved (or missed), based on a blue, red, amber, green (BRAG) status. When attributing benefits is difficult, as is the case here in respect of the 'increased sales revenue', the Benefits Map is one of the best vehicles to provide confidence that the benefit is attributable to the programme.

Often benefits at the right-hand end of the map are open to influence from activities, external to the programme (for example, from one of the other initiatives commissioned by the Sales Director) and sometimes external to the organisation (for example, a competitor going out of business), whereas those at the left-hand end are usually more directly related to the programme. If movements through the map, like the trains on the rail network, are monitored, their convergence on the end benefit should give confidence that the particular improvement in sales revenue is a consequence of the programme.

2.   CHOOSING WHICH BENEFITS TO TRACK

When considering benefit tracking we must not ignore the cost of measuring. Some benefits in the case example may be considered difficult to measure – this usually means that more elaboration is required (for example, what aspect of staff morale are we seeking to improve?) and/or the cost of measurement is high (for example, improved image).

At the other end of the spectrum, some benefits could be tracked at zero or low cost to the programme, because they are already being measured by the company (for example, errors, productivity, overtime and sales revenue). If a Measures Dictionary had been in operation, these would have been found there (see Section 10.10).

Because measurement may be time consuming and costly there may be pressure to measure only a few benefits – the key benefits. However sensible this seems, it can be a disastrous strategy. For instance, in the case example, which are the key benefits? Looking at the Benefits Map the key benefits must be: fewer errors, easier sales processing and better information on customers and sales profitability, since without these none of the other benefits will be achieved. Once they are achieved, the key benefits become those immediately to the right of those just achieved and so on.

Ultimately all benefits are key benefits, though some might look at the diagram and think that the key benefit is increased sales revenue. There are several reasons for this; it is the end benefit, it is clearly of great interest to the sponsor (the Sales Director), it is the only financial or cashable benefit and is easy to track because it was already being measured by the bank. The arguments seem impressive, but unfortunately if we only track this benefit we will be wasting our time, since it would not tell us anything useful. We would not have any idea whether any change in sales revenue is attributable to the programme; furthermore we would not know which parts of the programme are working and which are not.

So if possible all benefits should be tracked. If one or two are particularly difficult to measure, the best compromise would be to measure benefits either side of the difficult ones.

3.   IDENTIFYING A SUITABLE SET OF MEASURES FOR EACH BENEFIT TO BE TRACKED

Measures should relate as closely as possible to the way the benefit is described, but if a benefit description is a little vague (for example, improved quality of time spent with customers), measures can be used to make it more specific.

'Fewer errors' can straightforwardly be tracked by monitoring the number of errors (the metric); however, if sales were to increase (the intention of the programme) the number of errors is likely to increase; so a ratio, such as the number of errors per 100 sales, would be a suitable measure. In practice then we track the metric and report the measure.

'More quality time with customers' is more difficult. Note first its two dimensions – time and quality. Face-to-face time with customers is easily monitored but how would we measure quality? One suggestion is the 'value of sales generated' because the intention is to increase this. But 'value of sales generated' is a measure for the next benefit 'increased sales revenue'. An alternative might be 'lead conversion rate', which is an improvement. On its own, however, it is not direct enough, because the quality of the time spent with customers could improve significantly while sales might not increase because the price is far too high; monitoring the 'lead conversion rate' would hide this fact.

Here, quality may require a set of complementary measures such as:

- the preparedness of sales staff (staff view);

- the clarity of purpose for each meeting (sales managers' view);

- the customer's view of the quality of each meeting which could be assessed using a standard set of 3–5 questions at the close of each meeting, and more extensively using mystery shoppers;

- lead conversion rate – this can be useful alongside the other measures but would be misleading on its own.

A fuller treatment of measures and their identification is given in Chapter 10.

4.   DETERMINING IMPROVEMENT TARGETS FOR EACH MEASURE

For each definite or expected measure, based on the **sigma** Value Types (Section 9.4D), a target improvement must be determined in close collaboration with those who will be responsible for achieving the target. Targets should be realistic and owned and so should relate to the expected improvement for the specific benefit. Ideally these claims should be logged in the Measures Dictionary (see Section 10.10) so that overclaiming of benefits will be spotted quickly and appropriate action taken.

Before we can set a target, we need a baseline and alongside it a timescale over which the improvement is expected. In our case example, where the measure frequency was set at three months, the table in Figure 15.2 shows a subset of the measures, with baselines, targets and improvement timescales. This format could form the basis for a Benefit Tracking Report.

Measure	Baseline value	Start Period	End Period	Target Value	Period 1	Period 2	Period 3	Period 4
No. of errors per 100 sales	7.5	1	3	2.5				
No. of written complaints per week	9	2	4	2				
No. of phone complaints per week		2	4	5				
Customer service rating (%)	55	3	8	80				
No. of sales processed pp per day	8.5	2	4	12				
Value of sales processes pp per day	£480	2	4	£750				
Total overtime worked per week (hr)	55	2	4	15				
Staff morale rating (%)	68	3	6	80				
Time spent with customers (hr/wk)	450	3	6	1000				
No. of new customers per period	3	4	7	10				
No. of lost customers per period	5	4	7	2				
Lead conversion rate (%)	28	4	8	40				
Sales revenue	£300,000	4	9	£1m				

Period = 3 months

Figure 15.2   Measures with baselines, targets and improvement timescales

5.   DECIDING TO WHOM EACH MEASURE SHOULD BE REPORTED

Most stakeholders will want reports only for those benefits in which they are interested, for instance, in the previous banking example:

- Sales Director: sales revenue, and retained new customers;

- Sales Processing Manager: errors, easier sales processing and productivity;

- Customer Relationship Manager: errors, customer frustration, customer service and image;

- HR Manager: overtime and staff morale.

Reporting could be further reduced by reporting only on an exception basis – that is, when targets are not being achieved.

15.3   Case Example – Tracking and Reporting

1.   STARTING TO TRACK THE MEASURES AND REPORT THE RESULTS TO THE RELEVANT STAKEHOLDERS

Start tracking benefits as soon as each measure and its associated metric tracking mechanism have been identified, and certainly before any possible programme changes are likely to occur. This will provide a baseline (if not already available) and enable the identification of early benefits or quick wins.

To record the results, the values of the measures can be added to the table in Figure 15.2, providing values for all measures for each period, as in Figure 15.3. The horizontal shading indicates the stakeholder who should receive or experience the benefit and to whom the measures should be reported; in many situations this could also be the stakeholder who tracks and records the measure.

Measure	Baseline value	Start Period	End Period	Target Value	Period 1	Period 2	Period 3	Period 4
No. of errors per 100 sales	7.5	1	3	2.5	7	4	3	2.5
No. of written complaints per week	9	2	4	2	10	8	6	4
No. of phone complaints per week		2	4	5	25	21	15	9
Customer service rating (%)	55	3	8	80	55	60	70	82
No. of sales processed pp per day	8.5	2	4	12	8.5	9	10	12
Value of sales processes pp per day	£480	2	4	£750	£500	£600	£680	£770
Total overtime worked per week (hr)	55	2	4	15	56	50	35	20
Staff morale rating (%)	68	3	6	80	70	72	74	75
Time spent with customers (hr/wk)	450	3	6	1000	440	450	520	660
No. of new customers per period	3	4	7	10	3	4	3	7
No. of lost customers per period	5	4	7	2	5	4	4	3
Lead conversion rate (%)	28	4	8	40	25	33	33	33
Sales revenue	£300,000	4	9	£1m	£286,000	£275,000	£290,000	£350,000

Period = 3 months

Sales Processing Manager	
Customer Relationship Manager	
HR Manager	
Sales Manager	

Figure 15.3   Measure reporting – planned and actual – by stakeholder

2.   SETTING CRITERIA, TO DECIDE WHEN A BENEFIT WILL HAVE BEEN ACHIEVED, WHEN BENEFITS HAVE MULTIPLE MEASURES

The benefit 'improved customer service' could have several measures of which two might be – 'number of written complaints' and 'number of phone complaints'. We could add to these the 'number of email complaints' and the 'number of complaints made in person'. Each of these could be assigned a target and we could say the benefit is achieved only when all four targets have been achieved. But we may feel that the targets do not carry equal weights so we could say that the benefit is achieved once the target for 'complaints made in person' has been achieved provided the others have passed the 70 per cent mark.

This level of sophistication is difficult without suitable software to generate automatically the BRAG status, based on agreed criteria.

3.   USING THE BENEFITS MAP IN CONJUNCTION WITH A BRAG STATUS TO COMMUNICATE PROGRESS

Once criteria have been determined for the realisation of benefits with multiple measures (see 2 above), Benefit Maps may be used to communicate progress against target. The following diagrams (Figures 15.4 to Figure 15.7) show the results of tracking the benefits in the Case Study example, at each of four different stages.

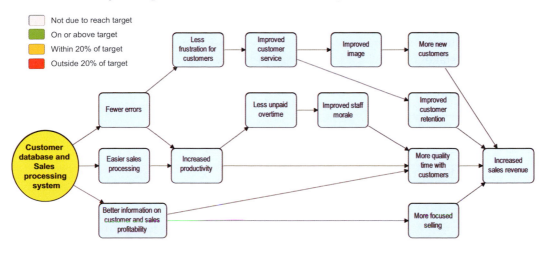

Figure 15.4   BRAG Report – Benefits Map immediately after implementation

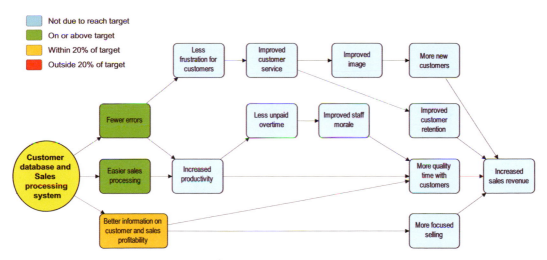

Figure 15.5   BRAG Report – Benefits Map three months after implementation

4.   INVESTIGATE MISSED TARGETS

Tracking and reporting can improve performance in two ways. Knowing that results are being monitored, people are usually motivated to perform better. The intelligence gathered from missed (including exceeded) targets should lead to one or more of the following:

- managing further change where this has not been adequately implemented;

- initiating mitigating action to compensate for any shortfall;

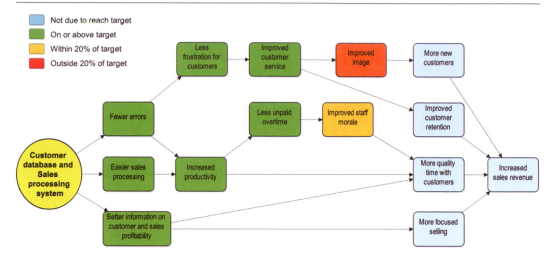

Figure 15.6   BRAG Report – Benefits Map one year after implementation

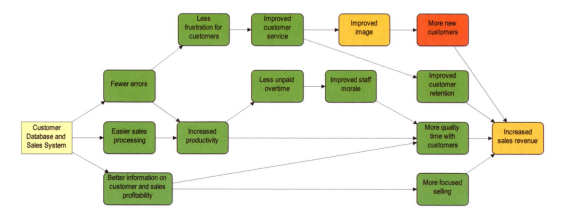

Figure 15.7   RAG Report – Benefits Map two years after implementation

- adjusting or forewarning any likely impacts on later targets;

- capturing any 'lessons learned' relating in particular to map creation, measure selection and target setting.

15.4   Generating Commitment to Tracking

Many organisations are reluctant to measure, as is borne out by the fact that only 35 per cent of organisations currently measure the expected benefits from planned changes. This reluctance is usually based on a combination of the following concerns:

- it is difficult to attribute improvements in a measure to a particular programme;

- measurement is unnecessarily bureaucratic, time consuming and costly;

- including imtermediate benefits there are to many benefits to track;

- the perception that only cashable benefits are taken seriously;

- it is difficult to identify suitable measures;

- measurement is unimportant;

- we don't want to be accountable for the improvement in a particular measure;

- we don't like the implications of benefit achievement (for example, budget cuts).

Consideration of the case example in the previous section has addressed most of these issues, though 'the perception that only cashable benefits are taken seriously' is so common a pitfall, that it is worth giving it further attention.

In the case example, the only benefit which would be measured in real money (that is, is cashable) is sales revenue, which happens also to be the end benefit and of greatest interest to the sponsor (the Sales Director). Many organisations would select this as the key benefit; we have also identified it as carrying a low tracking cost.

So should the Programme Manager simply report on this benefit and leave the others? – after all, the rest are all non-financial and some might be costly to track. There are at least four good reasons why it is important to track most if not all of the benefits in the diagram:

1. If sales revenue alone is tracked, there is no way of knowing whether an improvement in sales is a consequence of this programme, another programme or changes in the marketplace.

2. Even if sales revenue is known to increase as a result of this programme, it will be impossible to determine, without measuring all of the benefits, which path(s) have functioned to create the improvement. If this proves to be a single path, it is likely that only a small proportion (perhaps 10 to 20 per cent) of potential benefits has been realised. To ensure maximum improvement in the end benefit it is important to check that all paths are functioning, by measuring all benefits.

3. Interest in benefit tracking and reporting is not confined to the sponsor and other senior managers. Most staff are keen to see improvements and are interested to know whether or not they are on a pathway to success. Different stakeholders will be interested in different benefits and will want to see reports of measures relating to their interests.

4.   Each Benefits Map carries a timeline. To move to fewer errors, then less frustration for customers, then improved customer service, then improved image, then increased sales revenue will take some time, probably two years. The bank will not want to wait two years to find out whether or not they are being successful. It is much better to check whether the targets for errors, sales processing and better information are achieved within three months, targets for customer frustration and productivity within six months, and targets for customer service, unpaid overtime and staff morale within one year.

Another danger of the perception that only cashable benefits are important is that it puts pressure on organisations to give monetary values to benefits which are not cashable, thus distorting the facts and leading either to double counting and/or to putting at risk the true financial benefits.

In our case example: let us suppose that the profit margin from the increased sales revenue is £400,000 p.a. and the average productivity improvement for the sales team of 30 is 10 per cent. Some might argue that 10 per cent productivity improvement for 30 staff is equivalent to a saving of three staff and since the total cost of three staff is £100,000 p.a., this implies a total cash benefit for the programme of £500,000 (£400,000 + £100,000). But the £100,000 becomes real money only when the three staff are removed, and if that happens, three important benefits will not be achieved, namely: less unpaid overtime, improved staff morale and more quality time with customers. Without these benefits, increased sales revenue is at risk and it is quite possible that the profit margin from the increased sales revenue will drop to £200,000.

We therefore have two choices – (1) make three staff redundant, so making the £100,000 real, which then gives a total benefit of £300,000 (£100,000 + the new profit margin of £200,000); or (2) treat the improved productivity as non-cashable, which will result in a total benefit of £400,000. Any other option would involve double counting of financial values. The Benefits Map in its current form clearly supports the second choice.

This highlights two other uses for the maps – (1) the avoidance of double counting – if there is any path which passes through two financial benefits there will be double counting; and (2) as an aid to communication – the benefit 'improved productivity' often engenders staff anxiety about jobs, but the map clearly shows them that this benefit should give a shorter working day and more time with customers.

15.5   Benefit Trajectories

Against each measure (except 'number of phone complaints per week') in the table in Figure 15.8, there is a baseline value, a target value and the timescale over which the improvement is expected to occur. The improvement path is referred to as the trajectory or the benefit delivery profile. To avoid confusion with other uses of the term profile (for example, in Benefit Profile) I will use only the term 'trajectory'.

If a straight line trajectory is assumed, as described in Section 10.4, then the trajectories for five of the benefits from the above case example are given in the table in Figure 15.8.

Period	1	2	3	4	5	6	7	8	9
No. of errors per 100 sales	7.5	5	2.5	2.5	2.5	2.5	2.5	2.5	2.5
Customer service rating (%)	55	55	55	60	65	70	75	80	80
Value of sales processed p.p. per hour	£480	£480	£615	£750	£750	£750	£750	£750	£750
Lead conversion rate (%)	28	28	28	28	31	34	37	40	40
Sales revenue (£'000)	300	300	300	300	440	580	720	860	1,000

Figure 15.8   Five trajectories for benefits from the case example

If a benefit appears more than once (perhaps in different maps), an integrated trajectory can be obtained by adding together the related measure improvements – not the measure values – for each period.

Further refinements can cater for a baseline which is not static (horizontal), but has an upward or downward trend, and the expected improvement is not linear. The final trajectory could then be built up in the following way:

- take the trend line as the baseline;

- add the projected improvements for each occurrence of the measure;

- refine manually to take account of cyclical or other non-linear variations.

Based on the case example benefit 'fewer errors' this might look like:

Period	1	2	3	4	5	6	7	8	9
Baseline which is an upward trend	7.5	8	8.5	9	9.5	10	10.5	11	11.5
1st improvement trajectory		-2.5	-5	-5	-5	-5	-5	-5	-5
2nd improvement trajectory				-1	-2	-3	-4	-4	-4
Total	7.5	5.5	3.5	3	2.5	2	1.5	2	2.5
Refined total	7.5	5	3.5	3	2.5	2	2	2	2

Figure 15.9   Integrated trajectory for 'Fewer errors per 100 sales'

Or in graphical format:

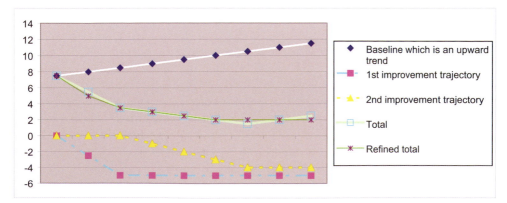

Figure 15.10   Integrated trajectory for 'Fewer errors per 100 sales'

Measurement motivates behaviour so gather the most pertinent intelligence and act upon it, as necessary adjusting future plans.

Risks and Issues

'The greatest risk is the risk of riskless living.'

(Stephen Covey)

'Two roads diverged in a wood, and I took the one less travelled by, and that has made all the difference.'

(Robert Frost)

16.1   Definitions and Scope

There is confusion in the use of the word 'risk', related perhaps to a lack of clarity of meaning. The *Oxford Dictionary* gives two definitions:

a)   a chance or possibility of adverse circumstances;

b)   a person or thing causing a risk.

MSP also provides two definitions:

c)   risks are things that may happen at some point in the future and require positive management to reduce their likelihood of happening, their impact on the programme, or both (MSP, P. 51);

d)   a negative threat (or potential positive opportunity) that might affect the course of the programme (MSP Glossary).

Between them, these four definitions appear to relate to five logically linked components, namely:

- the chance or probability of a future adverse situation occurring – definition (a);

- a description of this potential adverse situation – definition (c);

- the impact that this undesirable situation might have on a desired future outcome (that is, the reason why the situation is undesirable) – definition (d);

- a person or thing causing the adverse situation – definition (b);

- the desired future outcome.

A simple illustration may help to understand this:

There is an unprotected cliff path close to sheer drops (b). If you walk along the path there is a 0.001 per cent chance that you will fall over the edge (a). Falling off the cliff is an adverse situation (c). If you fall off there is a 10 per cent chance that you will live (d). Staying alive is your desired future outcome. So which of these five components is the risk?

We might say the path is 'risky' but not usually 'a risk'. We certainly talk about 'the risk of falling over the edge'. If we say 'falling over the edge is a risk', this is an abbreviation for 'falling over the edge carries a risk (that is, 0.001 per cent)'. We would not normally say there is a 10 per cent risk of living though we might say there is a 90 per cent risk of dying. So risk is the chance of a bad experience, not of a good experience (except when used ironically).

The common understanding of risk is closest to definition (a). In the context of projects, programmes and change, the ultimate adverse circumstances would be non-fulfilment of the vision, though en route to this it could be the failure to realise the benefits and achieve the objectives. Prior to these adverse circumstances could be enablers which are not fit for purpose and/or inadequate management of business change. In the end, risk always concerns benefits.

Definition (b) is closely related to a disbenefit, since any disbenefit is likely to demotivate stakeholders, thus causing a risk.

So the definition I propose for *risk* is 'a potential adverse circumstance which could lead to the non-achievement of the vision or non-realisation of the benefits'.

In contrast I will define an *issue* as 'a current adverse circumstance which could lead to the non-achievement of the vision or the non-realisation of the benefits'.

Issues and risks must, as part of good governance or due diligence and care, be identified, assessed and managed, in order to minimise their collective impact on the desired outcomes. Registers (sometimes called logs) of both issues and risks are useful tools for facilitating this process; they are described more fully in Section 18.4.

16.2   Risk Register or Log

Although the register is usually associated with a particular project or programme, it should really relate to a planned outcome, such as the achievement of a vision. On the other hand the disadvantage of relating it to a programme when that programme is specifically designed to achieve the vision is small.

Each entry in a Risk Register should contain:

- a description of the adverse circumstance;

- the chance of it occurring – which could be a probability or a percentage – or simply high, medium or low;

- the consequences of the adverse circumstance – its impact.

Risks are added to the register as and when they are identified. One reason for relating the Risk Register to the vision rather than the programme is that some risks may be identified before the programme has been established (one such risk is the chance that senior managers will not own the vision and the Strategy Map). So the Risk Register should be set up during Phase 1.

Since a BDM describes the path to fulfilment of the vision and each entity on the map (enabler, business change or benefit) represents a milestone along the path, the risk of not achieving the vision is a combination of the risks of not achieving each milestone. So in identifying risks, each entity along the path should be examined.

An issue (an existing adverse circumstance) should be logged in a similar manner but without the chance element. Against an entry for either a risk or an issue, you may wish also to record when, how and by whom the risk was identified and any actions taken to minimise or mitigate the impact of the adverse circumstance.

Although disbenefits are different from risks there will quite often be a relationship between them; for example, the disbenefit 'reduced career development prospects' may lead to 'demotivated staff' and so increasing the risk of stakeholder resistance to the required business changes, which in turn will increase the risk of failing to achieve the benefits.

16.3   Risk Management

An activity with no risks is probably not worth undertaking, and is unlikely to give an organisation a competitive edge. Positive management is necessary to reduce the probability of an adverse circumstance occurring and/or to reduce its impact on the programme. Responsibility for this may be shared between the Programme Director/ Manager and the SRO and Programme Board.

Don't seek a risk-free path. Focus on the vision and identify, log and manage the risks along the way.

Governance, Programme Assurance and Gateways

> 'The optimist see opportunity in every danger; the pessimist sees danger in every opportunity.'
>
> (Sir Winston Churchill)

> 'To govern is to serve.'
>
> (Edward Heath)

17.1 Levels of Governance

Governance is the act or manner of governing; in the context of benefit realisation it should be applied to the whole of an organisation's investment in change. It is usually undertaken by a body of people who:

- own or are custodians of the investment funding;

- are likely to be affected by the required changes;

- will experience, or at least appreciate, the value of the majority of the expected benefits.

Governance is likely to operate at two or three levels.

At the highest level, a management group would oversee the distribution of investment across the whole spectrum of change initiatives, in order to create and maintain a strategically balanced high-value portfolio which is aligned to the organisation's mission. This management group is likely to be a permanent body of senior people, possibly a subset of the main Board such as an executive committee. If it is a group established for this specific purpose it might be called a Portfolio Board, a Steering Group or the Change Management Executive. MSP refers to this board as The Sponsoring Group. The responsibilities of such a group are described in Section 6.5 and amplified in Chapter 24.

At the middle level, for a programme or significant stand-alone project, governance should reside with a group of senior representatives of the affected stakeholders. This is the sponsoring group for the specific change initiative and is normally referred to as the Programme or Project Board; it should exist only for the life of the programme or project. Unlike the above-mentioned Portfolio Board/Steering Group, this Board should be dedicated to a single programme or project and is likely to:

- sanction the release of approved funding;

- influence business units, including their own, in the acceptance of change;

- be accountable for the realisation of expected benefits.

The Programme Board should be set up during Phase 3 and is normally chaired by the principal sponsor or SRO. Prior to its existence (that is, during phases 1 and 2), reviews should be undertaken by the Sponsor and/or the Portfolio Board.

At the lower levels, Project Boards oversee smaller projects; User Groups oversee work packages and change requests once the main changes have been implemented and absorbed into BAU, and the programme has been closed.

It is also valuable to set up independent reviews by objective reviewers who may be more familiar with the detail of the processes. Reviews of this type include:

- peer reviews

- audits

- gateway reviews, as advocated by OGC.

Although independent reviews are valuable, they should not take precedence over the hierarchical reviews. The Programme Board must retain its accountability for programme success and should commission any independent review, receiving reports of its results. Otherwise there is a risk that accountability becomes dissipated.

17.2   Scope of Governance

Key elements of the governance process are choosing between options, realigning or refocusing activities and occasionally terminating the change initiative. Securing funding and resources and influencing stakeholders outside the control of the programmes are also important responsibilities.

The ultimate purpose of any investment in change should be the realisation of planned benefits, so, irrespective of the particular change delivery mechanism – programme, project or work package – the primary focus of any governance body should be benefit realisation. Instead the dominant focus is often on the procurement of enablers, probably because this is where the major part of the capital expenditure is incurred, and expenditure is generally easier to monitor than benefit realisation.

sigma was involved in helping a major insurance company with benefit realisation for a project for implementing a new company-wide Management Information System (MIS). After several months we realised that the BRM activity was becoming marginalised and there was a risk that the project would not deliver the expected business benefits. We discussed the situation with the Group Finance Director, the sponsor of the project.

Part of the problem lay in the governance structure. The Project Board, composed of senior managers from the major business functions, occupied itself in discussing technical issues relating to the MI software or contractual issues relating to the software supplier. In practice, no doubt because of the nature of these Board discussions, many Board members were missing meetings, sending junior substitutes instead. The Board's subcommittees (one of which was a subgroup on benefits) were composed of more junior people, who tended to follow the example set by the Project Board, also sending substitutes, yet more junior.

We suggested that the terms of reference for these groups were the wrong way round ('cart-before-horse' governance); the Project Board should focus on benefit realisation and subcommittees could look after the secondary matters of software and suppliers. Although this was a new way of thinking for the Finance Director, he saw its merits and instigated the necessary changes. He subsequently saw increased involvement by the senior functional managers and the project was eventually successful.

17.3   Key Review and Decision Points

Change initiatives, once started, are very difficult to stop. In particular, review mechanisms are rarely structured to include termination as a serious option, and review panels seldom have the teeth or appetite to call a halt. Each year considerable investment is wasted on changes which should have been stopped at a much earlier stage. A successful change process, such as BRM, must therefore include regular review points; these reviews should always include specific consideration as to whether or not the change activity should continue. The default should be to stop the change, proceeding to the next step of the process only when a suitable case for continuing is made. Such a case should always ignore the investment made to date and the benefits already realised, considering simply further benefits against further costs, and taking account of the assessed future risks.

Another weakness of many existing review processes is that their predominant focus is on the acquisition and implementation of enablers rather than the realisation of business benefits.

So regular reviews with a strong emphasis on benefit realisation are essential, the total number depending on the duration and complexity of the change. For larger programmes I recommend at least six reviews, one between each of the six phases of the process. These are marked R1 to R6 in Figure 17.1.

Ideally reviews should be a natural part of the management process and not exceptional activities requiring an enormous amount of preparation, much of which is only being done for the reviewing body. The aims of each of the envisaged six reviews are described as follows:

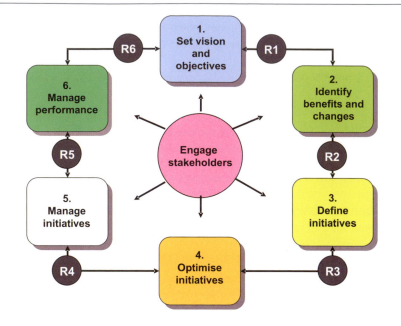

Figure 17.1   Change process with review points

FIRST REVIEW (R1)

- To confirm the vision, ensuring that it is a suitable response to the main drivers for change and that it is aligned to the organisation's mission;

- To endorse the Strategy Map of supporting objectives and the scope boundary for a feasible change initiative;

- To agree the stakeholders and assess their commitment to the vision and the scope of the proposed change initiative;

- To consider the case for continuing to step 2 and to approve the strategy to be adopted for the application of BRM.

SECOND REVIEW (R2)

- To consider the range of identified benefits and disbenefits, their distribution between the various stakeholders and some assessment of their importance or worth;

- To review the Benefits Maps confirming structure and path weightings for at least the right-hand ends;

- To agree the feasibility of any target improvements in benefit measures;

- To confirm the existence of BDMs, which have identified the dependent enablers and business changes;

- To approve the provisional business model or Blueprint for the future business state – at this stage this might be little more than the BDMs;

- To consider the case for continuing to step 3.

THIRD REVIEW (R3)

- To review the justification for investing in change, considering the provisional costs of the required new changes against the target improvements for the full set of benefits from the Benefits Maps;

- To agree the mechanisms for managing and implementing the changes and to approve the related Programme/Project structure;

- To endorse the proposed benefit tracking regime.

FOURTH REVIEW (R4)

- To select the most cost-effective solution options;

- To sanction the required funding;

- To approve Supplier Contracts for the required enablers and the strategy for mobilising stakeholders to undertake the required business changes;

- To approve the overall implementation strategy in order to minimise risk and maximise benefit realisation, using IAMs;

- To approve the BRP and the Full Business Case.

FIFTH REVIEW (R5)

- To review progress against plan, monitoring key milestones covering enabler development, change implementation and benefit realisation;

- To review strategies for overcoming stakeholder resistance;

- To continue to review benefit realisation and to instigate mitigating activities where targets are not being achieved.

SIXTH REVIEW (R6)

- To conduct post-implementation reviews with strong focus on the mechanisms for benefit tracking and reporting and the results to date;

- To conduct a portfolio review to assess how well the combined effects of the whole portfolio of programmes and projects are moving the organisation towards the achievement of its mission.

These aims are fully in line with the activities required for successful completion of the programme; they are unlikely to be undertaken merely to satisfy the review committee. The documents required to support this review process are described in Chapters 18–21

17.4   Relationship Between Review Structures and OGC Gateways

Many organisations have formal review structures for their investment in change. Review points are often called gates or gateways, suggesting that if certain criteria are not satisfied, permission to pass through the gate will not be granted. In practice this is often more fantasy than fact.

OGC's Gateway process is probably the most widely established review process. It was developed initially for procurement projects with five gates (1 to 5), to which gate 0 has subsequently been added, in an attempt to accommodate programmes. Gate 0 can be applied several times – at least after programme definition, programme execution and programme closure. A key aspect of this review is strategic alignment.

The table, in Figure 17.2 below, attempts to relate **sigma**'s process to OGC's programme and project processes.

OGC Programme Process	Sigma Process	OGC Project Process
Define programme	Set vision and objectives	
	R1 - Strategic alignment	
	Identify benefits and changes	
	R2 - Worth & stakeholder commitment	
G0 - Strategic assessment	Define initiatives	Develop business case
Execute programme	**R3 - Outline business justification**	**G1- Business justification**
	Optimise initiatives (incl. competitive procurement)	Develop procurement strategy
		G2 - Procurement strategy
G0 - Strategic assessment		Competitive procurement
Close programme	**R4 - Full business justification**	**G3 - Investment decisions**
	Manage initiatives	Award & implement contract
		G4 - Readiness for service
	R5 - Progress against all milestones	Manage contract
G0 - Strategic assessment	Manage performance	**G5 - Benefits realisation**
	R6 - Vision achievement & closure	Closure

Figure 17.2   Relationships between review structures

> **Establish a vision-focused governance structure which serves benefit realisation through wise choices.**
> **Ensure reviews aid and do not hinder programme success.**

18

Benefit Realisation Management (BRM)-related Documents

'A sketch is better than a long speech.'

(Napoleon Bonaparte)

'To succeed in business it is necessary to make others see things as you see them.'

(John H Patterson)

18.1   Transcending the Documentation Nightmare

Many of the innumerable methodologies for Project and Programme Management, and for the related review processes are based on either Prince 2 (for projects) or MSP (for programmes). There are also many adaptations to suit particular cultures, organisational environments or industry sectors. This diversity of approach has given rise to a plethora of recommended charts, tables and documents, so much so, that many project and programme managers feel overwhelmed by the number and range of reports they are required to produce.

In considering this myriad of requirements, we distinguish between a document and the charts and tables which form part of it, by defining a *document* as 'a text which contains several different views of the data usually connected by prose and analysis, and often containing conclusions and recommendations'. Even using this definition, we have identified as many as 25 documents in common parlance and have actually seen as many as 15 of them listed as part of a single Programme and Project Management methodology. While not all of these would be required for every programme, the number described can still seem overwhelming.

Sometimes the purposes of documents are unclear, and there may be serious overlap between them. This may indicate that a set of overlapping documents can be consolidated into one, which would then evolve over time. The separate names, previously given to the unconsolidated documents, would then relate to snapshots of the new document, each of which would have a particular purpose and emphasis, depending on the stage in the life-cycle at which it is taken. Although in theory one 'big book' could replace all the documents, this would probably go too far and might be impractical, bearing in mind the large number of contributors.

If the 'big book' is on the other hand an integrated electronic database it could be extremely practical. The separate documents referred to in various change methodologies become nothing more than sophisticated reports from the database. This approach is not only very efficient but increases the consistency and integrity of the documents, making programme management and governance more effective. The requirements for such a database are given in Chapter 29.

Whether or not the documents are individually handcrafted or just generated from the integrated database, it may be helpful to consider their prime functions and any logical groupings. As a compromise between the idea of a single 'big book' and the 25 plus named documents in the change management literature, at least one document should be expected for each of the five programme themes described in Section 5.7, namely:

- Benefit Realisation;

- Stakeholder Management;

- Solution Management;

- Programme Management;

- Governance.

Documents are for communication, providing a basis for decision making and ultimately leading to action. They can describe intentions or possible future paths, sometimes presenting options, and may report on progress to date. For high-quality, non-ambiguous communication, the use of pertinent visuals is recommended – maps, charts, graphs and so on. So before considering documents in more detail and attempting to rationalise them, I will describe some of the basic charts, maps and tables which can be regarded as a set of templates from which the documents draw their detailed information. Most documents will include several of these templates.

18.2   Some Useful Templates – Basic Charts, Maps and Tables

The main documents, described in Section 18.4, depend upon and generally incorporate a number of basic diagrams and templates. Those which are important for BRM include:

- Strategy Maps

- Benefits Maps

- BDMs

- Benefit Profiles

- Programme or Project Organisational Structure

- Governance Structure

- Investment Assessment Matrices (IAMs)

- Trajectories

- Cost benefit analysis calculations.

STRATEGY MAP

This is a map linking a set of objectives together in 'cause and effect' relationships. The objectives may relate to a single change initiative, such as a programme, or to the whole organisation, or to a major part of it.

Examples of Strategy Maps are included in Sections 4.7, 8.6 and 8.7. A diagram from 8.7 is repeated below (Figure 18.1), where the four bounding objectives are indicated by the brighter blue colour.

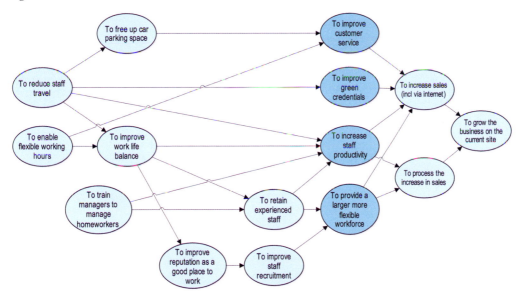

Figure 18.1   Strategy Map for growing a business on current site

BENEFITS MAP

This is a map linking a set of benefits in 'cause and effect' relationships. The benefits typically relate to a single project or programme and the map is often linked to one of the bounding objectives for the programme. A programme would usually have a separate

Benefits Map for each objective, though sometimes these would be combined into a single map.

Examples of Benefits Maps are included in Sections 3.5, 4.7, 9.5, 9.6, 9.7 and 15.2. A further example, based on the third of the four bounding objectives from the previous map, is given below:

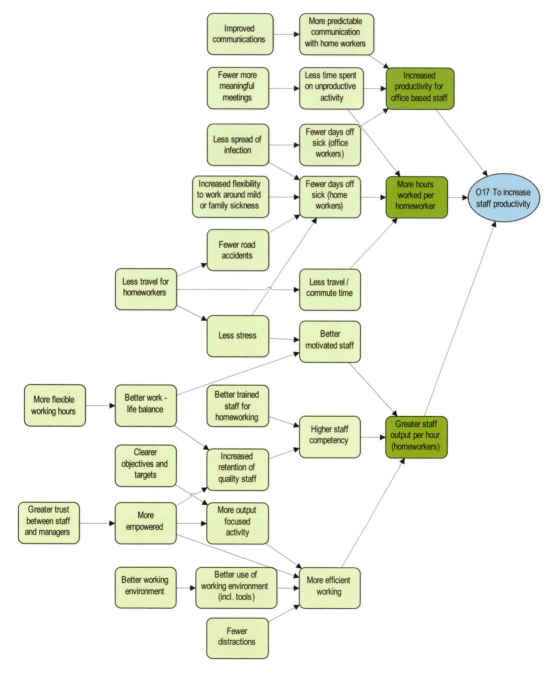

Figure 18.2   Benefits Map for 'Increasing staff productivity, from home-working'

BENEFIT DEPENDENCY MAP (BDM)

This map is essentially a Benefits Map with the addition of the changes – enablers and business changes – on which the benefits depend. Examples of BDMs are included in Sections 4.7, 6.3, 11.2 and 11.5. A further example, based on the previous Benefits Map, is given below:

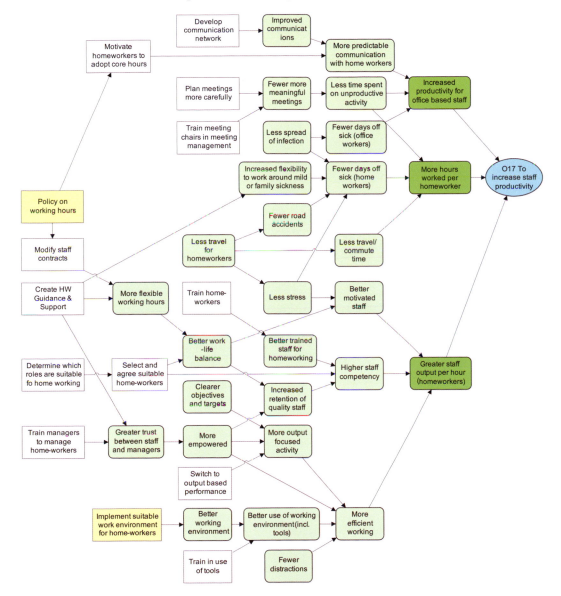

Figure 18.3   BDM for 'Increasing staff productivity, from home-working'

BENEFIT PROFILE

This is the document/template which holds the comprehensive description of a benefit with all its attributes and dependencies, a repository of all the information relating to an individual benefit which would aid its realisation. We recommend that the Profile for an individual benefit should occupy no more than a single page in length.

Benefit Owners may be responsible for benefits which are themselves dependent on changes outside their direct control, or even outside the control of the programme. The Benefit Owners must understand these dependencies and be aware of all the details pertaining to each benefit for which they are responsible and must know whom to chase and influence. For each benefit, this information is held within the Benefit Profile which contains:

Details about the benefit:

- number;

- description;

- programme or organisational objectives supported;

- other benefits to which this benefit contributes;

- impact of the benefit (for example, **sigma** Grid based on Boston Matrix);

- other classifications (for example, **sigma** Value Type, Balanced Scorecard Category).

Realisation issues for example dependencies:

- the enablers or enabler features on which the benefit depends, perhaps subdivided by: Information, Technology, People and Process;

- the business changes on which the benefit depends, perhaps subdivided into Culture, Process, People and Other;

- earlier benefits on which the benefit depends;

- risks of non-achievement of benefit;

- who is accountable for the benefit

- who will receive the benefit

Benefit tracking information:

- who is responsible for tracking the benefits;

- one or more measures with the following information for each measure:
    - description
    - how the measure is to be tracked

- baseline value
- target or predicted value
- time when improvement is expected to start
- time when predicted value is expected to be reached
- to whom the measure is to be reported
- frequency of reporting.

A suggested template for a Benefit Profile is given below (Figure 18.4):

Benefit Profile

MANAGEMENT COMMITMENT					
No:		**Benefit in Short:**			
Detailed Description:					
Benefit Category:			**Business Impact:**		
No:	**Business Objective Supported**		**No:**	**Other benefits contributed to:**	
sigma Value type:			**Scorecard:**		
Target Value:			**Change Type:**		

ENABLERS

Enablers – Features:

BUSINESS ACTION

Required Business Changes:

Culture	Organisational	Policy	Process

ACCOUNTABILITY

	Name / Job Title:		Function / Dept:			
Who receives the benefit:						
Who is accountable:						
Measures:	**Current Value:**	**Target Value:**	**Start Time**	**End Time**	**Frequency :**	
To whom are measures reported:						

ALL — **Issues / Risks**

Figure 18.4   Template for a Benefit Profile

A complete set of Benefit Profiles covering all the benefits for the programme could be regarded as the database of information relating to benefit realisation. From this core repository other information can be generated including:

- most of the information required for a Business Case (project cost and resource information would need to come from elsewhere);

- the information required for the two further tools described below – Benefits Maps and IAMs;

- the information required for the BRP.

This core document feeds and supports other documents, including those described below. It should be neither a static document nor a decision-making document (except perhaps for the individual who is responsible for the particular benefit to which the profile relates). It is a repository for all critical benefit-related information, and as such its content will grow and develop throughout the life-cycle of the change initiative.

ORGANISATIONAL STRUCTURES

The organisational structure for a programme must provide for the effective management of business change (see Chapter 12) and ensure responsibilities for benefits are clear. Governance structures should minimise duplication but ensure that key review responsibilities do not fall between two review bodies (see Section 16.1).

INVESTMENT ASSESSMENT MATRICES (IAMS)

The horizontal and vertical axes of these matrices are benefit attributes (for example, benefit classification and beneficiary) and the cells of the matrix contain the benefits. Examples, including how and when they might be used, are given in Chapter 13.

TRAJECTORIES

A trajectory, represented in tabular or graphical formats, is simply a series of projected values. In the context of BRM this can be applied to measures, benefits, costs and net value (the difference between financial benefits and costs).

Measure trajectories may span all the programmes which impact the particular measure, (see Section 15.5) whereas benefit, cost and net value trajectories are usually applied to a single project or programme, as illustrated in Figure 18.5.

COST–BENEFIT ANALYSIS

This is a calculation, which frequently forms part of a financial justification and enables all the financial or cashable benefits to be balanced against the financial costs. This can be done using a net value trajectory which shows the net flow of cash in each time period or as a single net NPV. The NPV is the sum of the individual net flows, after a discount

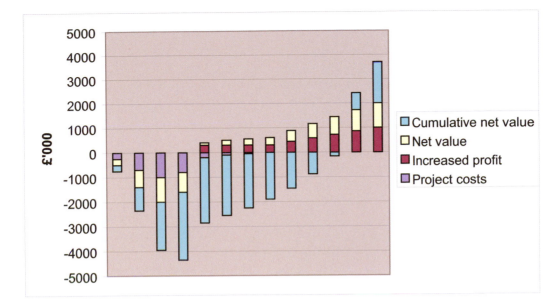

Figure 18.5   Cost, benefit and net value trajectories

factor has been applied to translate them into values at a common point of time (usually year 0). See Section 22.7.

18.3   Document Rationalisation

Five sets of documents, based on the five Programme Management themes, are required to manage change effectively and achieve full benefit realisation, namely:

1.   BENEFIT REALISATION

Documents which describe how BRM will be applied to the programme and provide all the details of the planned benefits, including how they support the vision, how and when they will be realised, how success will be monitored and reported, and naming those who will be accountable and responsible.

2.   STAKEHOLDER MANAGEMENT

Documents which define and classify the stakeholders, show how and when they will be engaged, and describe the techniques for involving them. The scope of the involvement should include:

- owning the vision;

- identifying the pathways to achievement, including the intermediate benefits;

- understanding, accepting and adopting the required changes;

- determining measures, and

- participating in the measurement process.

3.   SOLUTION MANAGEMENT

Documents which define the ultimate solution, including how any required enablers are to be integrated with business change, in order to generate the benefits on the way to the end goal and the fulfilment of the vision. This description of the future working model may include detailed specifications of enablers and process changes and the migration path into 'BAU'.

4.   PROGRAMME/PROJECT MANAGEMENT

Documents which help the Programme/Project Manager to manage the change delivery mechanism and ensure that the numerous activities are integrated effectively, to move everything towards the achievement of the vision.

5.   GOVERNANCE

Documents which are used to steer the programme through the series of formal reviews. At each stage they will provide the necessary justifications to continue the case for securing and releasing funding.

Using these five categories I have classified, in Figure 18.6, about 25 documents which are in fairly common use. These are also listed, by phase, and in approximately the order in which they are likely to be created.

Although some of these documents do not at first sight appear to be related to benefit realisation, all are in some sense so related. From this list I have distilled a set of essential documents (those that are necessary and sufficient for the realisation of the benefits); their structure and content are described in either this chapter or the following chapters.

This distillation recognises that many documents evolve through the change life-cycle, and are given different names at different stages (for example, the McCartney recommendation, as endorsed by the OGC includes a Strategic Outline Case, an Outline Business case and a Full Business case[1]). Wherever possible I prefer to view this as a single evolving document, the various names applying to snapshots taken at different times. This approach is usually welcomed by those who have to write business cases, and probably contributes to greater consistency.

---

1   www.ogc.gov.uk

Phase when created or started	Document	1 Benefit Realisation	2 Stakeholder Management	3 Solution Management	4 Programme Management	5 Governance
1	Strategy for Change – sometimes known as Programme Mandate					▓
1	Strategy for BRM – sometimes known as Benefits Management Strategy	▓				▓
1	Issues log				▓	
1	Risk Register / Log				▓	
	Review					
2	Stakeholder Management Strategy		▓			
2	Blueprint – sometimes known as Business / Target Operating Model			▓		
2	Programme Brief \ Strategic Outline Case (SOC)				▓	▓
	Review					
3	Benefit Realisation Plan	▓				
3	Stakeholder Management Plan (incl. Communications Strategy)		▓			
3	Requirements Definition Document			▓		
3	ITT / RFP			▓		
3	Programme Definition Document				▓	
3	Governance / Programme Structure				▓	▓
3	Project Initiation Document(s) – PID(s)				▓	
3	Programme Plan				▓	
3	Outline Business Case					▓
	Review					
4	Benefit Tracking Report	▓			▓	
4	Supplier contracts			▓	▓	
4	Change / Implementation Plan			▓		
4	Programme Management Strategy				▓	
4	Full Business Case					▓
	Review					
5	Milestone reports				▓	▓
	Review					
6	Post Implementation Review (PIR) Report				▓	▓
6	Post Programme Review (PPR) Report	▓			▓	▓
	Review					

Figure 18.6   Common documents grouped by theme and phase (table)

We will now consider each of the five Programme Management themes in turn, recognising that the scope for document rationalisation may be constrained by factors such as:

- the size of the change initiative – generally the larger the initiative the more separate documents are required;

- the purpose of the document;

- the primary recipients of the documents.

Ideally each theme would have a single document, but some themes need documents for different purposes and different audiences. In such cases it makes sense to have different documents.

BENEFIT REALISATION

Within this theme there are four distinct documents:

- *Strategy for BRM*. This document describes the way BRM is to be applied to the programme and is largely unrelated to the other benefit realisation documents. It is created early in the life-cycle and once agreed should remain fairly static.

- *Benefit Realisation Plan (BRP)*. This is the primary BRM document. It evolves throughout the life-cycle, or at least during the first four phases, and feeds or influences most of the other change management documents.

- *Benefit Tracking Report*. Although this will be based on the BRP it is a regular (probably monthly or quarterly) report of actuals, and so should be separate.

- *Post-Implementation Review (PIR)*. This documents reviews undertaken after all the changes have been implemented, often after programme closure, and focuses on the realisation of benefits, especially the effectiveness of benefit tracking.

STAKEHOLDER MANAGEMENT

The documents within this theme all share a common purpose with common recipients and so they should be integrated in a single document. The Stakeholder Management Strategy should evolve into the Stakeholder Management Plan which should include a communications strategy.

SOLUTION MANAGEMENT

Within this theme the primary evolving document is the Blueprint which describes the intended future state of the organisation, including how the various enablers will integrate with the necessary business changes to generate the planned benefits. There are several other documents which arise from or feed the Blueprint; they should be kept separate because they are required for specific purposes and for different recipients.

In particular, ITTs and any resulting procurement contracts for enablers and or services, which are legal documents with specific but limited purposes, must be separate. The Change Strategy, which describes how the Blueprint will be achieved, especially how the stakeholders will be motivated to change the way they work, is clearly dependent on the Blueprint but also has strong links with Stakeholder Management; it should probably be a separate document.

PROGRAMME MANAGEMENT

The Issues Log and the Risk Register, which are used on a day-to-day basis to gather information and feed actions or other documents, are largely self-contained and should probably be left as separate documents.

The more general programme management documents such as the Case for Change, the Programme Brief and the Programme Definition Document can be treated as a single evolving document perhaps called the Programme Management Strategy. The programme structure and programme plans can then be part of this combined document.

GOVERNANCE

The documents within this theme have a common overall purpose and are intended for the same recipients; they should therefore be treated as a single evolving document, which I will refer to as the Business Case. So Case for Change (Programme Mandate), Programme Brief, Strategic Outline Case, Outline Business Case and Full Business Case all become snapshots, taken at different stages, of the evolving Business Case.

Overlap between the Programme Management Strategy and the Business Case may make it possible to combine these into a single document.

18.4   Descriptions of Recommended Documents

Below is a schematic (Figure 18.7) showing a minimal set of documents for managing a large programme. The documents are grouped by the five programme themes, and show the phase when they are first created. A continuous line between documents indicates that they can be regarded as a single evolving document and the separate boxes would represent snapshots of the document, taken at different times for different purposes. A dotted line between documents indicates that the earlier document feeds and informs the later one, but the boxes represent distinct documents.

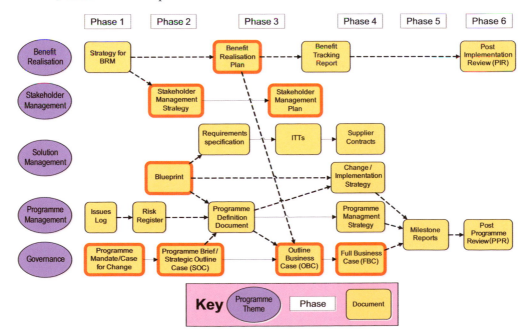

Figure 18.7   Common documents grouped by theme and phase (chart)

All the above documents are briefly described below in the order they appear in the diagram, where appropriate with cross-references to fuller descriptions in earlier sections. The core and evolving documents for four of the five themes, – the Benefit Realisation Plan, the Stakeholder Management Strategy, the Blueprint, and the evolving Business Case (highlighted by thick borders), are so important that fuller descriptions are also provided, respectively in Chapters 19 to 22.

All documents are to inform decisions and drive actions and the diagram below shows the documents required for the six review points in **sigma**'s change life-cycle.

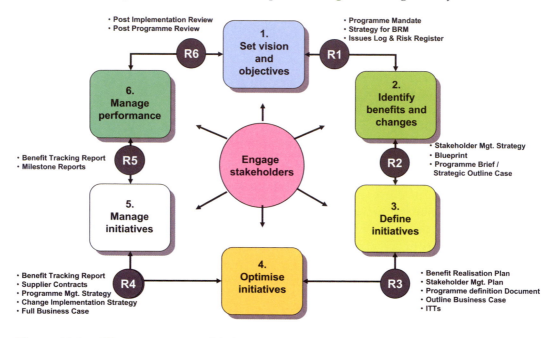

Figure 18.8   Change process with key review documents

STRATEGY FOR BRM

This document describes the approach to benefit management which is to be adopted for the particular change initiative. BRM is scalable and includes a very large tool-kit, from which careful selection is made to cater for each situation.

Often this will contain the plan for applying BRM, including an outline budget, high-level roles and responsibilities, an initial mechanism for engaging stakeholders, a schedule of events including workshops and review points and a communications strategy. It could also define the intended governance and review process since these should be benefit focused.

It should not be confused with a BRP, which describes how, when and where the particular benefits expected from the initiative will occur.

This document should be produced early in the change life-cycle, usually during Phase 1; it is sometimes referred to (for example, by OGC) as the Benefits Management Strategy.[2] For a fuller description see Section 7.10.

BENEFIT REALISATION PLAN (BRP)

Unlike the Strategy for BRM, which may include a plan for application of BRM, this is the plan for the realisation of the set of benefits specific to the particular change initiative. It would normally include:

- the vision;

- a Strategy Map of the objectives showing the programme boundary;

- Benefits Maps for each of the objectives, selected to bound the programme;

- an alignment check with the organisation's mission, direction and any strategic plans for change;

- measures which have been identified for at least the majority of the benefits;

- a set of trajectories for each of the benefit measures;

- a Benefit Distribution Matrix, showing benefits and disbenefits by stakeholder;

- BDMs showing the changes required to realise the benefits; and

- a full set of Benefit Profiles (usually as an appendix).

The BRP is a critical component of the Business Case at each review point, and the full BRP finally becomes a critical component of the full Business Case.

For further details of the BRP see Chapter 19.

BENEFIT TRACKING REPORT

This should report the values of the various identified measures against the target values for the reporting period. Where more than one initiative is contributing to the improvement in the measure, it may be necessary to assess and agree the respective contributions. The initiative managers should cooperate in this task, which may be moderated by the custodian of the Measures Dictionary. Possible reporting formats are shown in Figures 15.2 to 15.7 of Chapter 15.

---

2   MSP 2007 pages 68 and 198.

POST-IMPLEMENTATION REVIEW REPORT

This is produced after programme closure and assesses:

- the success to date of the programme in terms of benefit realisation; and

- the continuing effectiveness of the benefit tracking and reporting mechanism.

STAKEHOLDER MANAGEMENT STRATEGY

This strategy maps out how stakeholders are to be engaged throughout the change process so that they:

- share the vision;

- own the benefits;

- contribute to the design of the solution – the Blueprint;

- become committed to making the required business changes;

- are willing to measure and track the benefits.

The document defining the strategy should include sections on:

- stakeholders' interests and expectations;

- particular challenges;

- a plan for formal engagement, including a schedule of workshops;

- a plan to overcome specific stakeholder resistances;

- a communications strategy and plan;

- responsibilities for stakeholder management;

- measures to monitor the effectiveness of the Stakeholder Management Plans.

This is embodied in a strategy which becomes a plan and includes a communications strategy. It is described more fully in Chapter 20.

BLUEPRINT

This is a model of the future business environment necessary to achieve the vision. It describes the people, processes, information and technology capability that comprise this new business state. This combination of change entities should be capable of delivering all the expected benefits – the end benefits which relate to the vision, as well as the intermediate benefits which move the transformation in the right direction and at the right pace. An initial representation of the Blueprint is the Benefit Dependency Map (BDM) described more fully in Section 11.2. The BDM is a very valuable component of the Blueprint, not least because it maps the transition sequence through which the existing environment will evolve towards the vision.

As the programme develops, the Blueprint will evolve and is likely to include:

- new organisational structures;

- new processes and working practices;

- new job roles with job descriptions;

- how any new technology will become embedded in the changed environment;

- and is sometimes referred to as the New Business Model or Future Business State. For a fuller description see Chapter 21.

REQUIREMENTS SPECIFICATION

This is a document which should be based on the Blueprint; it defines in great detail the requirements of the solution, particularly the specification of enablers. It is needed to enable the creation or building of the enablers and is also required before any ITTs are issued.

Where organisations use their own or a proprietary technique for determining these specifications, it is important to ensure close ties with the Blueprint and the BDMs.

INVITATION TO TENDER (ITT)

The format and content of this formal document issued to potential suppliers depends on the procurement polices of the requesting organisation. In addition to the detailed requirement specification, it is helpful to offer access to the blueprint including the BDMs. Where possible it is helpful to share openly with suppliers the responsibility for benefit realisation.

SUPPLIER CONTRACTS

These are the legal documents describing the contract with the suppliers based on their responses to the ITTs. In choosing between suppliers who can meet the requirements, other services or features which they offer must be valued. This valuation must be linked to clear realisation of further benefits in support of the vision or end goal. See also Section 13.3d.

CHANGE/IMPLEMENTATION STRATEGY

This document describes the strategy for managing change, implementing the Blueprint and accomplishing the transition to BAU. For further information on the issues to be considered see Chapter 14.

ISSUES LOG

This is a log of all the issues identified during the life of the programme. The issues may relate to vision, objectives, benefits, disbenefits, measures, stakeholders, enablers, business changes, the integration of enablers and business changes, timing and so on. The log should be accessible to all those who may be involved in the programme, so that they can log issues as they arise, and see the resolution status of previously logged issues.

Against each issue you should log how, when and by whom the issue was identified and what action is planned or has occurred to resolve the issue. You may wish to record a degree of seriousness.

RISK REGISTER

A Risk Register is, as the name suggests, a register or log of risks. It is normally associated with a particular project or programme, though I would prefer to see it related to a planned outcome, such as the achievement of a vision. Each entry in a Risk Register would normally contain:

- a description of the possible adverse circumstance;

- the probability of its occurrence – which could be a percentage, but may be simply high, medium or low;

- the seriousness of the adverse circumstances – their impact.

Risks are added to the register as and when they are identified; another reason for relating the Risk Register to the vision rather than the programme is that some risks will probably be identified before the programme has been established.

Since each entity (enabler, business change or benefit) on the BDM represents a milestone along the path to the fulfilment of the vision, the risk of not achieving the vision is a combination of the risks of not achieving each of the milestones. So in seeking to identify risks, each entity along the path should be examined.

Against each entry you may wish also to record when, how and by whom the risk was identified and what actions have been taken to minimise or mitigate its potential impact.

THE PROGRAMME DEFINITION DOCUMENT

This is a detailed version of the Programme Brief which should include some solution options, with at least a high-level view of costs and related identification of potential projects. It should have links to or include summaries from:

- the Blueprint – what the programme is going to deliver;

- Programme Plan – how it will do it;

- BRP – what benefits to expect;

- Stakeholder Management Plan – who will be involved and how.

It should take account of registered risks and issues and provide a programme structure which will accommodate the potential projects and facilitate the management of business change.

PROGRAMME MANAGEMENT STRATEGY

Effectively an updated Programme Definition Document, this is the primary handbook for the Programme Manager. It includes programme organisation charts and terms of reference (TOR) for job roles and pulls together the key elements of the primary documents from the other themes.

CASE FOR CHANGE/PROGRAMME MANDATE

Normally produced at the end of Phase 1, this document describes the purpose, level of commitment and the Case for Change. It is a sketch of what is known about the programme under consideration, with sufficient detail, to support a recommendation to proceed to Phase 2.

My recommended structure, including some optional sections, is given below:

- Vision statement – (optional);

- Bounding objectives – preferably within a Strategy Map;

- Strategic fit – showing alignment with the organisation's strategy and balance with the rest of the portfolio;

- Value – high-level benefit ideas;

- Scope – context – market conditions and geographical/physical locations (optional);

- Boundaries – what is and what is not included – (optional);

- Timescales – critical windows or dependencies (optional); estimated duration;

- Stakeholders;

- Solution – ideas (optional);

- Dependencies (optional);

- Risks and options – any risks to the organisation from proceeding, including how these risks might vary for different options (optional).

This Case for Change is the earliest version (snapshot 1) of a Business Case and its approval by the Portfolio Board gives the mandate for proceeding to the definition phases of the programme. For document context see Section 8.8.

PROGRAMME BRIEF

The Programme Brief builds on the Programme Mandate, approved at the conclusion of Phase 1, and should include, with added detail where available:

- the vision;

- a Strategy Map of the objectives showing the programme boundary;

- Benefits Maps for each of the objectives, selected to bound the programme;

- an alignment check with the organisation's mission, direction and any strategic plans for change;

- a list of the primary stakeholders;

- a Benefit Distribution Matrix, showing benefits and disbenefits by stakeholder;

- BDMs showing the changes required to realise the benefits;

- a recommendation to proceed to Phase 3, or to discontinue the programme or whatever.

The Programme Brief should also include some comment on the stakeholder's appetite for the necessary degree of change.

It is unlikely that at this stage the benefits will be valued or the changes costed so the recommendation to proceed or not will be based on the general feel of the proposed programme, its alignment with the organisation's mission and direction, and evidence that thorough information gathering and analysis is being undertaken. The various maps should give confidence that the whole opportunity is being properly considered.

This information sets the scene for a controlled start-up of the programme. Once value and cost information is available in Phase 3, then a Programme Definition Document and an outline Business Case should be developed; these are essentially the next step on from the Programme Brief.

The Programme Brief is similar to OGC's Strategic Outline Case[3] and to **sigma**'s BOOST Report. The BOOST report was so named because its purpose is to launch the programme; its title is an acronym for its structure, namely:

- **B**usiness Vision and Benefits

- **O**perational Impact – including the stakeholder distribution of benefits and disbenefits

- **O**rganisational structure to make it happen (for example, proposal for programme)

- **S**olution – the Blueprint – at this stage in the life-cycle, the BDM

- **T**imescales – including any critical windows of opportunity.

STRATEGIC OUTLINE CASE

This is effectively a version of the Programme Brief suitable for the Sponsor and/or Portfolio Board – an early version of the evolving Business Case.

OUTLINE BUSINESS CASE

This is similar to the Programme Definition Document but is also part of the evolving Business Case.

BUSINESS CASES

A Business Case is a balance of benefits, costs and risks, intended to justify investment or further investment in pursuit of an end goal or vision. During a change life-cycle the Business Case should evolve, probably through several distinct stages. At each stage the case should justify investment for at least the next stage. Successive stages of the Business Case are likely to become more detailed as understanding of benefits, costs and risks increases.

---

3   OGC website.

Three of these stages usually correspond to the three types of Business Case referred to in OGC guidance,[4] namely:

- a Strategic Outline Case (SOC);

- an Outline Business case (OBC); and

- a Full Business case (FBC).

These cases may also cover various levels of work package or change management. For example, if a programme includes three projects, there may be a Business Case for each project and a business case for the overall programme, but sometimes it will be appropriate that only the programme has a business case.

A fuller consideration of the business case, as a single evolving document, is given in Chapter 22.

> **Use documents to focus actions on programme success.**
> **Include visuals, avoid duplication and automate production.**
> **Make documents work for you and not you for them.**

---

4   OGC website.

19

The Benefit Realisation Plan (BRP)

'A good plan is like a road map: it shows the final destination and usually the best way to get there.'

(H. Stanley Judd)

'Make no little plans. They have no magic to stir men's blood and probably themselves will not be realised. Make big plans. Aim high in hope and work. Remembering that a noble, logical diagram once recorded will not die.'

(Daniel H.Burnham)

19.1   How the Different Aspects of Realisation Match the Evolving Plan

As mentioned in Section 3.1, dictionary definitions of the word *realise*, in the order they are listed, are:

- *be fully aware, conceive as real;*

- *understand clearly;*

- *make realistic;*

- *convert into actuality, achieve;*

- *convert into money.*

Each can be applied to benefits and the sequence matches the logical stages through the development of the BRP. The benefit is first conceived as real, though at this early stage it is only aspirational and short on detail; it is then understood clearly – the detail is probed; it is then made realistic through the mapping of its dependencies – earlier benefits and required changes; then as the changes are implemented the benefit is achieved; finally in certain situations the benefit may be converted into money.

Although much of the content of the BRP has been described earlier it is repeated for completeness to give a full description of the plan.

19.2   Purpose of the BRP

The primary purpose of the plan is to facilitate the realisation of the planned benefits. So it should be created to enable the Programme Team and those involved in business change to keep track of anything and everything necessary to benefit realisation or that could put benefit realisation at risk; and to facilitate the tracking of benefits by Measure Monitors and Benefit Owners.

A secondary purpose is to support the Business Case, so the plan must tie in to the content and structure of the Business Case – see Chapter 22. For this purpose the BRP could be an attachment to the Business Case, or its component information, charts and templates could form part of the Business Case.

19.3   Structure and Content of the BRP

The BRP shows why, when, where and how all the benefits, for a particular change initiative, are expected to be realised. It draws on the information contained in the Benefit Profiles (see next Section 19.4), and often includes the full set of profiles as an appendix.

It should include, roughly in the following order:

1.   the Vision Statement for the programme or project to provide the context for the benefits and the overall purpose; it should also show, via a Strategy Map of objectives, how the bounding objectives or end benefits relate to the vision;

2.   a full set of Benefits Maps, probably one for each of the bounding objectives;

3.   the set of measures, each with its baseline value, target and timescale, for each of the benefits to be tracked, (which should be the majority of those appearing in the maps – see Sections 10.4, 10.8 and Chapter 15);

4.   selective inclusion of IAMs (see Section 13.3) to demonstrate alignment and/ or balance with respect to:

   • the organisation's mission and strategy;

   • stakeholders;

   • business impact (for example, **sigma** Grid); and

   • degree of transformation.

5.   a summary trajectory showing when all the benefits are expected to be realised. Benefit trajectories when combined with cost trajectories form a key element of the justification section of a Business Case (see Section 22.7);

6.   details of all the dependencies, generally best presented in the form of a BDM (see Section 11.2);

7.   the mechanism to be employed for tracking and reporting benefit realisation – this should include a description of the mechanism for attributing improvements in measures which impact more than one programme;

8.   the accountabilities and responsibilities relating to benefit realisation, naming specific individuals, and perhaps including signatures confirming acceptance of responsibility for specific benefits.

19.4   The Information Source for the BRP – Benefit Profiles

This document/template holds the comprehensive set of information relating to a single benefit so a complete set of Profiles is the primary source of information for the BRP. A single Profile is especially useful to the person who is responsible for the realisation of its benefit so it is sometimes referred to as a Benefit Realisation Proforma. It would normally include:

- identifier information – number, title and perhaps fuller description;

- its impact and contribution to business/programme vision, objectives and goals;

- categorisation(s) to check for balance and alignment;

- dependencies – internal and external to the particular change initiative;

- stakeholder information, including benefit beneficiaries and owners;

- measures and measure attributes, including baseline, target, realisation timescales, measurement frequency and reporting mechanism;

- assumptions and risks related to the realisation of the benefit.

A fuller description of content with an example template is given in Section 18.2.

19.5   The Core of the BRP – Maps

Maps should be a fundamental part of a BRP. Their visual nature aids communication, reducing ambiguity, confirming chronology and increasing clarity of purpose. A single BRP is likely to contain the following maps:

- a Strategy Map, linking objectives in cause-and-effect relationships through to the end goal or vision, and highlighting the two or three bounding objectives which summarise and bound the change initiative (see Sections 8.6 and 8.7);

- a Benefits Map for each of the bounding objectives and possibly a consolidated Benefits Map (see Section 9.5);

- BDMs corresponding to each of the Benefits Maps (see Section 11.2).

Of these, the most static is the Strategy Map which is unlikely to change as a consequence of more detailed analysis or programme performance. In contrast, the status and content of both Benefits Map and BDM will change with progress. Initially the Benefits Map is a wish list, then a set of feasible options, then a prioritised set of options, then the plan (as some paths are chosen and perhaps others rejected), then a vehicle for communicating expectations and finally a report of actual progress towards the achievement of the vision.

These maps are extremely useful for:

- managing benefit realisation, especially the dependent changes;

- assessing the impact of unexpected changes – internal and external;

- communicating expectations;

- tracking benefits;

- avoiding double counting of benefits;

- attributing benefits to their source;

- maximising benefit realisation.

Benefits Maps are more fully considered in Section 9.5, and are used throughout this book.

19.6   Developing the BRP

In developing this plan it is important to remember the basis for benefit realisation. In the context of implementing and managing change, benefits are realised as people do things differently, as they change:

- their attitudes;

- the way they work;

- the way they communicate; and

- the way they make decisions.

Realisation is the opposite of forcible extraction (see Section 3.2); it is not a question of simply adjusting budgets, but rather of engaging with stakeholders to encourage and motivate them to change. Often team effort is required.

So the BRP should be developed through a process of stakeholder engagement, consultation and negotiation.

19.7   Who Owns the BRP?

The BRP should be owned by the Programme Director/Manager on behalf of the Sponsor/SRO who has the overall accountability for benefit realisation. This is very clear in OGC's MSP,[1] which states that the SRO is ultimately accountable for the overall realisation of benefits from the programme. In a sense the SRO owns the plan on behalf of the major stakeholders and beneficiaries of the plan. Senior representatives of these stakeholders usually sit on the Programme Board, of which the SRO is a member, normally the chair.

Benefit Owners will have an interest in the BRP and may like a copy but their special interest will be in the Benefit Profiles pertaining to the particular benefits for which they are responsible. These owners, if they have not actually been engaged in the BRM Process, should certainly have agreed the content of their specific profiles.

Document and share bold intentions and visionary expectations.

'Aim high in hope and work, remembering that a noble, logical diagram once recorded will not die.'
(Daniel H. Burnham)

---

1   MSP page 41.

The Stakeholder Management Strategy and Plan

'The shepherd always tries to persuade the sheep that their interests and his own are the same.'

(Henri B. Stendhal)

'It is not the strongest of the species that survive, nor the most intelligent, but the one most responsive to change.'

(Charles Darwin)

20.1 The Purpose of Stakeholder Management

It is important to build and maintain trust between the Programme Team and the different stakeholder groups, and to encourage productive relationships between stakeholders. Stakeholders must be engaged throughout the change process so that they:

- share the vision;

- own the benefits;

- contribute to the design of the solution – the Blueprint;

- become committed to making the required business changes;

- are willing to measure and track the benefits.

Although stakeholder involvement is always important, the longer the duration and the broader the scope of a programme, the more critical a formal stakeholder management process becomes.

20.2 Responsibility for Stakeholder Management

The overall responsibility for stakeholder management lies with the Programme Manager, but since all members of the Programme Team are likely to be dealing with stakeholders, each carries responsibility in this important area. The Programme Manager may delegate specific responsibilities to certain roles such as that of the Business Change Manager.

The Programme Manager may need help from the Programme Director, if such exists, the Sponsor or SRO, and the members of the Programme Board in dealing with stakeholders outside his or her direct sphere of influence.

20.3 The Content of the Stakeholder Management Strategy and Plan

This is a single evolving document which should cover the following topics:

STAKEHOLDER INTERESTS AND EXPECTATIONS

Stakeholders must be identified and grouped or classified (see Section 2.3), and their interests and concerns determined, through both formal and informal engagement, which should cover:

- their general areas of interest;

- the benefits and disbenefits they are likely to experience;

- the benefits for which they will be responsible;

- the changes they will experience;

- the changes for which they will be responsible.

This information will develop over the life of the programme. Areas of interest should be determined in Phase 1 and can be represented in a Stakeholder Interest Matrix (sometimes referred to as a Stakeholder Map), an example of which is given in Figure 20.1 below:

	Strategic Alignment	Competition	Customer relations	Operational changes	Financial	Safety	Legality
Customers			X			X	
Partners		X	X		X	X	
Suppliers				X			
Shareholders	X				X		X
Senior Managers	X	X			X	X	X
Staff		X	X			X	
Unions				X		X	X
Regulatory bodies						X	X

Figure 20.1   Stakeholder Interest Matrix

Benefits and disbenefits which the stakeholders are likely to experience should be determined in Phase 2 and are represented in a Benefit Distribution Matrix, an example of which is given in Figure 20.2.

Key Benefits and Disbenefits by Stakeholder	Board	Sponsor (e.g. SRO) & Programme Board	Programme Director/Manager	Business Change Manager	Programme Team	Enabler Project Teams	Business Manager	Business User
Benefit								
More optimum programme portfolio	G	G					G	
Earlier recognition of ineffective programmes	G	G						
Improved stakeholder engagement			G	G	G		G	G
Clearer sense of direction			G	G	G			G
More effective programme management			G	G	G			
Better use of resources		G		G	G			
Improved management of risk		G			G			
Reduced Enabler costs		G				G		
More financial benefits realised	G			G				
More non-financial benefits realised				G			G	G
Greater visibility of realised benefits		G						
Improved Programme image			G					
Disbenefit								
Extra effort by the business							R	R
Slower start to the programme					R	R	R	R
Enabler project targets threatened						R		

Benefit	(green)
Disbenefit	(red)

Figure 20.2   Benefit Distribution Matrix for embedding BRM within an organisation

Change-related information will be added from Phase 3 onwards. A change-stakeholder matrix (see Figure 25.5 in Section 25.2), showing how the stakeholders are impacted by the potential changes, should facilitate management of the changes.

PARTICULAR CHALLENGES

Any special challenges should be identified. These might appear as a result of:

- the stakeholder analysis (for example, if a stakeholder is expecting disbenefits and insufficient compensating benefits);

- cultural differences;

- informal intelligence gathering.

A PLAN FOR FORMAL ENGAGEMENT, INCLUDING A SCHEDULE OF WORKSHOPS

Workshops engage stakeholders efficiently and effectively (see Sections 2.5 and 2.6) and, provided they are well structured and facilitated, participants generally find them enjoyable and valuable. Stakeholders are, however, generally busy people and it is easy to overdo a good thing, so it is important to plan well ahead and to schedule a varied, appropriate and chronological series of formal engagement sessions. Each session should be designed to capture stakeholder needs and aspirations, ideas for change and concerns, in the process securing buy-in and commitment.

A PLAN TO OVERCOME PARTICULAR STAKEHOLDER RESISTANCE

However carefully stakeholders are involved, situations of resistance to the direction of the programme may arise. These may result from concern about a particular change leading to people feeling threatened or vulnerable, disbelief in certain benefit targets or lack of understanding as to why change is necessary. Specific plans to 'sweeten the pill' will be required, and the first requirement is that the concerns are clear.

A specific technique for identifying, assessing and responding to resistance is described in Section 14.6.

COMMUNICATIONS STRATEGY OR PLAN

The above engagement plan relates to formal events; a much wider communications strategy is necessary, covering: informing, involvement, intelligence gathering and enthusing. So, in addition to formal events, such as workshops and focus groups, newsletters, marketing literature, user groups and social gatherings may also play a part. The strategy and plan for comprehensive communication must be disseminated to the stakeholders, as well as being included in this document.

RESPONSIBILITIES FOR STAKEHOLDER MANAGEMENT

If the Programme Manager's responsibility for stakeholder management has been delegated or shared, the Stakeholder Management Strategy should define how and to whom it has been devolved.

MEASURES TO MONITOR THE EFFECTIVENESS OF THE STAKEHOLDER MANAGEMENT PLANS

The Stakeholder Management Strategy should also include the measures by which the success of stakeholder management is to be monitored.

20.4   Developing the Strategy and Plan

This evolving strategy starts with the identification and assessment of stakeholders in Phase 1 and continues throughout the life of the programme. The stages of the document are illustrated in the schematic in Section 18.4, Figure 18.7.

> **Document how you intend to work with stakeholders so as to: engage them in the process, build on their interests, encourage flexibility, engender commitment and celebrate success.**

21

The Blueprint

'The great successful men of the world have used their imagination. They think ahead and create their mental picture in all its details, filling in here, adding a little there, altering this a bit and that a bit, but steadily building.'

(Robert Collier)

'Cherish your visions and your dreams, as they are the Blueprints of your ultimate achievements.'

(Napoleon Hill)

21.1   What is a Blueprint?

It is *'a model of the future business environment which is needed to achieve the vision'*; it is similar to an engineering plan showing how all the parts fit and work together. It describes the people, processes, information and technology capability that comprise this new business state. This combination of change entities should be capable of delivering all the expected benefits – the end benefits, which relate to the vision, as well as the intermediate benefits, needed to move the transformation in the right direction and at the right pace.

It is sometimes referred to as the Target Operating Model, New Business Model or Future Business State.

21.2   Why have a Blueprint?

A fundamental weakness of many projects and programmes is that enablers are acquired or built and then implemented, but their actual use by the user population and their place in the fulfilment of the vision have never been thought through. Project Managers then complain that the users are not using the new enabler in the intended manner, or are not using it all. Users complain that the enablers do not meet their needs or do not fit with their existing processes. No benefits can be realised until this stalemate is unblocked, a process which at such a late stage, when it has not been planned as part of the Blueprint, will be costly; in addition the solution is likely to be far from optimum.

So without a Blueprint – the picture or plan as to how enablers should fit with the business changes – benefits are likely to be significantly curtailed and delayed.

Some years ago **sigma** was involved with a UK retail bank which was introducing a suite of new IT applications throughout their branch network. After they had installed many of the applications, including one to handle standing orders and direct debits, we discovered they were running two separate training courses covering this area. One course taught staff about the concepts, principles and some of the processes related to standing orders and direct debits, the other course explained how to use the particular computer application which dealt with standing orders and direct debits. Amazed that these courses had not been integrated into a single training module, we were not surprised to learn that one of the biggest sources of errors made by branch staff was in their handling of standing orders and direct debits.

21.3   Creation and Ownership of the Blueprint

The Blueprint is a description of the desired future business state and as such should be created with and owned by the business. Although business managers may need help from relevant experts to shape and define the Blueprint, abdicating their responsibilities, with regard to its creation, has serious consequences.

On two occasions I have been involved in commissioning significant domestic changes – one was a major redevelopment and extension of our house and the other the transformation of the field behind our house into a beautifully landscaped garden. On both occasions my wife and I had strong ideas about the benefits we were seeking but worked closely with relevant experts to design and document feasible solutions which matched our aspirations. Several iterations were involved but eventually agreed plans (Blueprints) were drawn up. In both instances this was done before potential suppliers were approached and the projects to deliver the Blueprints were commissioned.

Creating at least a high-level Blueprint before engaging those who will deliver it reduces the risk of being side-tracked and going down inappropriate paths. Inevitably as each project proceeded there were occasions when small changes to the Blueprints were discussed and agreed. I believe this sequence of events, which fits well with the recommended change life-cycle (Figures 4.9, 7.3, 17.1, 23.1 and 24.1), delivers the best value for money. So in the business environment I believe the high-level Blueprint is best developed, with help from the Benefit Facilitator, before the Programme Team has been established and certainly before projects to deliver enablers have been commissioned.

21.4   The Content of the Blueprint

An early and high-level representation of the Blueprint is the diagram of overlapping fried eggs, an example of which is given in Figure 21.1.

This shows how three sets of enablers, which could be delivered through three projects, integrate with groups of business changes, in support of the three programme objectives. Although the content of the business change is not specified in the diagram, the picture

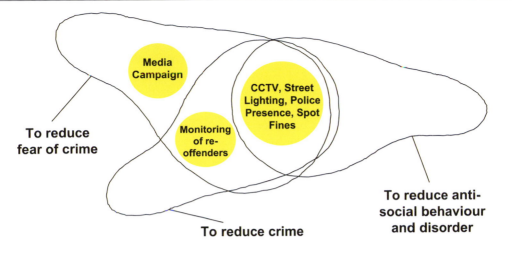

Figure 21.1   An early high-level view of the Blueprint

nevertheless highlights that business change is required to nurture and bring to life the power and potential of the three yolks.

Another early, but more detailed, picture of the Blueprint is the BDM, which is described more fully in Section 11.2. The BDM is a very valuable component of the Blueprint, not least because it maps the transition sequence through which the existing environment will evolve towards the vision.

As the programme develops, the Blueprint will continue to evolve and is likely eventually to include:

- new organisational structures;

- new processes and working practices;

- new job roles with job descriptions;

- how any new technology will become embedded in the changed environment.

At a detailed level it must map the transition from the 'as is' to the 'to be' and can be subdivided by function, business unit, job role and/or location as best fits the size and complexity of the transition.

21.5   Maintaining and Developing the Blueprint

The initial high-level version of the Blueprint should be created early in the life-cycle, usually in Phase 2, since many other documents depend upon it, especially enabler specifications and requirements analysis. The BDMs, which are initially created in Phase 2, provide an early picture of the Blueprint. This initial picture of the Blueprint will therefore generally be created, before the programme or project has been formally established, by senior business stakeholders assisted where possible by the Benefit Facilitator.

Once the programme or project has been formally established and a Programme/Project Manager is in place, they should take responsibility, in conjunction with the business, for the maintenance and further development of the Blueprint and ultimately its implementation.

> **Apply your imagination to the vision to create the Blueprint.**
> **Refine, adapt and implement it until vision becomes reality.**

22

The Business Case

'A goal without a plan is just a wish.'

(Antoine de Saint-Exupery)

'The secret of success is constancy of purpose.'

(Benjamin Disraeli)

22.1   Purpose of the Business Case

The purpose of the Business Case is:

- to steer programme activity towards the eventual achievement of the vision;

- to enable periodic reviews to assess whether the programme should:
  - proceed to the next phase
  - be terminated or
  - be held pending further analysis.

The Business Case must be seen as a living document, not something which simply sits on a shelf. It should drive programme activity and take account of changes within the external environment (goalposts are no longer fixed) as well as adapting to learnings from within the programme arena, so that it can be used to judge whether the programme is, and continues to remain, desirable, viable and achievable.

For each formal review, within a programme or project life-cycle, documents must be presented, describing progress to date and mapping out future expectations, including costs, benefits and risks. Future expectations should be the basis of any justification for continuing with the project. In many formal review structures, such as the Gateway Process recommended by OGC, these documents have specific names, such as: Programme Mandate, Programme Definition, Strategic Outline Case, Outline Business case and Full Business case. Many Programme and Project Managers are understandably overwhelmed by the thought of having to produce a whole sequence of different formal documents, which is one of the reasons why we prefer to think of the Business Case as a single evolving document (see Figure 18.7), or at least a single database of evolving information from which required documents can be automatically generated.

If an integrated software system is not available (see Chapter 29), we recommend that for any particular change initiative there should be a single Business Case which brings the programme or project into being, and then takes it through its various phases and reviews. The case will evolve through the life-cycle as more detail becomes available. As it is used for different reviews at the conclusion of the different phases, it might be given different names, snapshots of a single evolving document, such as those mentioned in the previous paragraph.

All programmes, and any stand-alone projects which are not part of a programme, should have a Business Case.

22.2   Structure of Business Case

The basic structure of the evolving Business Case should include sections on the following:

- purpose of the change, including how it supports the organisation's mission;

- a realistic assessment of the value or worth of the investment, including assumptions and risks;

- the future business state or Blueprint;

- how the Blueprint is to be delivered and the vision achieved, including maps, options and costs;

- the financial assessment – ROIs, payback and NPVs;

- proposed mechanisms for benefit tracking and reporting;

- programme organisation and governance structures;

- opinions and details of the stakeholders who have been engaged and the method of engagement;

- summary of issues for consideration and decisions by the Review Board, including a recommendation as to whether or not to proceed further.

The content for this structure is described in the following sections of this chapter; references to the sections, which describe how the information is generated, are included.

22.3   Purpose of the Change, and How it Supports the Organisation's Mission

This should cover the following topics:

THE VISION

Start with a Vision Statement, which provides the context and purpose of the proposed change and is sometimes the ultimate goal. The source of the vision, or an outline of the process by which it was determined or received, must be included. Ideally the Vision Statement will be sufficiently explicit to make it clear when the vision is fulfilled (for example, by the end of the decade to put a man on the moon and bring him safely back again). On occasions it may have to be more general (for example, to be recognised as the leading player in a particular field), so success criteria may need to be defined in terms of the supporting objectives. A good vision is unlikely to change in response to external influences; though once it is achieved it may be replaced by other visions.

OBJECTIVES, STRATEGY MAP AND SCOPE BOUNDARY

The objectives which support the vision and provide a fuller explanation for the change should be clearly stated. For clarity and consistency we suggest that these should all start with the word 'to'. It is helpful to include a list of some of the main drivers for change, perhaps grouped by objective.

In addition to listing the objectives, possibly linked to their drivers, it is important to present them in a Strategy Map – a 'cause and effect' relationship diagram. This diagram should link the objectives in a left to right flow with the vision at the right-hand end.

Although the map should represent a set of logical paths, of which all or most will lead to the vision, some of the objectives may lie beyond the scope of the proposed change. It is helpful therefore to mark the recommended scope boundary, and the two or three end objectives for the programme or project, on this Strategy Map (see Figure 22.1).

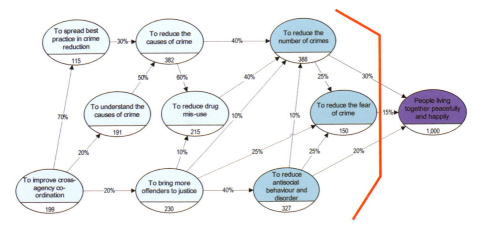

Figure 22.1   Bounded and weighted Strategy Map linked to a vision

Not all paths through the map are of equal importance. Some make a greater contribution towards vision achievement than others; this can be represented by weighting the paths and scoring the objectives possibly before determining the scope boundary. This additional information should be included in the Business Case.

STRATEGIC ALIGNMENT

It is possible to come up with a worthwhile vision and clear supporting objectives which are not in line with the organisation's mission and direction. I have heard of several companies whose investment in change was not aligned to their business strategy and direction; consequently and not surprisingly they ended in bankruptcy. It is vital therefore that the Business Case shows the alignment between the proposed change and the business direction. Although there are a variety of possible expressions for this alignment, the best is probably a simple matrix relating the objectives for the change with the organisation's objectives, strategies or KPIs, where the cells of the matrix will hold an indication of the degree of contribution, as a percentage value or as high/medium/low. See Figure 22.2 for the contribution to business objectives from the programme to embed BRM within an organisation.

Business Objective Programme Objective	To create and maintain an optimum portfolio	To improve programme ROIs	To change to a more benefit focused culture
To develop and grow the business			
To improve service to customers			
To increase profitability			
To develop staff towards greater agility and openness to change			

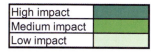

High impact	
Medium impact	
Low impact	

Figure 22.2   Programme alignment/contribution to business objectives

STAKEHOLDERS

Although a proposed change may be very advantageous for an organisation, supporting a clear vision and aligned with the organisation's objectives, some people may not view it as such. So it is essential to consider the stakeholders – those who will be affected by the proposed changes – and to assess, from an early stage, their degree of commitment to the proposal. It may be helpful to include signatures of senior representatives of some of the key stakeholders, indicating their support, at least to the vision and direction. Any strong opposition to the programme should also be documented in the Business Case.

22.4   The Value or Worth of the Investment, Including Assumptions and Risks

The value of the investment need not be financial although it often has a financial component. Experience shows that approximately 10 per cent of benefits are financial, in the sense that they represent real money, so 90 per cent of the value of an investment is likely to be represented in non-financial terms.

A primary representation of worth is the Benefits Map which contains not only all the benefits but also an indication of the sequence if not the time in which they should be achieved. One or more measures, each with a target improvement, should be attached to each benefit on the map. This detail will not all be available initially (for example, very little of the benefit-related information will be available for Review 1 and very little measure information for Review 2), but it will build up gradually as the programme progresses through the phases.

The initial Benefits Maps, as generated in Phase 2, are aspirational and effectively represent wish lists. As the changes required to deliver the benefits in these maps are identified and added so the maps are transformed into BDMs. These BDMs represent a set of feasible options so in Phase 3 it is possible, by weighting the paths and scoring the benefits, to select the higher value routes – the 'super highways' – ignoring or postponing the rest. In Phase 4 these BDMs (perhaps with some routes removed) become a plan and, in Phases 5 and 6, a report of actual progress towards the achievement of the vision.

The Benefits Map describes the overall worth of the programme. Net worth – benefits less disbenefits – for individual stakeholders can be shown in a Benefit Distribution Matrix.

The Benefit Distribution Matrix is an example of an IAM; it may be helpful to include other examples in this section of the Business Case. These matrices are easily generated from the Benefit Profiles and can aid assessment of the worth of the investment. An example of such a matrix, previously given in Section 13.3, is given below – Figure 22.3

Value type / Business Impact		Speculative	Strategic	Key-operational	Support
Definite	Financial			Reduced salary costs	Reduced telephone bill
	Non-financial			Greater administrative productivity	
Expected	Financial		Increased sales revenue from other products		
	Non-financial		Improved responsiveness to clients		
Logical	Financial		Improved management of insurance risk		
	Non-financial	Improved image	Greater client satisfaction		
Intangible		Increased client confidence			

Figure 22.3   IAM – by business impact and value type

This matrix holds all the identified benefits showing both their **sigma** Value Types and their Business Impact, thus indicating (from the vertical dimension) the degree of confidence in any targets set, and (from the horizontal dimension) those benefits with high potential but also high risk, those which will develop and take the organisation forward, those which solve some of today's critical problems, and those which are merely 'nice to have'.

For a fuller consideration of Investment Assessment Matrices see Section 13.3.

The Business Case should state clearly any significant risks especially risks pertinent to the non-realisation of the benefits.

22.5   The Future Business State or Blueprint

Alongside the vision, a description of the future business state or business model is necessary, including how and where the required enablers will be embedded, their related changes to business practice and some indication of the transition path. This is the Blueprint; it is likely to be a separate document (see Chapter 21), though the main elements of the Blueprint may be included here.

As the programme progresses and more detailed aspects of the business change are planned, the Blueprint will take on additional dimensions, including:

- organisational structures;

- staffing levels;

- skill requirements;

- technology and information needs;

- required facilities, including accommodation and buildings.

A fully developed Blueprint will help define the transition to 'BAU' and should provide a basis for calculating whole life costs.

22.6   How the Blueprint is to be Delivered and the Vision Achieved, Including Maps, Options and Costs

While the Blueprint describes the future business state, including enablers to be acquired and how they will be embedded into the new organisation, there are likely to be several possible acquisition or procurement options. These may carry different costs, risks, timescales and cashflow implications. So it is often helpful to present options within the Business Case, especially where significant procurement is involved. Options for business change may also be available and should also be presented, with their impacts on different stakeholders and related risks.

The main source of this information will be the set of BDMs, particularly if their paths are weighted and the options are scored. These maps fill the void which so often exists between the enablers and the end objectives or vision and so represent a realistic and practical path to move the business environment from the 'as is' to the 'to be'. The analysis in this section should therefore cross-reference these maps, which will appear in the BRP, but could also be included within the appendices to the Business Case.

I would always question the credibility of any Business Case which does not include a set of maps (Strategy and Benefit Dependency) and strongly encourage the rejection of the related programme or project.

22.7   The Financial Assessment – ROIs, Payback and NPVs

The financial assessment is a key part of most business cases. It will include a schedule of costs, which is generally straightforward to compute; it is important to include the cost of the business change and any variations in the BAU costs, for example the running costs of a new facility such as a computer system or building. This cost schedule must be integrated with a schedule of the cashable financial benefits, as illustrated in Figure 22.4, to give the net benefit trajectory.

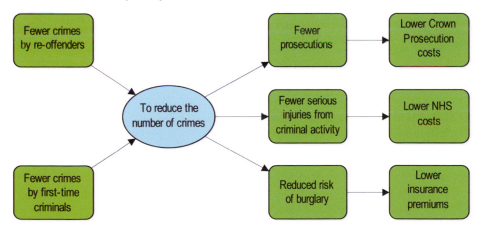

Figure 22.4   Consequential benefits resulting from 'reduced crime'

The cashable financial benefits will probably appear at the right-hand end of the Benefits Map, often to the right of the bounding objective(s) to which the map relates. If we consider the example in Section 9.5 where a bounding objective was 'to reduce crime', consequential benefits might be as illustrated in Figure 22.4, which include at the far right the following financial or economic benefits:

- lower Crown Prosecution Service (CPS) costs;

- lower insurance premiums (for house and car owners);

- lower NHS costs.

I refer to these three as economic benefits as they do not represent real money to the police force that was sponsoring the programme and the computation of their value is based on economic data.

Taking the costs of the programme to reduce crime together with the three consequential financial benefits we get the following trajectories over a nine-year period:

£m	2005	2006	2007	2008	2009	2010	2011	2012	2013
Cost of reducing crime	-3.0	-3.5	-3.2	-2.2	-0.8	-0.4	-0.4	-0.4	-0.4
Reduced CPS costs		0.5	1.2	1.8	2.0	2.3	2.2	1.7	1.5
Lower insurance premiums				0.5	0.7	0.8	0.8	0.8	0.8
Reduced NHS costs			0.5	0.9	1.1	1.0	0.9	0.9	0.9
Total benefits	0.0	0.5	1.7	3.2	3.8	4.1	3.9	3.4	3.2
Net benefit	-3.0	-3.0	-1.5	1.0	3.0	3.7	3.5	3.0	2.8
Cumulative net benefit	-3.0	-6.0	-7.5	-6.5	-3.5	0.2	3.7	6.7	9.5

Figure 22.5   Net benefit trajectory for 'reduced crime'

The break-even point, the point at which the cumulative net benefit becomes positive (that is, where the cumulative net benefit curve crosses the x-axis), occurs in mid 2010, giving a five-year pay back period (see Figure 22.6).

In a volatile economic environment, many organisations, especially in the private sector, will invest only in changes which have short payback periods (for example, of less than three or even two years).

The payback calculation has only considered the economic benefits and has summed them to obtain the above results. Apart from the difficulty in attributing improvements in the economic benefits to this programme, the summation has little meaning, since each of the three financial benefits is of value to a different stakeholder and probably none of these stakeholders has made the investment in the programme.

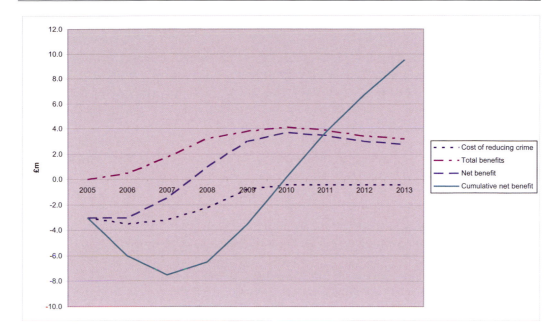

Figure 22.6   Net benefit trajectory for 'reduced crime'

A third measure which is frequently used in financial assessments is the NPV of the investment. This takes the stream of future costs and discounts them back to a common point in time (usually Year 0), where the discount factor may be based on some combination of the projected rate of inflation and cost of borrowing. They can then be simply summed to give a single value in current money. This value is generally referred to as the Discounted Cash Flow (DCF). A similar process can be applied to the future benefits stream. The NPV is the difference between the DCF for benefits and the DCF for costs. The ROI is the return expressed as a percentage of the investment.

So

$$ROI = 100 \times NPV/Costs\ DCF$$

These computations are mechanistic and so straightforward. The challenge lies in valuing the benefits.

Often in order to obtain an NPV which is positive and sufficiently attractive, artificial financial values are given to non-financial benefits. This practice distorts the truth and generally leads to a variety of problems (see Chapter 27). I prefer to evaluate the true cash position and if this gives a negative NPV, to promote the worth of the non-financial benefits.

It is worth remembering that securing funds, by deliberately overstating benefits or giving them unreal financial values, is tantamount to fraud.

22.8   Proposed Mechanisms for Benefit Tracking and Reporting

It is vital that the Business Case covers details of the proposed mechanism for benefit tracking and reporting, which should include:

- one or more Benefits Maps;

- at least one measure for each, or at least the majority, of the benefits;

and for each measure:

- baseline value;

- target improvement expected from this particular programme;

- time period over which the improvement is expected;

- measurement frequency;

- how the underlying metrics are to be tracked;

- person responsible for the measurement;

- stakeholders to whom the measurements will be reported.

The reporting mechanism should include a definition of what represents an acceptable deviation from plan, especially when a RAG status is used. Where a benefit has several measures, a combined tolerance should be defined.

22.9   Programme Organisation and Governance Structures

The Business Case should document the programme organisation structure (see Chapter 12), naming key players and their roles. Standard TOR for these roles across the organisation avoids the need to give them within the Case. A recommended set of roles with brief descriptions is given in Chapter 6.

This section should also include the programme review schedule, details of the Review Boards, their different functions and responsibilities. Again standard TOR for the reviews and the Review Boards across the organisation are helpful.

22.10 Progress to Date – Milestone Achievement

Programmes often run over several years and while the case is being made for investment in the later tranches of a programme, progress should also be reported on the achievement of early milestones. A milestone can be any significant point, event or target in the plan, embracing enablers, changes and benefits.

Benefit tracking should start as soon as the measures have been identified; in many programmes this will be early in the programme life-cycle. So benefit reporting will already be under way by the time later versions of the Business Case are presented to Review Boards. In these situations benefits should be included among the milestones reported.

An excellent way to monitor and report progress is to use the maps themselves, in either Benefits or Benefit Dependency formats, in conjunction with the normal RAG conventions. For further details see Figures 15.4 to 15.7 of Chapter 15.

22.11 Issues for Consideration and Decision by the Review Board

As the Business Case evolves through the programme life-cycle, content develops, is refined, approaches completeness and becomes more accurate. Although the review of the Business Case will vary, depending on the review point and the information the case contains, there are some fundamental questions which should always be answered, including:

- Should the programme be terminated or mothballed?

- Should there be any major changes to scope or direction?

- Are there several routes to the end goal – different options to choose from?

- What resources – funding, Programme Team, third party suppliers, business staff time – are required for the future plan, in particular the next phase?

- Are there actions to be taken by members of the Review Board (for example: open doors, secure the cooperation and commitment of stakeholders outside the control or influence of the Programme Team)?

The information available to answer these questions will be different for each review point or gateway as the Business Case becomes steadily more comprehensive and approaches completion. The particular form these questions take, at each of the six recommended reviews, is summarised below, and should support the aims of the six reviews as described in Section 17.3.

1ST REVIEW

- How well do the bounding objectives align to the organisation's mission and strategies?

- Are the key stakeholders committed to the vision and overall direction?

- Does adding this investment to the existing portfolio enhance the balance?

- Is the Strategy for BRM comprehensive and realistic and is funding available?

2ND REVIEW

- Is there a comprehensive set of benefits related in one or more Benefits Maps?

- Do the benefits outweigh the disbenefits?

- Does the distribution of benefits and disbenefits by stakeholder highlight any potential problem areas?

- Will the Blueprint support the fulfilment of the vision?

- Does the initial programme structure seem suitable for its scope?

- Are the anticipated outcomes – benefits – of sufficient worth to justify the anticipated scale of required change – enablers and business changes?

3RD REVIEW

- Is the Blueprint achievable? In particular: is there a realistic assessment of the organisation's ability to cope with the scale of change envisaged? Do the key stakeholders have the energy for the required change?

- Does the programme demonstrate 'value for money'? (that is, are the benefits worth the anticipated costs?)

- Was the consideration of options based on the weightings of paths through the relevant maps?

- Will the benefit measures motivate the desired behaviours?

4TH REVIEW

- Has the necessary funding been secured?

- Has a project structure been set up to manage the acquisition of the required enablers?

- Is the Blueprint achievable and does it include an optimised portfolio of changes?

- Is the programme still affordable?

- Select from tenders and commission third-party work.

- Review and initiate mechanism for benefit tracking and reporting.

5TH REVIEW (MAY BE REPEATED)

- Is the programme structured appropriately to manage all the business change?

- Are benefit considerations being used to overcome stakeholder resistance?

- Is there a benefit-driven implementation plan?

- Are key milestones being achieved, covering: enabler acquisition, enabler implementation and integration with business change, benefit realisation?

6TH REVIEW

- Has the Blueprint evolved into BAU?

- Are benefits being reported in line with expectations?

- Is remedial action, including new initiatives, under consideration for any shortfalls in target achievement?

- Has the planned contribution to vision achievement been accomplished?

- Have 'lessons learned' been captured for future use?

- Will the benefit tracking and reporting mechanism survive programme closure?

- Has the programme been closed?

> **The Business Case should be a living and evolving document, which steers programme direction towards the vision, maintaining constancy of purpose – a handbook for the Programme Director/Manager.**

The Change/Benefit Realisation Management (BRM) Process

'Choose always the way that seems best, however rough it may be. Custom will soon render it easy and agreeable.'

(Pythagoras)

'Though no one can go back and make a brand new start, anyone can start from now and make a brand new ending.'

(Carl Bard)

23.1   The Scope of the Process

Benefits are the reason for change and change is the mechanism for delivering benefits, so the Change Process and the BRM Process are really one and the same. Most organisations have processes for managing projects and some have processes for managing programmes, fewer have processes for managing benefits. Since many programme/project activities should be driven by benefits and benefit-related information, an effective BRM process cannot function as a simple addendum to the company's normal change management systems. What is required is a single integrated process.

sigma has several times customised its BRM process to create cohesive and consistent attachments to clients' existing programme or project management processes. While this approach can produce good results, they rarely compare with the outcome of a single integrated process as described above and in the example which follows.

The UK arm of a US oil company asked **sigma** to provide them with a process for managing IT projects and change. Since the company had no previous standard process for project management, we started with a 'clean sheet' plus the advantage of their wanting us to start with our BRM process, building the project/change management methodology around it. The result was a single integrated process with BRM as its core; it is no coincidence that it became one of the most effective methodologies for managing IT and change.

In a similar way, the process described in this book is a single integrated process, showing how the specifically benefit-related activities drive many of the other activities. Greater detail is provided for the benefit-related activities than for other aspects covered. The process, which is cyclical, is divided into six phases with review points between each of them. The diagram, introduced in Section 4.6, which outlines this six phase life-cycle is repeated in Figure 23.1 but with the phase descriptions amplified.

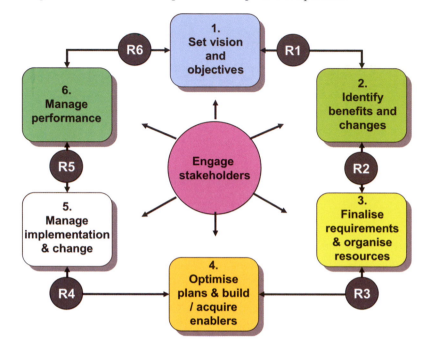

Figure 23.1   Change Process with review points

As the process is cyclical it can be entered at any phase, and although Phase 1, 'setting vision', is the optimum entry point, this flexibility enables the application of BRM to initiatives which are already well under way. It is also iterative, enabling return to a previous point, which is useful when more detailed analysis prompts refinement of earlier definitions and plans. A change in the external environment may also require a reworking of earlier phases.

Engaging stakeholders throughout the change process is a CSF.

Organisations and methodologies use varied terminology and boundaries for dividing up the benefits or change life-cycle. Figure 23.2 relates this six-phased approach to some of these.

This approach is also applicable at any level within an organisation. For instance, it can be applied at:

- Corporate or Group level to determine business direction and strategy;

- Divisional level to determine the optimum portfolio of change investments;

- Programme level, which can be within a single division or cross-divisional;

- Project level.

1	Set vision & objectives	Identifying a Programme	Define	What and Why? (Team Building)
2	Identify benefits & changes			
3	Define initiatives	Defining a Programme	Establish	How? (Business Commitment)
4	Optimise initiatives			
5	Manage initiatives	Governing a Programme	Direct	Do it (Local action)
6	Manage performance	Closing a Programme	Deliver	Realise benefits (continuous improvement)

Figure 23.2   How sigma's six-phased approach relates to other schemes

Each phase is described in more detail in the following sections and includes:

- an elaboration of the process with references to earlier sections of the book;

- suggestions for involving stakeholders;

- details of information to be generated with reference tools and templates for recording the information;

- reference to commonly used documents, useful for grouping and communicating the information, including that for formal reviews;

- a flowchart of the phase;

- who should manage the phase.

The purpose and scope of the reviews between each phase are considered in detail in Section 17.3. Reviews R3, R4, R5 and R6 should be undertaken by the Programme Board, sometimes complemented by an independent review such as an OGC Gateway Review. R1 and R2 will often occur before the formal creation of the Programme Board and so should be undertaken by a business sponsor and or the Portfolio Board, supported by a Benefit Facilitator, where such exists.

23.2   Phase 1 – Set Vision and Objectives

Phase 1 sets vision and objectives, positioning them within the overall mission and direction of the organisation. In a logical sequence of steps, it:

- identifies the primary stakeholders;

- establishes, with senior stakeholders, a 'vision' for change;

- identifies/confirms the supporting 'objectives';

- selects a subset of objectives to summarise the intent and bound the change;

- checks stakeholder commitment to the proposed direction and change;

- checks alignment with the organisation's mission;

- checks fit with other existing or planned change initiatives;

- summarises findings and recommendations in a 'Case for Change' document;

- defines the strategy for applying BRM;

- initiates a formal review to confirm conclusions and to decide whether to proceed to Phase 2.

The actual sequence of steps depends on the starting point. It may be a vision or end goal passed down from above (usually senior management), an idea for improvement or a pressing need for change. Whatever the starting point, stakeholders should be identified and involved as early as possible.

Irrespective of whether a vision or end goal has been set, a set of objectives should be determined by considering the drivers for change. This is best undertaken working with senior representatives of the stakeholders within a well-facilitated workshop – see Section 8.6. The objectives are then linked in a cause-and-effect map, the Strategy Map. The paths of the map can be weighted, working right to left and a suitable boundary for the change initiative determined (see Sections 8.7 and 9.7).

To complete the foundation laying (Phase 1) three other checks should be undertaken, namely:

- check that the bounding objectives are strategically aligned with the organisation's mission;

- check that the senior representatives of key stakeholders are committed to this way forward;

- check that the proposed investment in change complements existing change initiatives, providing a balanced portfolio of change.

The results should be summarised in a Case for Change (Programme Mandate), which is the mandate for proceeding to more detailed analysis in Phase 2. This Case for Change (see Section 18.3) together with a Strategy for BRM (see Sections 7.10 and 18.3) provide a suitable basis for the first formal review. These two documents (with their clear picture of the end in view, and the strategy for maintaining focus on benefits) should be the starting point for any investment in change. Providing senior stakeholder representatives are involved in formulating these documents, they should launch the change initiative on a potential voyage to success.

The following flowchart (Figure 23.3) provides a summary of Phase 1:

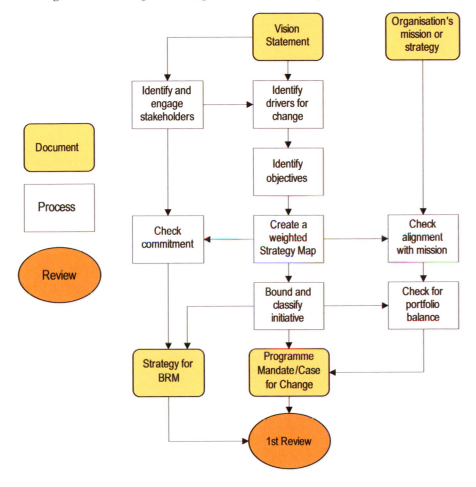

Figure 23.3   Phase 1 – Set vision and objectives

White boxes represent activities and lightly shaded brown boxes represent documents. Documents are created by and used to drive activities. Since a Programme Manager is not normally appointed until Phase 3, activities of this phase are likely to be managed or facilitated by the Benefit Facilitator. This first review (see Sections 17.3 and 22.11) is usually undertaken by the Sponsor and/or the Steering Group/Portfolio Board.

23.2   Phase 2 – Identify Benefits and Changes

Phase 2 builds on the agreed vision and objectives and works with the stakeholders to scope a potential change programme and position it within the overall mission and direction of the organisation. In a logical sequence of steps, it:

- determines a set of benefits which relate to the stakeholders and supports each of the primary (bounding) objectives;

- validates and classifies the benefits;

- identifies and analyses any disbenefits;

- creates a Benefits Map for each of the bounding objectives;

- weights the paths and calculates scores for each benefit;

- determines measures for each benefit, where possible setting target values;

- identifies the enablers and business changes required to realise the benefits, and creates a case to justify progressing, if appropriate, to Phase 3.

Stakeholders should be involved in each of the above steps and during this phase a strategy for their ongoing engagement should be developed.

Techniques for identifying, validating and classifying benefits, including the generation of Benefit Distribution Matrices, have been described in some detail, in Chapter 9.

Disbenefits should also be analysed in this phase, often leading to:

- the registration of one or more risks in the Risk Log;

- the determination of actions for stakeholder engagement;

- the identification of actions to mitigate the impact of the disbenefits; or even

- the termination of the change initiative.

Identifying and setting targets for measures was considered in depth in Chapter 10. It is an iterative process, involving small groups of those stakeholders who are likely to feel positively about the realisation of the related benefits. Measures should be sought for all benefits with high scores in the weighted maps, and for most others. Subsequently baselines, targets and improvement timescales will be required for the measures, especially those classified as 'definite' or 'expected', using the **sigma** Value Types. This measure activity may begin in Phase 2, and is likely to continue well into Phase 3.

The identification of enablers and business changes, based on the Benefits Maps, should be reasonably comprehensive, even if details are sketchy at this stage. Much further elaboration and analysis, which depends on the use of BDM(s) and the ongoing involvement of stakeholders, will be required; it is described in detail in Chapter 11. This time-consuming and costly process is best postponed until Phase 3, after the review of the initiative at the close of Phase 2.

The involvement of stakeholders throughout Phase 2 is most effectively achieved through well-structured and facilitated workshops. The identification and classification of benefits, the creation and weighting of Benefits Maps and the subsequent development of a BDM are extremely demanding requiring at least a full day's workshop. Identifying measures is best undertaken in separate smaller workshops with stakeholders who are closer to the area of change. Many of these participants will become Benefit Owners or Measure Monitors. The identification of baselines and the setting of targets are best done outside the workshop environment.

At the end of the phase it is important to ensure that all the findings have been recorded in appropriate documents, such as:

- the BRP;

- the Stakeholder Management Strategy or Plan;

- the Blueprint; and

- the Risk Log;

with the main messages summarised in the Programme Brief, sometimes referred to as the Strategic Outline Case, for submission to the review body. These documents are described in Chapters 18 to 21, and are initial versions of those required to support the five programme themes (see Section 5.7), namely:

- Benefit realisation – BRP;

- Stakeholder Management – Stakeholder Management Strategy;

- Solution Management – Blueprint;

- Programme Management – Risk Log and Programme Brief;

- Governance – Programme Brief/Strategic Outline Case;

though, as recommended, the Programme Management theme may not formally begin until Phase 3.

The flowchart in Figure 23.4 brings together the main steps of the phase with the documents that they create, as represented by the lightly shaded brown boxes. Since a Programme Manager is not normally appointed until Phase 3, activities of this phase are likely to be managed or facilitated by the Benefit Facilitator.

Establishing and resourcing a programme should normally begin in Phase 3, after the vision and objectives are agreed, some benefits have been identified, and the nature and size of the required changes are understood. It may, however, be useful to confirm the sponsor or SRO during this phase.

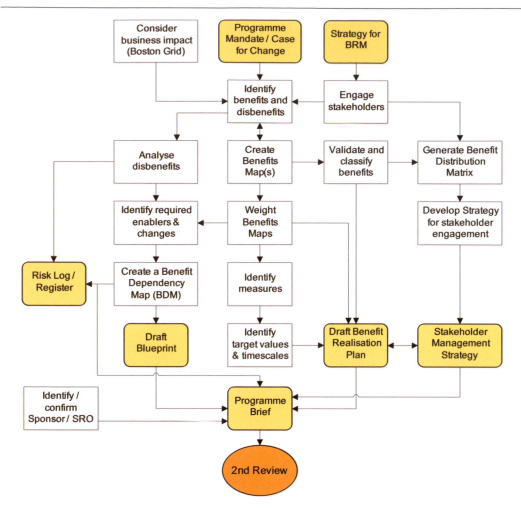

Figure 23.4   Phase 2 – Identify benefits and changes

The second review should be undertaken by the Portfolio Board; the proposal to proceed should be presented by the Sponsor or SRO.

23.4   Phase 3 – Define initiatives

This is the beginning of the change activity. Phases 1 and 2 have determined the vision, scope, strategic alignment and a high-level view of how it can all be achieved. This phase will:

- formally establish the programme (if this has not already happened);

- identify further measures including baselines, targets and timescales;

- set up a benefit tracking mechanism;

- prioritise, process and cost the required changes;

- develop options for the acquisition of the enablers (procurement strategy) and the implementation of the business changes, identifying potential projects;

- update the Blueprint;

- develop Business Cases for the projects if required;

- assess funding requirements and possible sources of funding;

- analyse options and present case for continuing (Outline Business Case), including justification for required funding.

At this stage, the programme must be formally established, including nomination or appointment of key personnel, including:

- A sponsor or SRO, if not already appointed;

- A Programme Board;

- A Programme Manager and/or a Programme Director;

- A Business Change Manager (BCM).

The structure of the programme will depend on its scope and complexity (see Chapter 12), so it may evolve through its life-cycle. The team will grow as the programme develops.

To help bring these new players up to speed, the Benefit Facilitator should involve the Business Change Manager (and possibly the Programme Manager) in:

- the identification of further measures;

- setting targets;

- establishing Benefit Owners;

- processing the changes.

During Phase 2, a large number of changes have probably been identified and this number could be augmented during this phase. Generally these will be high-level changes and the distinction between enablers and business changes may not be accurate. So before they are accepted and put into plans, the changes must be processed through several further stages. This further analysis is described more fully in Chapter 12, but the basic steps are listed below, in a suggested chronological sequence:

- categorise;

- consolidate;

- prioritise;

- specify in much greater detail;

- match against existing change initiatives to check whether they are already being worked on;

- cost if new;

- integrate them into appropriate change delivery mechanisms.

Once change delivery mechanisms have been determined, options for the acquisition of the enablers must be assessed and compared. Solutions having been selected, the Blueprint must be updated and the solutions grouped into potential projects. If required, business cases should be developed for these projects and overall funding requirements determined.

These options and the case for continuing (Outline Business Case), including justification for the necessary funding, plus project business cases if these are required, should be presented to the Review Body.

The set of documents created or updated in this phase support the five main themes in the following way:

- Benefit Realisation – BRP and Benefit Tracking Report;

- Stakeholder Management – Stakeholder Management Plan;

- Solution Management – Blueprint;

- Programme Management – Issue and Risk Logs, Programme Plan and Programme Definition Document;

- Governance – Outline Business Case for the programme and, if required, business cases for individual projects.

The Programme Definition Document should include all that was included in the Programme Brief but in greater detail, especially with respect to the changes. It should also include details of the programme structure, high-level cost estimates for the changes, including their groupings, and a suggested structure for the candidate projects.

A flowchart for Phase 3 showing how the activities link with the documents is given in Figure 23.5.

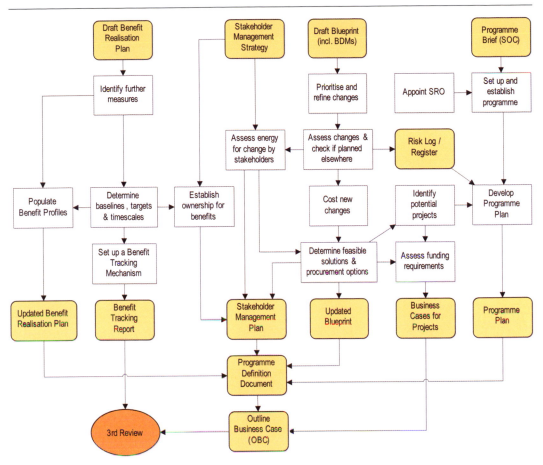

Figure 23.5   Phase 3 – Define initiatives

23.5   Phase 4 – Optimise Initiatives

This is the final major planning phase before the commitment of major expenditure and the start of significant change, and the last phase to include significant choices.

It will:

- optimise portfolio of changes;

- finalise enabler requirements and issue ITTs;

- evaluate tenders and select suppliers;

- secure funding;

- structure the delivery within projects and work-streams;

- secure ownership of business change;

- track and report benefits;

- analyse options and present case for continuing (if appropriate), including a justification for the required funding.

Benefits remain a key driver for change and their influence is probably best mediated through use of IAMs as described in Chapter 13.3. These should facilitate optimisation of the portfolio of changes, checking for balance and alignment, and the evaluation of tenders. Benefit tracking and reporting should commence, if this has not already begun, and significant effort should be devoted to securing commitment to the required business change.

A flowchart for Phase 4, showing how the activities link with the documents to be generated, is given in Figure 23.6 below:

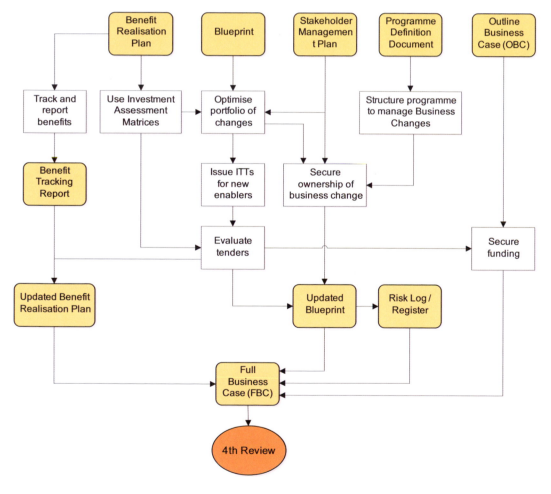

Figure 23.6   Phase 4 – Optimise initiatives

23.6   Phase 5 – Manage initiatives

This is the phase which makes it all happen. Usually the longest and highest cost phase in the programme, it can sometimes span several years. The more effective the planning of the previous four phases, the more successful this one will be. It will:

- place contracts and manage enabler acquisition;

- structure programme activity to manage business change;

- plan to overcome stakeholder resistance;

- plan to optimise benefit realisation during implementation;

- continue benefit tracking;

- plan to compensate for missed targets;

- implement enablers and business change based on the updated plan;

- provide Milestone Reports to the review body.

The relationships between these activities are described in the flowchart in Figure 23.7.

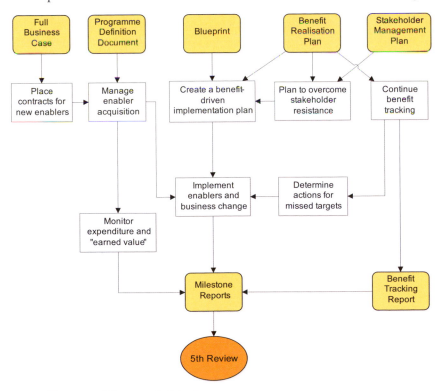

Figure 23.7   Phase 5 – Manage initiatives

Although the flowchart is less busy, the phase can be very long, as enablers are built and acquired, and subsequently embedded into the organisation through business change. During the phase the five main documents:

- BRP;

- Stakeholder Management Plan;

- Blueprint;

- Programme Definition Document; and

- Business Case

will continue to be updated. The BRP will be accompanied by Benefit Tracking Reports and the Blueprint by ITTs and Supplier Contracts.

23.7   Phase 6 – Manage Performance

Although this phase formally closes the programme, benefits will continue to be tracked and reported and the results related to vision achievement. These results should also be consolidated with results from other initiatives, from the portfolio (see Chapter 24), to measure the overall impact on business performance.

This phase will:

- manage the transition to BAU;

- monitor progress towards vision achievement;

- continue benefit tracking and reporting;

- consolidate performance with other initiatives;

- spawn any required new initiatives;

- capture lessons learned;

- manage programme closure; and

- undertake a PIR.

The relationships between these activities are described in the flowchart in Figure 23.8.

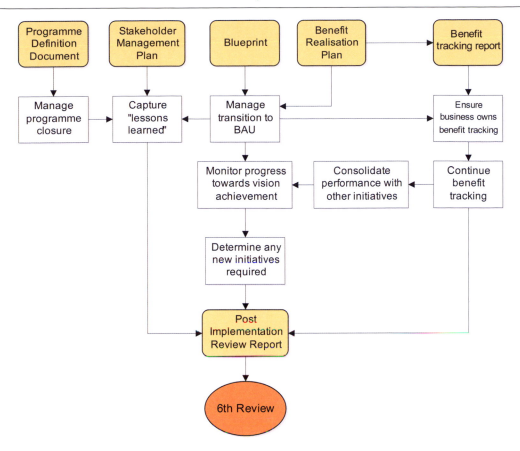

Figure 23.8   Phase 6 – Manage performance

Taking BRM as the backbone/core, integrate all your other change processes.
Use the flowcharts as a guide – adapt as required – but adopt a process in which
you believe.

PART III
The Application of Benefit Realisation Management (BRM) to Portfolio Management

Part I examines the fundamentals of benefit realisation, providing a good overview of Benefit Realisation Management (BRM).

Part II expands this summary, with specific application to individual Programmes or Business Projects.

Part III is a single chapter which considers the application of BRM to a portfolio of programmes or projects. It considers how an optimal portfolio is created and maintained, who should be responsible and how this responsibility is best exercised.

For this to work effectively senior managers need to buy in to BRM and the approach must fit with other management performance-monitoring processes. This is best achieved by embedding BRM within the practices and culture of the organisation and this is considered in Part IV.

24

Maintaining an Optimum Change Portfolio

'Don't be afraid to give up the good for the great.'

(Kenny Rogers)

'Often he who does too much does too little.'

(Italian Proverb)

'Never mistake activity for achievement.'

(John Wooden)

24.1   The Scope and Purpose of Portfolio Management

Most organisations already have significant portfolios of investment in change, often comprising hundreds of programmes and projects. Their problem is unlikely to be lack of activity or vacillating inertia or shortage of funds, but lack of focus. Does the organisation have an optimum portfolio, taking account of its mission, goals, values, human resources, funds and attitude to risk? Is the organisation doing too much and achieving too little? This question is never more pertinent than in a time of recession, such as we experienced in 2009 following the 'Credit Crunch'.

It is vital that the change portfolio, like any investment portfolio, is actively managed in order to optimise the flow of benefits for the whole portfolio, relative to the degree of risk the organisation is prepared to accept. As such active portfolio management becomes a key part of the embedding of BRM within an organisation (see Chapter 25) and embedding BRM within an organisation is a key part of portfolio management.

Portfolio management can and should be applied to any portfolio of change activities, including:

- the organisation's complete portfolio of programmes and projects;

- the portfolio of Information and Communication Technology (ICT) projects;

- the portfolio of projects within a programme;

- a package of changes from within 'BAU'.

The most frequent application is to all change programmes and projects within an organisational area or within a logical grouping. We will focus at the highest level – all change programmes and projects within an organisation as this raises the widest range of challenges. These considerations can then be scaled down for other portfolios.

Although most aspects of managing a portfolio of changes are very similar to those for managing a portfolio of shares there is one significant difference. Within a business environment there is an additional responsibility – that of creating and maintaining an overall environment in which the portfolio will thrive.

I suggest therefore that the primary objectives of portfolio management are:

1.   To maximise the benefits realised from investment in change.

2.   To help deliver the organisation's vision and goals as cost effectively as possible.

In support of these primary objectives I recommend the following supporting objectives:

3.   To define and communicate the environment for change – business strategy, values, guidelines, constraints, appetite for risk and so on.

4.   To create and maintain a high-value portfolio acceptable to the organisation.

5.   To ensure appropriate guidance and support to those managing change – SROs, Programme Managers, Project Managers, Benefit Facilitators and Business Change Managers.

6.   To ensure that the overall resource pot is distributed to generate the greatest return.

7.   To ensure stakeholders are engaged, involved and committed and not overwhelmed by change.

Achieving objectives 3, 5, 6 and 7 should create the environment in which the portfolio will flourish and achieving objective 4 should optimise the composition of the portfolio; so that together they should enable the fulfilment of the two primary objectives. These two aspects – environment and portfolio – are considered in detail in the following two sections.

24.2   Creating an Environment in Which a Change Portfolio Will Flourish

Before programmes or projects can be selected for the portfolio, the business and change environment needs to be defined. This includes:

- the business imperatives – direction and targets;

- influences and constraints;

- processes and governance.

In order to align and consider the contribution of changes to business priorities, the organisation's direction and targets need to be known and understood. It is then possible to consider how and to what degree a programme will contribute to these goals. This assessment of alignment and contribution may be related to:

- statements of strategic direction;

- KPIs;

- specified benefit categories or 'benefit baskets' (see Section 9.4B);

- Balanced Scorecard indicators.

Other influences or considerations might include:

- the organisation's values;

- the organisation's attitude to or appetite for risk;

- the business impact balance (based on the Boston Matrix – see Figure 24.1) considered appropriate for the organisation;

- acceptance and monitoring criteria for programmes and projects (see Section 24.4);

- pain thresholds – acceptable levels of change for stakeholders;

- resource constraints.

In order that Programme and Project teams can operate effectively they will need a good understanding of governance arrangements and the processes they need to follow. In particular this will include the organisation's:

- change life-cycle, perhaps the one described in Figures 4.9 and 7.3;

- methodology for BRM; ideally a standard approach for the whole organisation based on the ideas contained in this book;

- methodology for programme and project management, perhaps based on the Office of Government Commerce (OGC) guidance;

- defined roles and responsibilities (see Chapter 6 and Section 24.4).

Although this whole framework will need to be reviewed and updated from time to time its initial definition is a once off activity. Unlike the portfolio itself, it should not be dynamically changing.

24.3   Active Management of the Portfolio of Change Initiatives

Active management of the portfolio should involve:

- regular monitoring of the current portfolio;

- terminating non-performing or poor performing investments;

- closing programmes which are no longer in line with the organisation's strategy;

- sanctioning only those new investments which will increase the overall value of the portfolio and maintain an appropriate risk balance;

- encouraging creative and innovative thinking to generate a steady flow of good new proposals.

Unlike the environmental considerations in Section 24.2, all of the above have a direct equivalent in the management of a shares portfolio, where, for instance, the last bullet could be undertaken by the research department of a good stockbrokers. It is for this reason I have included this fifth bullet in this list, though in a business change context it could easily be placed in the environmental Section (24.2).

As each of the above activities is undertaken in pursuit of the creation and maintenance of an optimum portfolio, the following nine factors must be regularly reviewed and balanced:

- degree of alignment with the organisation's mission, strategy and policies;

- potential reward – desired benefits – financial and non-financial;

- benefit timescales;

- how well BRM is being applied;

- risk – especially of not achieving the benefits;

- business impact;

- organisational impact – especially the degree of change involved;

- resource requirements – especially business expertise;

- dependencies between investments.

Within a portfolio, the investments will be at different stages of their life-cycles, and so assessment of the above factors, especially how well BRM is being applied, must take this into account. The assessments should be undertaken at least briefly for each regular review, and especially when new investments are being added to the portfolio. Additional in-depth annual reviews may be undertaken by an independent review body.

When using these criteria to assess a programme, particularly a potential new programme, there are two considerations:

- Does it stand up on its own, as a worthwhile investment which supports the business strategy and direction?

- How does it score relative to other candidate (or possibly existing) programmes?

For the comparative assessment it may be helpful to create a score for each of the nine factors listed above and then compute a weighted total. This total should be considered in conjunction with some exception reporting (for example, a RAG Status) for each factor, in case it hides a catastrophic change in a single factor (for example, degree of alignment with mission).

24.4   Portfolio Review Factors

DEGREE OF ALIGNMENT WITH THE ORGANISATIONS MISSION, STRATEGY AND POLICIES

Although each investment should make a contribution to an organisation's mission and objectives, the total portfolio must support the organisation's mission in a balanced manner (for example, if an organisation has four main objectives, it is not good if all the investments support the first two objectives, with none contributing to the other two).

A balanced portfolio at one stage does not guarantee balance at another. In addition to the effects from investments entering and leaving the portfolio, an organisation's strategy might change (for example, in response to changes in the external world). Active portfolio management must respond to these changes.

In addition to alignment to objectives some organisations expect all their programmes to contribute to specified corporate goals – KPIs, benefit categories/buckets or scorecard indicators. One set of benefit categories/buckets, used by a local authority (see case example Section 30.2), are:

- improved customer satisfaction;

- improved quality of life;

- improved job satisfaction;

- net cost reduction;

- improved environmental impact.

POTENTIAL REWARD – DESIRED BENEFITS – FINANCIAL AND NON-FINANCIAL

Again there are two considerations:

- Is the anticipated return (not just in monetary terms) worth the proposed outlay, taking account of risk?

- How does the ROI compare with other proposals contending for a share of the same limited resources?

Reviewing the relative worth of portfolio investments would be easy if each of them could be reduced to a single value (for example, a NPV); sadly life isn't like that. The reality is that a range, including many non-financial benefits, must be considered. Converting them to pseudo-financial values distorts the truth and misleads. In considering the complete range of benefits, IAMs can be useful (see Section 13.3).

BENEFIT TIMESCALES

The expected timing for the realisation of benefits is important. In a balanced portfolio, benefits are being generated all the time. Some of this 'harvest' will probably be reinvested in 'future plantings'.

Once, while we were reviewing a portfolio of 11 programmes on behalf of a senior manager in one of the high street banks, he suddenly told us that he needed some cost reduction benefits in the fourth quarter of the year. We had mapped all the benefit realisation timescales and the earliest projected realisation of cost reductions was 18 months further on. Although surprised that the portfolio was not better aligned to the needs of the business, we recognised that the 18-month window, when no benefits would be realised, was probably a consequence of its newness.

Nevertheless we were able to help the bank with its requirement to reduce costs. We had identified two projects whose termination we recommended on the grounds that they carried too high a risk; the consequent savings were sufficient to meet the needs of the manager. He was pleased that we had found a solution, though sorry to see one of his pet projects disappear!

HOW WELL BRM IS BEING APPLIED

Since the primary purpose of any programme must be the realisation of benefits, a key review criterion for assessing or optimising a portfolio should be how well the individual programmes are applying BRM. These criteria should also be weighted more highly than many of the other criteria since a programme with a potential ROI of 40 per cent and an excellent application of BRM should be far more desirable than a programme with a potential ROI of 100 per cent with an appalling or non-existent application of BRM.

To assess how well BRM is being applied the review criteria need to reflect the stage of the programme within its life-cycle. Responsibility for each review is indicated in the diagram (see Figure 24.1).

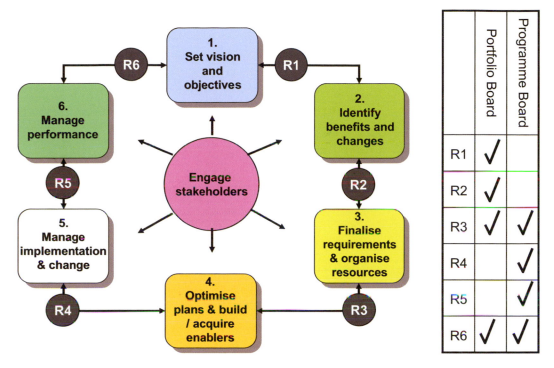

Figure 24.1 Change life-cycle with review points and reviewers

Suggested criteria for each of the six reviews are listed in Figure 24.2. I suggest marks out of five for each question and the total expressed as a percentage. At any stage earlier, questions, especially any with low scores, might be repeated. The questions for each review assume that there is a recommendation to proceed to the next phase.

Clearly, in the later reviews, the quality with which BRM is being applied is unlikely to influence programme termination, though it should be a major consideration in the earlier reviews.

RISK – ESPECIALLY OF NOT ACHIEVING THE BENEFITS

The primary risk is that associated with the non-achievement of benefits, which must be balanced against the risk of doing nothing. Most other risks relate to these two, though situations can be conceived where change could trigger some potential new risks (for example, of staff fatalities) which might outweigh the non-realisation of benefits.

Review 1	Score
· Is the potential programme following the agreed Change Management Cycle?	
· Have relevant stakeholders been engaged?	
· Did the programme start with the identification of a vision or objectives and benefits?	
· Is there a Strategy Map of linked objectives?	
· Have bounding objectives been determined and agreed?	
· Is there a sponsor for Phase 2 – a potential SRO?	
· Is there an agreed Strategy for BRM?	
· Does the potential programme fit with the existing portfolio based on Boston Matrix / Cranfield Grid?	
Review 2	
· Have relevant stakeholders been engaged?	
· Is there a quality Benefit Dependency Map (BDM) for each bounding objective?	
· Have the paths in the maps been weighted and the benefits scored?	
· Are the stakeholders broadly comfortable with the envisaged changes?	
· Is there a Benefit Distribution Matrix?	
· Are there meaningful measures for the majority of benefits?	
· Are there draft Benefit Profiles?	
· Is there a Stakeholder Engagement Strategy / Plan?	
Review 3	
· Have relevant stakeholders been engaged?	
· Have the changes identified in the BDMs been consolidated, prioritised and built into action plans, projects?	
· Are non-financial benefits treated as seriously as financial?	
· Have benefit targets and timescales been set?	
· Is there a defined mechanism for tracking and reporting benefits?	
· Is there a draft Benefit Realisation Plan?	
· Has benefit reporting started?	
· Has a Programme structure been formally established, with SRO, Programme Manager and Business Change Manager?	
· Is there a Business Case and does the justification to proceed satisfy the necessary criteria?	
Review 4	
· Have relevant stakeholders been engaged?	
· Is enabler development / acquisition proceeding to plan?	
· Is change being implemented in line with plan?	
· Is roll-out being benefit driven?	
· Is there a finalised Benefit Realisation Plan?	
· Are benefits being realised in line with expectations – on target?	
· Is remedial action being taken where targets have been missed?	
Review 5	
· Have relevant stakeholders been engaged and any resistance overcome?	
· Is enabler development / acquisition proceeding to plan?	
· Is change being implemented in line with plan?	
· Is roll-out being benefit driven?	
· Are benefits being realised in line with expectations – on target?	
· Is remedial action being taken where targets have been missed?	
Review 6	
· Has the Blueprint been delivered?	
· Are benefits being realised in line with expectations – on target?	
· Is remedial action being taken where targets have been missed?	
· Has the vision or bounding objectives been fully achieved?	
· If not, has remedial activity been identified and proposed?	
· Have lessons learned been documented and communicated?	

Figure 24.2   Portfolio review questions relating to the application of BRM

BUSINESS IMPACT

The commonest approach to balancing a portfolio, in respect of business impact, is to use the Cranfield Grid (Figure 24.3), which was the origin of the grid introduced in Section 9.4c, where it was applied to benefits within a programme. When applying this grid to the whole portfolio of programmes and projects the definitions of the four quadrants are as follows:

The Cranfield Grid

Strategic	Speculative
Programmes which primarily support **future business opportunities** – business development, growth	Programmes with a **high achievement risk,** but often high reward – e.g. arising from experimenting with the way we do things
Programmes which will deliver **critical improvements to today's operations** – e.g. increased efficiency and effectiveness	**"Nice to have"** programmes, in the sense that the organisation's growth or survival will not depend on them. Usually related to improvements to non-critical activities. **Often quick wins.**
Key operational	**Support**

Figure 24.3   Programmes/projects by type of organisational impact

In order to use this grid to keep the portfolio balanced, the appropriate balance for the organisation must first be defined by senior management, probably the Portfolio Board.

ORGANISATIONAL IMPACT – ESPECIALLY THE DEGREE OF CHANGE INVOLVED

As well as mapping expected benefits against time in order to achieve a smooth and steady flow of benefits, it is important, probably more important, to do the same for business changes, this time by stakeholder across the portfolio, rather than by programme. This will highlight future potential change overload, so that mitigating action can be taken well in advance – this might include postponing the approval of a new proposal.

This assessment of change impact on stakeholders should be balanced against some of the pluses – for example, the benefits they should expect to receive – and increased responsibilities. These considerations are best brought together in a Stakeholder Profile as illustrated in Figure 24.4.

It may then be helpful to extract the business change elements into a summary matrix as illustrated in Figure 24.5.

Figure 24.5 shows the impact of change from the whole portfolio for each stakeholder. In this example there should be concern for stakeholders C and F, who will experience overwhelming change. As a consequence it may be decided not to proceed with programmes P1 and/or P9. This simple matrix does not take account of the timing of the change and ideally a three-dimensional model is required, with time as the third dimension. An alternative would be to produce the above matrix for each half year or year.

This consideration emphasises the importance of stakeholder engagement throughout the process.

Stakeholder Profile

Stakeholder role / name				

Benefits to be received				
Ref. No.	Description	Due date		

Disbenefits expected				
Ref. No.	Description	Due date		

Benefits which stakeholder is responsible for achieving				
Ref. No.	Description	Measures	Target	Timescale

Benefits which stakeholder is responsible for tracking and reporting				
Ref. No.	Description	Measures	Target	Timescale

Changes which stakeholder is responsible for delivering				
Ref. No.	Description	Actions	Start date	End date

Changes which stakeholder is likely to experience				
Ref. No.	Description	Actions	Start date	End date

Figure 24.4   Stakeholder Profile

Programme	Stakeholders									
	A	B	C	D	E	F	G	H	I	J
P1	Low		High		Low	High			Low	
P2		Low		Low		Low				Low
P3			Medium					Low		
P4			Medium			Low	Low			
P5		Low								Medium
P6						Medium				
P7			Low					High		
P8		Medium	High		Low				Low	
P9			Low			High			Medium	

High impact	
Medium impact	
Low impact	

Figure 24.5   Impact of change by stakeholder and by programme

DEPENDENCIES

Dependencies between investments in a portfolio must be recognised and marked. This factor is different from the other eight, in that it affects more than one investment; so in considering the removal of one, all dependent investments should be taken into account.

24.5   Responsibility for Portfolio Management

Responsibility for portfolio management is spread across many different roles including those responsible for the individual components of the portfolio – Programme, Project and Change Managers. In this chapter I will focus on the key roles of Portfolio Board and Portfolio Management Office, an illustrative overall governance structure is shown in Figure 24.6.

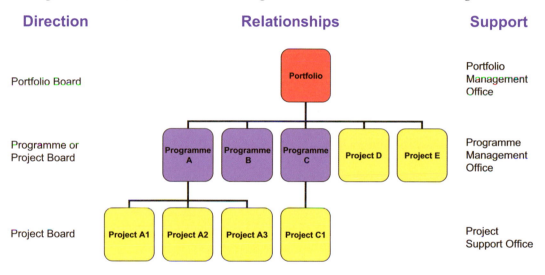

Figure 24.6   Portfolio Governance Hierarchy

PORTFOLIO BOARD

In many organisations the complete portfolio of change activities will affect the majority of staff from within the organisation and impact many stakeholders from outside the organisation. So effective management of this portfolio will involve a large number of staff in a variety of professional disciplines and require top-level leadership. The leadership must come from the top, perhaps the main Board, in view of:

- the number and diversity of stakeholders who must be influenced;

- the magnitude and source of the required funding;

- the enormity of the potential rewards;

- the related risks and change impacts.

Although I believe that the leadership should start with the main Board, active monitoring and management of the portfolio may be delegated to a subset of the Board or to a group one below Board level. The toughness of some of the decisions to be taken (for example, killing a pet project) also demands such seniority. I refer to this group as the Portfolio Board, though other names are often used including Steering Group, Sponsoring Group (MSP), and Change Management Executive.

A portfolio containing several hundred investments is almost unmanageable, especially by a single Portfolio Board. So in this situation projects should be synergistically grouped into a much smaller number of programmes and/or a hierarchy of Portfolio Boards should be used.

The main responsibilities of the Portfolio Board are:

- Define and communicate parameters of the change environment (once off);

- Encourage a culture of new ideas – creativity, continuous improvement;

- Identify and sponsor initiatives needed to deliver the organisation's vision;

- Review and reject/sanction new proposals;

- Monitor continuously the whole portfolio;

- Terminate programmes and projects that are not performing or no longer fit.

Composition of the Board:

- Director level, including SROs of major programmes;

- Chaired perhaps by the Director for Business Improvement or the Director for Transformation or Change Management, if such exist.

Frequency of meetings:

- Usually monthly, but will depend on the size of the portfolio.

To be effective this Portfolio Board will need practical support from a group of analysts, administrators and facilitators, normally referred to as the Portfolio Management Office, plus the commitment of many other professionals, such as Programme, Project and Business Change Managers, together with the support of a much wider group of stakeholders.

PORTFOLIO MANAGEMENT OFFICE (PMO)

An adequate definition of this office is that provided by the OGC[1] namely: 'Permanent office set up to support the definition and delivery of a portfolio of change across the entire organisation or enterprise'.

---

1   OGC's P3O page 8.

So its primary roles are:

- Support for the Portfolio Board in its decision making;

- Support for the Portfolio Board in its wider influence, especially with stakeholders.

Possible secondary roles include:

- Centre of Expertise, source of guidance/standards and internal consultancy for:
  - BRM
  - PPM methods
  - Change Management.

- Resource Pool for Programme and Project Managers.

Even when these secondary roles are not part of the PMO, the PMO must maintain close relationships with the groups responsible for these activities. In summary the main PMO interfaces are indicated in the diagram in Figure 24.7.

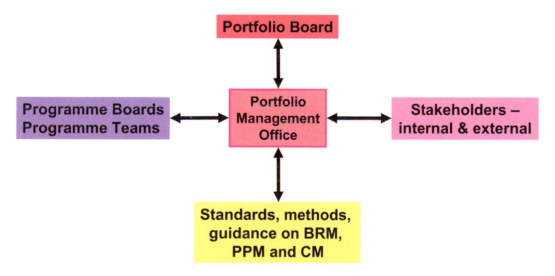

Figure 24.7   Interfaces for the Portfolio Management Office (PMO)

In its primary role of supporting the Portfolio Board, the PMO will need to:

- Evaluate new programme and project proposals using agreed criteria:
  - checking alignment and contribution to corporate strategy and goals
  - ROI

   - proposed application of BRM (for example, Strategy for BRM)
   - risks.

- Check mix/balance with existing portfolio:
   - Cranfield Grid
   - resource requirements
   - stakeholder impact.

- Oversee and consolidate performance reporting of existing portfolio;

- Investigate those which are missing targets for change or benefits;

- Identify candidates for removal from the portfolio;

- Prepare reports and recommendations for the Portfolio Board.

Several of these responsibilities require input from the Benefit Facilitator role so it makes sense for the Benefit Facilitator role to sit within the PMO.

24.6   Useful Analytical Templates, Tools and Techniques

There are a number of templates useful in the overall support of portfolio management and they fall broadly into four categories:

- Diagrams and templates which describe characteristics of a single programme or project. These are described elsewhere in the book and summarised in the sections on the Benefit Realisation Plan (Chapter 19) and the Business Case (Chapter 22).

- Tables and matrices which help to balance the portfolio, in respect of business impact (Figure 24.2) and stakeholder impact (Figures 24.3 and 24.4).

- Matrices which enable the comparison of programmes and projects based on two related criteria, for example – potential value to the business v quality of application of BRM. This vital comparison is discussed below and this and other matrices are considered in the case example in Section 24.7.

- A hierarchy of maps starting with a Portfolio Strategy Map.

A key assessment factor must be the value to be delivered to the business relative to the costs incurred (net value); however at a planning stage both value and costs are estimated and so:

$$\text{net value} = p1 * \text{potential value} - p2 * \text{estimated costs}$$

where p1, the proportion of potential benefits that are likely to be realised, is often very much less than 1 and depends on the quality of the application of BRM, and p2 is often greater than 1, especially where the costs of business change have not been included in the planning calculations or Business Case.

This highlights the importance of assessing how well BRM is being applied, as described in Section 24.4, and to relate this to the potential net value in a matrix. This should help to determine the appropriate portfolio management actions as indicated by the matrix in Figure 24.8.

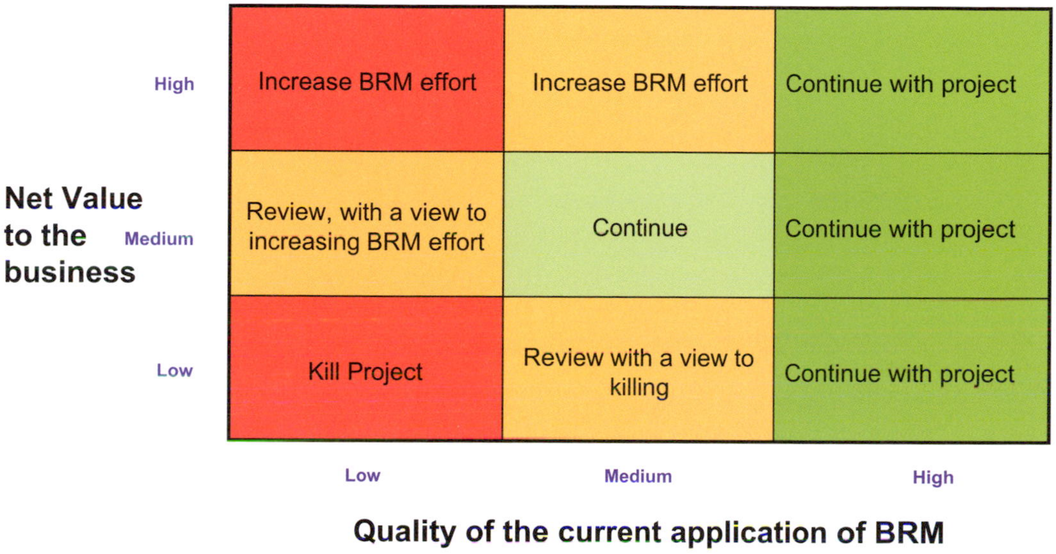

	Low	Medium	High
High	Increase BRM effort	Increase BRM effort	Continue with project
Medium	Review, with a view to increasing BRM effort	Continue	Continue with project
Low	Kill Project	Review with a view to killing	Continue with project

Net Value to the business

Quality of the current application of BRM

Figure 24.8 Portfolio evaluation matrix for assessing actions for different situations

A hierarchy of weighted and scored maps can be very effective in prioritising the implementation of change. At the highest level there would be a Portfolio Strategy Map of linked objectives, where the end objective might be: 'To deliver the business strategy'. Programmes and major projects could then be added to this map and the weighting algorithm applied in order to prioritise the programmes and projects.

Alternatively a set of bounding objectives could be determined using the Portfolio Strategy Map and a BDM developed for each bounding objective. Weightings can then be applied to the hierarchy of maps and individual changes can then be scored and prioritised. This process can be very effective for selecting and prioritising a large number of changes or projects and has been used to great effect prioritising and selecting from a large number of improvement opportunities identified using the Lean Process.

Sometimes combining the messages from different matrices can help in the assessment of programmes and projects and in determining those that need to be removed from the portfolio. This is best illustrated by considering the following case example. We had been asked to review a portfolio of 11 projects for the IT department of a high street bank. We assessed each of the projects considering a range of characteristics related to their ultimate purpose – the generation of benefits for the business departments of the bank.

We assessed how well they were already applying BRM or planning to apply BRM, depending on the stage the project was at, and mapped the results against the extent of BRM required, recognising that the required sophistication in the application of BRM will vary depending on the nature of the project. The projects were then colour coded, using a RAG status, where green was acceptable, amber was borderline and red needed attention, possibly removal from the portfolio. The results are displayed in the matrix in Figure 24.9.

Figure 24.9   Matrix showing the required v observed application of BRM

We then positioned the projects in a matrix whose axes were 'value to the business' and 'complexity of required change' but also carried forward the colours determined from the last matrix. The results are shown in Figure 24.10.

Figure 24.10   Matrix showing business value v complexity of required change

In this matrix, projects in the top left quadrant are good candidates for the portfolio while those in the bottom right quadrant are bad candidates. If this information is combined with the colour code determined from the previous assessment, it shows that 'workflow' is an excellent candidate for the portfolio, while 'reuse' and 'distributed application development' are very bad candidates. We later linked this information with the projected timing of benefits and as a consequence both 'reuse' and 'distributed application development' were removed from the portfolio.

24.7   Getting Started

If your organisation already has a Portfolio Board and a PMO then you may wish to use this chapter to check for any gaps in responsibilities or activities. If these are not in place, establishing them is a significant task involving perhaps considerable changes to the way the organisation functions. I therefore recommend managing this transition as a programme with an SRO, Programme Board, Programme Manager and appropriate funding. An alternative would be to manage these changes within the wider programme of embedding BRM within the organisation (see Chapter 25), perhaps as a distinct project.

In either situation it would be appropriate to apply BRM to this change activity, engaging stakeholders, identifying and mapping the benefits and then the changes, managing the changes and tracking and reporting the benefits. A simplified example of a BDM for this programme is given in Figure 24.11.

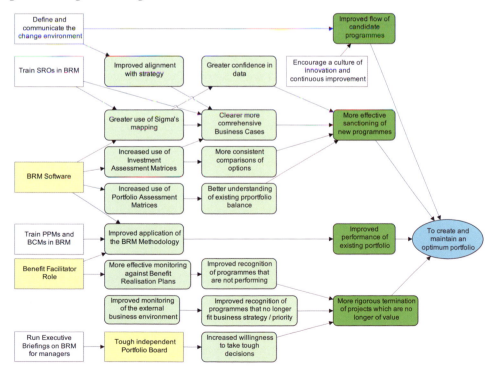

Figure 24.11   BDM for objective: 'To create and maintain an optimum portfolio'

So activities within this programme/project are likely to include:

- agree scope of portfolio management;

- identify current change initiatives;

- assess current change initiatives;

- agree corporate approach to BRM;

- agree corporate change life-cycle;

- define roles and processes;

- fill roles;

- engage and educate stakeholders.

24.8   Enablers for Portfolio Management

To enable the Portfolio Board to monitor and so manage the portfolio, the following are extremely useful:

- the adoption of a consistent BRM methodology for all programmes in the portfolio;

- the adoption of a consistent change process life-cycle;

- a corporate or portfolio-level Benefit Facilitator Role and a Portfolio Management Office , to provide expertise and support and to process and report the monitoring information;

- the adoption of a Measures Dictionary;

- the ability to generate Portfolio Assessment Matrices;

- software to support BRM and Portfolio Management – for details see Chapter 29.

Do less but make it count for more.
Cut those programmes/projects which are likely to deliver little or no value, and focus the released resources on high-value achievement.

PART IV
Embedding Benefit Realisation Management (BRM) Within an Organisation

Part I examined the fundamentals of benefit realisation, providing a good overview of Benefit Realisation Management (BRM).

Part II expanded this summary, with specific application to individual Programmes or Business Projects.

Part III considered the application of BRM to a portfolio of programmes or projects.

Although limited application of the tools and techniques of BRM can yield a very positive return, for best results it is desirable to embed BRM within the thinking, practices and culture of the organisation. Changing the mindset and winning the hearts and minds is a challenging task and is addressed in Part IV in chapters that consider:

- the practicalities of embedding BRM within an organisation;

- prerequisites – culture and leadership;

- dangers of giving financial values to non-cashable benefits;

- how BRM fits with other approaches;

- requirements for software to support the process;

- four very different case examples;

- in a nutshell – a summary of 20 critical success factors.

Embedding Benefit Realisation Management (BRM) Within an Organisation

'I would rather fail in a cause that will ultimately triumph than triumph in a cause that will ultimately fail.'

(Woodrow Wilson)

'The real voyage of discovery consists of not in seeking new landscapes but in having new eyes.'

(Marcel Proust)

25.1   Recognising it as a Programme

Embedding BRM within an organisation is not a trivial activity; it is a programme in itself. It will involve a broad cross-section of stakeholders, including:

- senior managers;

- investment sponsors, including SROs;

- Programme and Project Managers and staff;

- Programme Support Office;

- Business Change staff;

- other stakeholders who are likely to be affected by change.

The vision might be 'to see a dramatic improvement in the benefits realised from the organisation's investment in change'. One bank with whom we worked had the vision to be world class at benefit realisation. Although their enthusiasm for benefit realisation was encouraging, we were unsure whether this was an appropriate vision for a bank.

The primary objectives are likely to be:

- to create and maintain an optimum portfolio of programmes and projects;

- to increase the ROI of programmes and projects;

- to progress towards a more benefit-focused culture.

A high-level picture of the change initiative, using the fried egg model, might be:

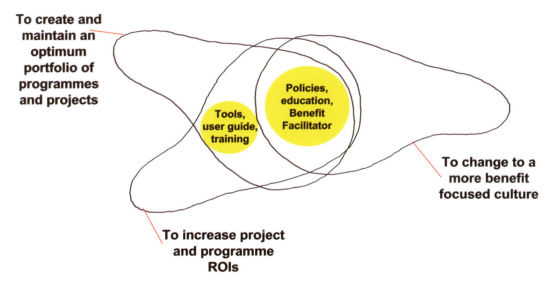

Figure 25.1   Embedding BRM within an organisation

This is a journey whose duration will probably be at least two to three years. Activities will include acquiring or developing some specific enablers, then managing a large amount of business change to embed these enablers within the organisation. These activities will require resources and a budget.

In view of the above, I believe this activity should be set up as a programme, with a clear sponsor (or SRO), a Programme Manager and team, a budget and a timescale. BRM should then be applied to this programme.

25.2   Programme Scope and Content

Programme scope will be dependent on the vision and the consequential bounding objectives. A Strategy Map for such an investment is given in Figure 25.2 and shows the three bounding objectives with the scope boundary.

Content will be determined by applying BRM and creating Benefits Maps and BDMs working from the bounding objectives. Illustrative BDMs for two of the

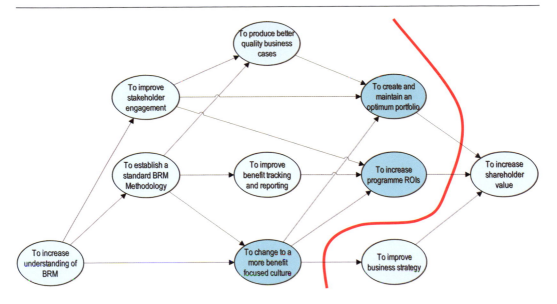

Figure 25.2   Strategy for embedding BRM within an organisation

bounding objectives are included, one in Section 24.7, Figure 24.10 and the other below (Figure 25.3):

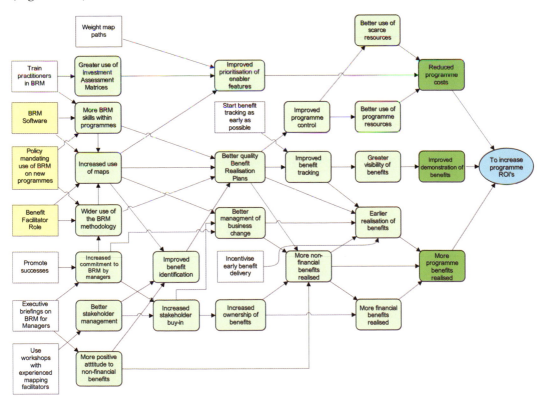

Figure 25.3   BDM for objective: 'To increase programme ROIs'

The key enablers and business changes from the three maps fall into eight main activity themes, or tranches, which are of four types:

- implementing enablers;

- implementing business changes;

- once off activity within the programme;

- transition into BAU.

These activity themes are represented in the following diagram – Figure 25.4.

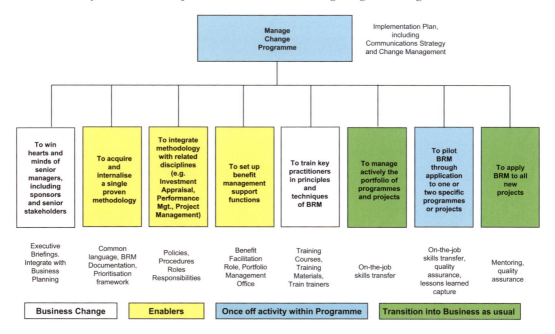

Figure 25.4   Activity themes for embedding BRM within an organisation

The matrix in Figure 25.5 opposite shows how some of the changes will impact some of the primary stakeholders.

25.3   Interfaces with Other Initiatives

Fully embedding BRM and making it robust and effective requires careful and sensitive interfacing with existing procedures in all of the following areas:

- performance management;

- portfolio management and investment sanctioning;

Stakeholder	Board	Steering Group	Sponsor (e.g. SRO) & Programme Board	Programme Director/Manager	Business Change Manager	Programme Team	Enabler Project Teams	Business Manager	Business User	Benefit Facilitator
Change										
Undertake training in BRM	X							X		
Refine processes to integrate with BRM	X	X								
Appoint benefit facilitator	X		X							X
Establish benefit focused review/gateway process			X		X					
Facilitate scoping workshops										X
Participate in scoping workshop			X					X		
Apply BRM to Portfolio Management		X								
Facilitate benefit workshops										X
Participate in benefit workshops								X		
Create Benefits Maps										X
Create and use BDMs					X					
Participate in measures workshops					X			X		
Use weighted BDMs to prioritise enablers					X		X			
Use benefits to drive change agenda					X					
Effect business change					X				X	
Track and report more benefits					X					X
Review benefit achievement and initiatiate actions			X	X	X					X

Figure 25.5   Stakeholder-change matrix

- programme management;

- project management;

- requirements analysis;

- staff performance appraisal;

- change management;

- risk management;

- review/gateway processes.

The content of this book should provide the information needed to establish effective interfaces, which may require changes to existing procedures.

25.4   Support for BRM

Once there is corporate support in terms of senior management commitment, it is important to establish a Centre of Expertise for BRM to provide more detailed support, to ensure a consistency of approach across projects and programmes, to coordinate experiences and to capture and disseminate 'good practice'.

This function could incorporate the previously recommended roles of:

- Benefit Facilitator;

- custodian of Measures Dictionary.

Effective application of BRM is dependent on the following:

- a supportive culture;

- an enlightened view of non-financial benefits;

- integration with other initiative and methodologies;

- software to support the process;

and these four issues are considered in the next four chapters.

> **Applying almost any of the techniques described in this book will deliver value, but to achieve significant and lasting value it is necessary to embed BRM within the culture and practices of the organisation.**
> **This non-trivial transition is best managed as a programme.**

Prerequisites – Culture and Leadership

'Leaders establish the vision for the future and set the strategy for getting there; they cause the change. They motivate and inspire others to change in the right direction.'

(John Kotter)

'No matter how good you get you can always get better and that's the exciting part.'

(Tiger Woods)

26.1   Importance of BRM – Acknowledgement Without Understanding

Benefit realisation is far from automatic. Although BRM may be common sense it is seldom common practice, frequently requiring a change of mindset, which will adopt the required new practices. It is therefore much more likely to blossom and bear fruit if the soil is fertile and the organisation's culture is supportive and in line with the BRM way of thinking.

Although organisations are coming to appreciate the importance of benefit realisation (so much so that in some, benefit realisation has become mandated for all programmes and projects), culture and mindset often remain unchanged. Acknowledgment of the importance of BRM does not always stem from the top and, even when it does, sufficient understanding to make available the necessary time, resource and funding, is often lacking.

A test of soil fertility, or how ready the culture is to embrace BRM, is provided by the degree of belief in the following 15 myths:

1.   The primary purpose of benefits is to justify a proposed investment.

2.   If the enabler (for example, a computer system) is specified and delivered correctly then we will definitely get the benefits.

3.   A shared vision/end goal is a luxury we can postpone or dispense with.

4.   BRM is secondary to the task of delivering the programme – the enabler(s).

5.   Benefit identification is the responsibility of the Programme Team.

6.   Disbenefits may be an inconvenience but they should never kill a project.

7.   Maps such as a Benefits Maps are complicated and unnecessary.

8.   A good Business Case is one that just shows that the anticipated return is worth the proposed outlay.

9.   Senior managers don't need to bother about benefits or understand BRM.

10.   At the end of the day stakeholders will just have to do what they are told.

11.   Measurement is for the benefit of managers to justify their decisions.

12.   You only need to measure and report key (usually end) benefits.

13.   The only benefits that count are hard financial ones.

14.   BRM is too bureaucratic and at best is only applicable to large programmes and projects.

15.   We don't really have a problem as we have always done a cost-benefit analysis and then taken what has been claimed from future budgets.

Personal or organisational belief in these myths seriously hinders benefit realisation. So if you want to score yourself or your organisation using the above list, give 2 for any statement where there is strong or fairly widespread belief, 1 if the belief is mild or patchy, and 0 if there is definite disbelief. Judge belief by action and not just by what people might say.

If you scored yourself before reading the book you may want to see how much your score has changed. If your organisation's score is greater than 10, this book should have provided you with sufficient ideas, material and motivation to begin the necessary culture change.

26.2   Overcoming Attitudes Which Hinder Benefit Realisation

I hope that what you have read in earlier chapters will have dispelled the myths which have been listed in the previous section, as belief in them will seriously hinder benefit realisation. For easy recollection I have included some summary comments against each one.

1. The primary purpose of benefits is to justify a proposed investment.

The primary purpose of benefits should be that people want to realise them. If people are not serious about achieving the benefits, stop the project and reinvest the resources where there is commitment to realise benefits.

2. If the enabler (for example, a computer system) is specified and delivered correctly then we will definitely get the benefits.

History is full of enabler implementations which have not delivered business value. Most benefits arise as people do things differently, changing the way they work, communicate and make decisions. So enablers must be integrated with appropriate business change to achieve benefits – the 'fried egg' principle.

3. A shared vision/end goal is a luxury we can postpone or dispense with.

If there is no documented vision or end goal which the whole team are working towards, factions will pull in different directions wasting resource and slowing progress and the focus is likely to drift to the enablers.

4. BRM is secondary to the task of delivering the programme – the enablers.

As enablers are usually very visible, often requiring large investment, they normally receive considerable management attention. Since benefits – the reason for the investment – are rarely an automatic consequence of the enablers, their realisation requires at least the equivalent attention of management.

5. Benefit identification is the responsibility of the programme team.

Because a programme needs benefits to justify its existence it might seem reasonable that the Programme Team should identify them. Unfortunately the nature of most programmes today makes this infeasible without significant engagement of the business community. Besides, the benefits should have been identified by the business before the programme is set up – we need to reverse the 'cart before the horse' mentality.

6. Disbenefits may be an inconvenience but they should never kill a project.

Disbenefits can carry significant costs and risks and so could outweigh any potential benefits. When this occurs we need the courage and commitment to kill the project even after it has started and in spite of the fact that it may be someone's pet project.

7. Maps such as a Benefits Map are complicated and unnecessary.

Quality Benefits Maps are only complicated if the nature of the change is complicated and/ or the duration of the change spans many years. A long complicated journey needs a good map. If the business community are engaged in map creation, with strong and experienced facilitation, they invariably see the value of the process and buy in to the results.

8. A good Business Case is one that just shows that the anticipated return is worth the proposed outlay.

A good Business Case should certainly show that the anticipated return is worth the proposed outlay, but if it does not also show how the return is to be achieved, then it is not a good Business Case. Quality maps are probably the best way to show this.

9. Senior managers don't need to bother about benefits or understand BRM.

Benefits should ultimately link in to business performance and so, if senior managers are concerned about business performance, they need to be concerned about benefits. It also seems incomprehensible that managers can occupy themselves with expenditure and then give little or no consideration to the return they should expect from this investment. Since benefits are never automatic they need to understand BRM.

10. At the end of the day stakeholders will just have to do what they are told.

This may be true and it could be a useful last resort, but success is likely to be easier and greater if stakeholders become motivated to change through engagement and involvement.

11. Measurement is for the benefit of managers to justify their decisions.

Measurement should motivate behaviour, influence decisions and drive action and so should be for everyone. Measuring only to enable managers to feel comfortable is a luxury most organisations can ill afford.

12. You only need to measure and report key (usually end) benefits.

Measuring only 'end' benefits is usually a waste of time as the information obtained is of little or no value. It will not tell you what has worked and what hasn't, and will not help you to know whether or not the change has been successful. It can also involve waiting a long time before knowing anything. It is much better to measure the full set of benefits, monitoring target achievement through the whole life-cycle and to use the gathered intelligence to steer subsequent activity.

13. The only benefits that count are hard financial ones.

Most financial benefits are a consequence of the realisation of a whole series of linked, non-financial benefits. So if these are ignored, it is very unlikely that the financial benefits will ever be realised.

14. BRM is too bureaucratic and at best is only applicable to large programmes and projects.

BRM is scaleable but the principles can and should be applied to all investments in change.

15. We don't really have a problem, we have always done a cost-benefit analysis and then taken what has been claimed from future budgets.

The 'we' is often the 'Programme Team' whereas it should be 'the business'. 'Done' implies a historic snapshot – with everything changing so quickly a more dynamic process is required. 'Cost-benefit' is the wrong way round ('cart before the horse') – it should be 'benefit-cost'. Success needs more than 'analysis' – managed change with stakeholder engagement is needed. Taking what has been claimed from future budgets is not benefit realisation – it is forcible extraction, which can lead to serious problems if the benefit has not genuinely been realised.

26.3   How to Change the Culture

The most effective way to change the culture is to:

- make senior management aware of the issues and opportunities;

- move to using programmes rather than projects as the primary vehicle for benefit realisation;

- integrate BRM processes and practices into existing frameworks and guidelines for selecting and managing programmes and projects; and

- embed BRM within the culture of the organisation.

Embedding BRM in an organisation, which embraces the first three bullets, is fully discussed in the previous chapter; however, it may be difficult to secure the commitment and the funding necessary to embed BRM in an organisation without previously changing the culture, or at least winning the hearts and minds of the senior managers.

Some tips for breaking into this vicious circle, are:

- Gather internal evidence for changing, by researching some of your company's significant failures.

- Use war stories from other organisations.

- Be ready to use ad hoc challenges, for example, if someone asks you – what benefits are expected from a new office block or computer system? – you reply – none. This will usually stop them in their tracks, when they might say – why are we then spending £2m if there are no benefits? You can then explain that they are purely enablers, and then go on to describe the principle of the fried egg.

- Start to use some of the BRM techniques on any project or programme for which you are responsible. Presentation of maps, IAMs and use of the **sigma**

Value Types in business cases will capture the attention of senior managers. In some organisations this approach has generated a very positive response.

- Seek an early opportunity to arrange an Executive Briefing on BRM, for senior managers, ensuring that the briefing is provided by an external organisation with appropriate track record and experience. Senior managers tend to take more notice of external consultants, who themselves can be more objective and challenging and have a wealth of war stories to support their challenges.

26.4   The Benefit Maturity Index

However desirable it is that the organisation's culture is supportive of the philosophy, process and practices of BRM, organisations show very different levels of maturity when it comes to benefit realisation. These differences can be expressed in terms of a **Benefit Maturity Level Index**, where in organisations at:

Level 1: The primary purpose of benefits is to support a programme/project justification, but once justified the programme/project focuses on the delivery of capabilities/enablers and largely forgets about the benefits.

Level 2: Benefits are used to justify programmes and projects, possibly via business cases, and the benefits are then tracked and reported post-implementation.

Level 3: The dominant focus of all investments in change is benefit achievement. Benefit realisation is the central theme of any change programme and all other activities are subservient to this overriding focus.

Level 4: Benefits are used not only to define the name, scope, enablers and changes of each programme, but also to determine and balance portfolios and to set/validate business strategy and direction.

Organisational culture may include a mixture of the above, though one level is usually dominant. Based on the experience of **sigma**'s clients, the higher the level of maturity of the organisation, the higher the levels of benefit realisation achieved. It is encouraging that many large organisations are endeavouring to increase their Benefit Maturity, based on the above index. A more sophisticated index is the myth index discussed in Section 26.1.

For tips on how to change the culture and improve on these indices see previous section.

> **The mandating of the application of BRM by senior managers is a positive step, but it is no substitute for understanding BRM and then leading by example.**

Dangers of Giving Financial Values to Non-Cashable Benefits

'Everything that can be counted does not necessarily count; everything that counts cannot necessarily be counted.'

(Albert Einstein)

'A hundred objective measurements didn't sum the worth of a garden; only the delight of its users did that.'

(Lois McMaster, A Civil Campaign, *1999*)

27.1   Why Do People Distort the Truth in this Way?

In most organisations there is a strong drive, sometimes a mandate, to find ways to give financial values to non-cashable benefits. This practice generates far more problems than it solves and has become such an important issue that I have gathered into this single chapter comments and considerations from several other chapters.

So why do people distort the truth in this way? The most common reasons, each of which will be addressed below, are:

- to prioritise between investment options;

- because non-financial benefits are felt to be inferior;

- to rank benefits in some order of importance for comparison purposes;

- by only considering truly cashable benefits, many programmes and projects would arrive at a negative NPV, which is considered unacceptable.

TO PRIORITISE BETWEEN INVESTMENT OPTIONS

Equating everything to money makes some decision making – for example, choosing between investment options – much easier.

John, a student on an Executive MBA Programme at which I was speaking, explained that he thought BRM made complete sense but it would never work in his company. The senior level Steering Group in this large multinational organisation met monthly to consider proposals for new investments in change. Since these meetings lasted about eight hours, John felt that the Group would never have time to consider some of the broader factors I had been talking about. With each proposal they wanted a simple measure of value, such as an NPV, and little else.

Initially I felt sympathetic towards this pressurised and over-worked group of executives until I suddenly realised how ridiculous the situation sounded. It seemed that the Steering Group were spending a day selecting and sanctioning those proposals which had the largest NPVs, a job more appropriate for a school leaver or a computer system, than for a group of highly paid executives. Surely we pay top executives enormous salaries to use their experience to make difficult decisions and to examine a whole range of non-financial factors when comparing options.

NON-FINANCIAL BENEFITS ARE GENERALLY FELT TO BE INFERIOR

The success of most private sector organisations is measured in financial terms such as profit and cash, so it is not surprising that financial benefits are favoured in that arena. It is much more of a mystery in the public sector, where in most instances the quality of the service provided should be the best measure of success (see Section 27.3). In either situation a dominant focus on financials often relates to short-term thinking and is generally counter-productive, since most financial benefits are dependent on earlier non-financial benefits. In the banking case example, considered in Section 15.2, and again in Section 27.2, only one of the fourteen benefits is financial/cashable – the end benefit, 'increased sales revenue'. Unless most, if not all, of the non-financial benefits are realised, there will be no increase in sales revenue, at least not as a result of the programme – which makes the non-financial benefits as important as the one financial benefit. If we attempt to put a financial value on some of these non-cashable benefits such as 'improved productivity', not only is there a risk of double counting, but such activity will be detrimental to the realisation of the true financial benefit.

A few years ago a Finance Director from a large pharmaceutical company attended one of my seminars on BRM. Early in the day he made it clear that he had no time for non-financial benefits. By the end of the day, after considering some of the issues raised in this chapter, he had completely changed his viewpoint and returned to his company to make some quite radical changes.

TO RANK BENEFITS

Organisations often want to rank benefits to gain a sense of relative importance. Achieving this by giving every benefit a pseudo-financial value is like putting up a smoke screen which hides the true nature and value of each benefit. For example, a 10 per cent improvement in productivity for a large team of people could carry the same financial value as an annual reduction of two in the number of fatalities – but are they really equivalent, and would we want to lose sight of the actual benefits?

Ranking benefits is better achieved using classifications such as business impact assessment based on the **sigma** Grid, or Benefits Map Scores based on weighted paths.

In Section 13.3, Figure 13.2, I showed how the **sigma** Grid classification could highlight the relative significance of reduced postage and fax costs, and fewer dangerous drivers on the road, without using pseudo-financial values.

BECAUSE NEGATIVE NPVS ARE CONSIDERED TO BE UNACCEPTABLE

Why in business are we obsessed with NPVs and in particular find negative NPVs unacceptable? Expenditure on change is an investment; irrespective of whether in a business or in a personal context, we spend for a return. In the personal realm we are comfortable investing to achieve non-financial returns (for example, we buy food to enjoy eating it and to stay healthy), yet this seems less acceptable in business.

Some would say that without financial indicators like NPVs we cannot choose between options, yet we manage to do this satisfactorily in domestic situations. With £8000 to spend, I could choose a new kitchen, a new car or an exotic foreign holiday for the family, without trying to compute artificial NPVs. Reaching a decision might involve family discussions and negotiations but dubious arithmetic would not feature.

An NPV, based on pseudo-financial values for the non-cashable benefits, is likely to include some double counting, and will be based on time- and environment-dependent conversion assumptions; its worth is limited. Often these facts are not recognised and decisions are made assuming the figures to be robust and timeless.

On one occasion to which I previously referred, during **sigma**'s work on a large programme for a pharmaceutical company where a major benefit was getting drugs to market one month sooner, the Development Director said he did not want us to give this benefit a financial value. He appreciated its value as it had been expressed and, if in a particular situation he needed to give it a financial value, he believed he could do this more accurately taking account of the drug, the market and the year. Although this kind of enlightenment is increasing, it is still too rare.

27.2 Some Case Examples

ILLUSTRATION

A programme has identified as a benefit, 'fewer steps in a process'. In many organisations there would be pressure to give this a financial value. In Section 9.6, I showed, as an example, the small part of a Benefits Map which is repeated in Figure 27.1.

This map shows a set of possible paths, of which not all may become part of the Change Plan, emanating from the benefit 'fewer steps in a process'. Of the eleven benefits, only the two end benefits in the brighter green are financial. Apart from the other two end

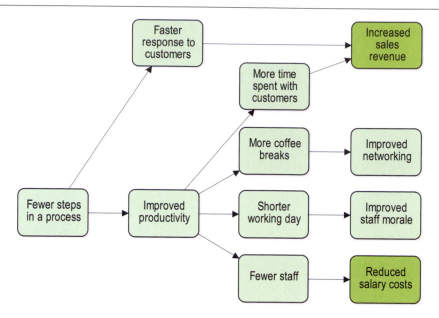

Figure 27.1   Why 'fewer steps in a process' should not be assigned a financial value

benefits, the remainder would all be easy to measure and in ways directly related to their descriptions (for example, the number of steps for 'fewer steps in a process').

To give a financial value to 'fewer steps in a process' implies a consequence, usually that represented by the lowest path in the diagram. There are four reasons why assigning a financial value to 'fewer steps' is unhelpful, even dangerous, namely:

1.   the implied path has not been made explicit and documented, so the basis of the financial value might be lost over time and the reduced salary costs never achieved;

2.   there may be a six-months' time difference between achieving the fewer steps and achieving the reduced salary costs;

3.   moving from fewer steps to reduced salary costs is not automatic, it requires the management of change – for example, making staff redundant;

4.   there is a risk that financial values could be given to both 'fewer steps' and 'reduced salary costs', which would be double counting.

By giving financial values only to cashable benefits and using maps to describe and communicate intentions, the above dangers are avoided. This map can also be used to communicate the intention that the time saved from the improved productivity could be used for more than one purpose – for example, 30 per cent for more time with customers, 20 per cent for a shorter working day and 50 per cent for fewer staff.

BANK CASE EXAMPLE

Section 15.2 considered the following example from a high street bank programme designed to increase sales revenues (Figure 27.2):

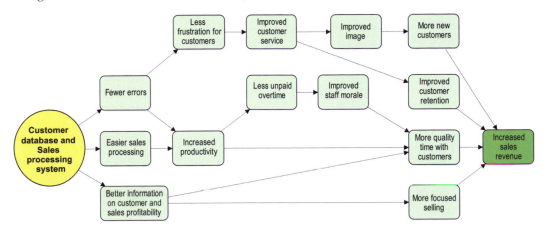

Figure 27.2   Benefits Map for 'increased sales revenue'

If you consider which benefits would be measured in real money (that is, are cashable, more money in or less money out) – the only one is sales revenue, which happens also to be the end benefit and the one of greatest interest to the sponsor, the Sales Director. This is the one that many organisations would single out as the key benefit.

So why don't we just report on this benefit and leave the others? After all, the rest are all non-financial and some might be costly to track. There are at least four good reasons why not – in fact four good reasons why you need to track all or at least most of the benefits in the diagram.

1.   If only sales revenue is tracked there would be no way of knowing whether an improvement in sales was a consequence of this programme, another programme or changes in the marketplace. However, if each benefit is achieved in turn (moving left to right) in its allotted time then it is like a ripple through the diagram from left to right. So when sales revenue increases, there is reasonable confidence that it is at least partly a consequence of this programme.

2.   Even if there was some other way to know that sales revenue was increasing as a result of this programme, without measuring all of the benefits, it would not be possible to determine whether the improvement is a result of a single path or multiple paths functioning. If a single path it is likely that only a small proportion (perhaps 10 to 20 per cent) of potential benefits are being achieved. To ensure maximum improvement in the end benefit it is important that all paths function and to check that this is happening, all benefits need measuring.

3.   Benefit tracking and reporting is not just for the Sponsor and other senior managers. Most staff are keen to see improvements and are interested to know whether or not they are on a pathway to success. So different stakeholders will be interested in different benefits and will want to see reports of measures relating to their interests.

The Sales Processing Manager would like the report on errors, sales processing and productivity. The Customer Relationship Manager is interested in complaints, customer frustration, customer service and company image. The HR Manager may be interested in the unpaid overtime and staff morale. The Sales Director (and Sponsor) will be interested in customer retention, new customers and the sales revenue.

4.   Each Benefits Map carries a timeline. To move to fewer errors, then less frustration for customers, then improved customer service, then improved image, then more new customers then increased sales revenue will take some time, perhaps two years. It is unlikely that the bank would want to wait two years to find out whether or not they have been successful.

It is much better to check whether the targets for errors, sales processing and better information are achieved within three months, targets for customer frustration and staff productivity within six months, and targets for customer service, unpaid overtime and staff morale within one year.

This perception, that only cashable benefits are important, is also dangerous because it puts pressure on organisations to give monetary values to benefits which are not cashable, thus distorting the truth and frequently leading either to double counting or to putting at risk the true financial benefits.

In our case example let us suppose that the profit margin from the increased sales revenue is £400,000 p.a. and the average productivity improvement for the sales team of 30 is 10 per cent. There may be pressure to put a financial value on the improved productivity and the argument might run – 10 per cent productivity improvement for 30 staff is equivalent to a saving of three staff and the total cost of three staff is £100 000 p.a. This implies a total cash benefit for the programme of £500,000 (£400,000 + £100,000); however, the £100,000 only becomes real money when the three staff are removed. If, however, the three staff are removed, three important benefits will not be achieved, namely: less unpaid overtime, improved staff morale and more quality time with customers. Without these benefits, increased sales revenue is at risk and it is quite possible that the profit margin from increased sales drops to £200,000.

We therefore have two choices: (1) make three staff redundant, so making the £100,000 real, which then gives a total benefit of £300,000 (£100,000 + £200,000), or (2) treat the improved productivity as non-cashable resulting in a total benefit of £400,000. Any other option would involve double counting of financial values. The Benefits Map in its current form clearly supports the second choice.

INTERNATIONAL SHIPPING SUPPLIES COMPANY

This company had been growing rapidly, mainly through acquisitions, and was keen to grow further but was concerned that because it now included varying systems, reporting procedures and cultures, it was losing control and might even be at risk of going under. In response to this situation the IT Director proposed to the Board a project which involved acquisition, customisation and implementation of a single management information system; it was expected to cost $28m and take two years, and was approved by the Board. Two years later the project was in serious difficulties and **sigma** was asked to review the benefits.

Because we had only ten days to produce an initial report, we were unable to involve the Board in the process described in this book, so we decided to start by examining the benefits in the original Business Case. We took these, initially ignoring their expected values, and put them into the IAM shown in Figure 27.3 below:

Business Impact / Value type	Productivity/ Internal Improvement	Risk minimisation/ survival	Growth
Definite £	Reduced systems costs Reduced manpower Reduced debtor days		
Expected £	Reduced stocks		Profit from increased sales volume and margin
Logical £			
Non-financial			
Intangible			

Figure 27.3   IAM showing benefits by business impact and value type

This was very illuminating, showing a complete lack of alignment with the intended strategic direction of the Board. Had this matrix been presented to the Board as part of the original project proposal, I have little doubt that the outcome would have been very different; however, in the original proposal the IT Director claimed annual benefits of $20m after year three and the whole decision to proceed was based on a sizeable, though not necessarily realistic, NPV.

The matrix is largely empty because the IT Director perceived that the Board was only interested in financial benefits whose value could be predicted with reasonable confidence. So the benefits which would have fitted into the bottom three rows of the matrix were either never identified or subsequently ignored. This resulted in no benefits for 'risk minimisation' and only one for 'growth' because benefits of these types were mainly 'logical', 'non-financial' or 'intangible'.

With help from **sigma**, the Board gradually came to appreciate the problem and restructured the project as a programme, giving it a much stronger business and benefits focus, while acknowledging the worth of the many non-financial benefits.

27.3 Benefits in the Public Sector

I would expect the majority of benefits from public sector/government projects to be non-financial, so negative NPVs should be quite acceptable.

I pay taxes, not to get money back, but to receive a service or improvement in society – for example, less crime, shorter hospital waiting lists, better care for the elderly and reduced fear of terrorism. These are all valuable in their own right; they are the positive outcomes for which most people are happy to pay taxes. In order that these outcomes are delivered in a cost-effective manner, there will need to be some investment in change to improve efficiency and possibly reduce costs; however, one would expect the majority of government investments in change to deliver improved services for the public.

It can of course be argued that some of these improvements might eventually lead to financial benefits (for example, shorter hospital waiting times leading to fewer working days lost through sickness leading to greater tax revenue). These links are tenuous and should be unnecessary – shorter hospital waiting times are valuable in their own right. If we pursue this tenuous linkage, we need to take into account that some improvements might lead to increased costs for government (for example, better care for the elderly leading to an increased state pension bill).

To take this kind of thinking to its logical conclusion, we need an economic model of the UK (or even the world) and a single all-encompassing programme aimed at making the world a better place. It would probably involve giving every human life a financial value which may need to take account of the person's life expectancy, abilities, earning potential, likely contribution to society or even the cause of death. Although this seems an absurd idea, considerable effort is being expended trying to move in this direction, including putting economic costs on unpleasant outcomes.[1]

I wonder how the values so computed compare with the amounts people might be prepared to pay to avoid the unpleasant outcome. If one has to put a financial value on these outcomes, this approach might give a more realistic value.

---

1   For example, the Home Office website puts an average economic cost of £12 000 on the emotional and physical impact on victims from sexual offences. In 2000 this was £12,000 and in 2003/4 this was £22,754.

27.4   Consequences

In summary, this smoke screen of pseudo-financial benefits often hides or distorts the truth, which frequently leads to unwelcome outcomes, such as:

- confusion and lack of motivation;

- undesirable behaviours;

- double claims;

- double counting;

- implicit assumptions that are often not made explicit;

- increased risk of programme failure;

- a portfolio of lower quality investments.

Not only are the above consequences extremely serious, but those bodies, including government departments, that require business, programme and project managers to give financial values to non-financial benefits are effectively asking them to commit fraud in order to secure funding (often from public funds) under false pretences.

> Financial values are great when they are real; but money is not the only form of worth. Experienced managers can and should weigh quality information and choose between options without reducing everything to financial numbers.

How Benefit Realisation Management (BRM) Fits with Other Approaches

'There is nothing new under the sun.'

(Ecclesiastes 1.9)

'Aviation is proof that given the will, we have the capacity to achieve the impossible.'

(Edward Vernon Rickenbacker)

28.1 Is BRM New?

Most of BRM is common sense and so by virtue of this fact cannot be new; it is not, however, common practice and so is new to many organisations, at least as a cohesive and comprehensive process. Although some people feel they have been practising benefit realisation for many years, most would acknowledge that they struggle with it and that their experience is at best limited to one or two aspects.

The underlying needs have certainly existed for a long time – the need for a clear end point, a practical pathway to get there, stakeholder commitment to the route, measures to monitor progress and herald success. It is therefore not surprising that various methodologies have emerged that address some or all of these issues, including:

- OGC's MSP;

- Balanced Business Scorecard;

- European Foundation for Quality Management (EFQM);

- Value Management.

28.2   BRM and MSP

Because of the importance of the OGC Publication, MSP, I have referred to MSP or made comparisons at each of the relevant stages within this book; however, I believe a few more general comments may help to put the situation in context.

The version of MSP published in September 2007 is a great improvement on the earlier versions, particularly the benefits chapters, and so as more organisations adopt MSP as respected guidance on programme management, there ought to be an overall increase in the benefits realised from change.

However in spite of all the good efforts of OGC and the publication of MSP, I believe the big challenge for the public sector is to create a focus on benefits which is rooted in a desire to achieve them. The existing strong culture of 'we will do benefits because we need a Business Case to secure the funding and/or because OGC or the Treasury say we must and we have to face a series of Gateway Reviews' is narrow and restrictive.

The current focus within the public sector on implementing enablers, rather than on realising benefits and achieving the vision or end goal, is so widespread and deep rooted that it will need more than MSP guidance to improve performance across the public sector.

Gateway Reviews would help if they were to give appropriate focus to benefits but perhaps the reason they often don't is that many of the reviewers are not experienced in BRM.

I hope this book may make some contribution towards changing this culture and helping organisations to increase their benefit maturity rating (see Section 26.4).

28.3   Balance Business Scorecard (BBS)

The Balanced Business Scorecard (BBS) is a scorecard of measures, which, in its generic form, is divided into four measure categories:

- client

- innovation and learning

- internal improvement

- financial.

This is a very useful technique, which is consistent with BRM, and is fairly widely known. In my view its strengths are:

- its strong focus on measurement;

- measurement is coordinated within a single model for the whole organisation;

- it encourages a scope of measurement which is much broader than just financials;

- its advocates have generally been successful in securing commitment from senior managers.

Although I have encountered many organisations that use the approach, application is sometimes patchy and rarely drives the change agenda. Unfortunately, in several of these organizations, the benefits planned from investment in change are not linked to the relevant scorecard categories and targets.

One of **sigma**'s clients, a large insurance company, recently asked me to help them develop a measure for their scorecard, to monitor their progress embedding BRM within the organisation. I was encouraged by this request but concerned that they had not linked the expected outcomes of their investments into the scorecard. Fortunately this was soon remedied.

28.4   EFQM[1]

This useful tool also focuses strongly on measurement, covering a broad range of topics. Its link to accreditation gives it added impetus. In practice it can suffer from a weakness, similar to that observed for some of the applications of BBS, namely that the activity doesn't seem to drive the change agenda.

Strategic measures are identified for the EFQM areas:

- leadership

- people management

- policy and strategy

- resources

- process

- people satisfaction

- customer satisfaction

- impact on society

- business results

---

1   EFQM is an abbreviation both for the European Foundation for Quality Management and for the process which they have championed. The above refers to the process.

and improvement targets are identified but rarely become the basis for the organisation's change portfolio. In contrast, BRM first identifies the end goal and the intermediate benefits, and then determines and manages the changes necessary to achieve them.

28.5   Other Techniques

Various other techniques exist including Best Value, Six Sigma, Lean, Value Management and Root Cause Modelling which appear to have similar or related aims to BRM, but are less comprehensive. Both Best Value and Root Cause Modelling begin by focusing on current problems rather than looking at future opportunities.

BRM's emphasis on starting with the end in view (see Chapters 1 and 8) provides focus both for fixing problems and exploiting opportunities, now and in the future, and so gives it a more positive emphasis leading to greater returns.

28.6   Does BRM Replace These Other Techniques?

BRM could replace all the other techniques since it includes an equivalent of most of their key elements; if your organisation has none of the above then I strongly recommend that you start with BRM. Even if your organisation is already committed to one or more of the above approaches, you are likely also to need BRM, and so it should be sensitively integrated with what you already have.

I recently worked with an organisation which had embarked on a major transformation programme. Over about nine months, it had invested heavily in 'Lean' thinking and had identified many hundreds of potential process improvements – far more than it was able to resource. Although the improvements were clearly useful – for example, in reducing duplication and eliminating waste – they were not clearly linked to benefits or the organisation's strategy and so there was no meaningful way of prioritising and selecting which ones to implement and in which sequence. The application of BRM helped fill this gap with **sigma**'s mapping providing the framework to transform the myriad of potential improvements into a benefit-driven prioritised and measurable implementation plan. In conclusion, many of the senior managers said how much they wished they had started with BRM as they could see it would have given them a faster, less painful and slightly higher-quality result.

So BRM should fill the gaps inherent in some of the approaches and tie everything together. A number of organisations, with experience of several of the above techniques, regard BRM as the glue that binds everything together (see Figure 4.3 in Section 4.1).

> **Integrate your current business improvement processes by adopting BRM.
> In themselves the components may not be new or radical but the cohesive and
> robust result should create a new opportunity for competitive edge.**

Requirements for Software to Support the Process

'Build a system that even a fool can use, and only a fool will want to use it.'
(George Bernard Shaw, 1856–1950)

'The least flexible component in any system is the user.'
(Lowell Jay Arthur)

29.1 General Requirements

Software to support the process is never more than an enabler, nevertheless a comprehensive integrated software system can provide a high degree of support to the concepts, processes, techniques and mind-set changes which are central to BRM.

In fact, it is difficult to imagine how large programmes or portfolios of projects and programmes can be effectively managed without sophisticated software. This chapter gives a brief description of the fundamental requirements for such software.

Over the years **sigma** has used standard Microsoft products and other systems to support different parts of the overall change management process. But lack of a single integrated product has given rise to frustration, inefficiencies, inconsistencies and loss of quality. So the software should fully support, in a cohesive and integrated manner, all the BRM processes and techniques described in this book, with the ability to integrate activities at different levels – organisation, portfolio, programme and project. Since BRM should form the core of any change process, the software should also support, at least at a basic level, the related management disciplines, as shown in Figure 29.1.

As well as covering the basic elements of these disciplines (as discussed in earlier chapters), the software should also provide a simple interface with any existing systems, particularly in the following areas:

- performance management;

- personnel systems for stakeholders;

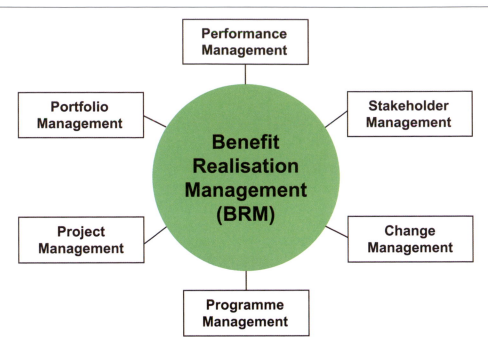

Figure 29.1   The relationship between BRM and other management disciplines

- project management;

- benefit tracking.

A schematic of the software structure from a user's perspective is illustrated in Figure 29.2 opposite.

The software should also be easy to use, intuitive and include options for hiding features based on user role (for example, a Programme or Project Manager might not see all the portfolio options). Navigation might also be role dependent.

The software should be able to support several hundred users, and up to a thousand change initiatives, with a security system that will allow varied access rights. This level of activity should be possible without significant degradation in response times. The system should maintain audit trails and include facilities to restore data that has been erroneously deleted.

It should also be capable of effective use in workshops, to support and even to drive the facilitation process, and to streamline data capture.

29.2   Scope and Architecture

The software operates at a variety of levels in terms of:

- goals – vision, objectives and benefits; and

- delivery structures – portfolios, programmes, projects and work packages.

It should be possible to enter it at any of these levels. The underlying system architecture is likely to look similar to the structure in Figure 29.2 below:

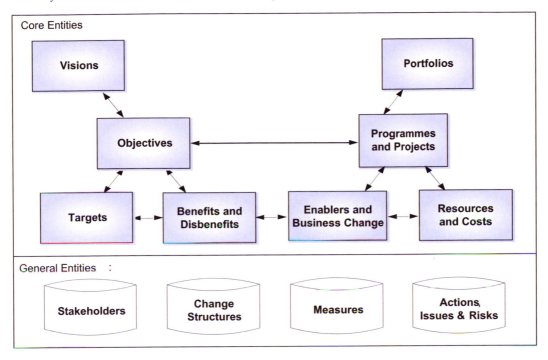

Figure 29.2   Possible architecture for the BRM software

29.3   Compatibility with the BRM Process Including Reviews

Navigation options in the software should be compatible with the six-phased cyclical process used by **sigma** and which is amplified with flowcharts in Chapter 23. It should be able to generate automatically the documents required for reviews, as described in Chapters 18 to 22. To accommodate this a report generation and/or customisation facility will be required.

29.4   Mapping Requirements

The software must include sophisticated, flexible, easy-to-use mapping facilities which can handle several hundred entities in each map and which is fully integrated with its central database where more detailed information can be held, including owners, scores, measures, targets, timescales, costs, resource requirements and responsibilities.

The mapping facilities should:

- utilise shape and/or colour to distinguish between different entity types;

- include flexible and easy-to-use linking options;

- contain an ability to weight paths and calculate scores for the complete range of map entities – objectives, benefits, enablers and changes;

- provide for different views of a map including version control;

- include an ability to 'drill down' on any entity to view or amend related details.

All the maps in this book have been generated with software meeting these requirements.

29.5   Change Delivery Mechanisms

The software must be able to hold a detailed picture of each change identified, whether via the BDM or some other process, including resource requirements, planned delivery timescales and costs.

The ability to group changes into change delivery mechanisms, such as programmes projects, using a 'drag and drop' facility on a delivery breakdown structure, is very useful and facilitates 'what if' analyses on solution options.

29.6   Analysis and Consolidation

The software should include analytical ability to enable:

- sensitivity analysis covering weightings and map scores;

- comparisons between options, including resource requirements and costs, for grouping changes into delivery packages such as projects and programmes;

- the generation of IAMs – see Section 13.3;

and a facility to consolidate entries (for example, when duplicates have been identified), merging and adjusting the relevant attributes and links. The system should produce an audit trail of any consolidations made.

29.7   Measurement and Tracking

Ideally the software should include provision for the recommended Measures Dictionary, where each measure could contain:

- dimensions (for example, by product, function, geographic region);

- historic data;

- baseline value (based on historic data but could be frozen at the start of a project);

- predicted improvement profile for each benefit, programme or project;

- change measure contributions;

- how frequently, by whom and how the measure is to be tracked;

- actual values as these are tracked;

- an ability to apportion actual improvements between benefits, projects and programmes.

29.8   Reporting – Dashboard

The system should incorporate a variety of reporting and display mechanisms, including dashboard facilities and the ability to use maps in conjunction with a BRAG Status (see Section 15.3), to monitor business performance, programme and project milestones, and benefit realisation.

It should also be able to generate all the standard reports for managing the programme and for review bodies.

29.9   Portfolio Management

The software should include a facility to generate comparisons between different investments within a portfolio, using:

- financial measures, such as NPV;

- consolidated scores based on a weighted set of attributes;

- Portfolio Investment Matrices.

29.10 Security

Since the system will be used by several hundred people, with different roles and responsibilities, from a variety of stakeholder groups, access must be controlled by sophisticated security, with restrictions on both update and view, depending on user or role.

29.11 Available Software

New software products in the portfolio/programme/project and benefits space regularly come on to the market; though at the time of going to press, few are able to support BRM adequately and through the whole change life-cycle, including the monitoring and reporting of actuals.

sigma seeks to monitor the marketplace for relevant products and so for up-to-date information on those which most closely deliver the functionality outlined in this chapter, please visit the **sigma** website at www.sigma-uk.com

> **A fully integrated system for BRM and Programme Management is a valuable aid, releasing time and energy for analysis, innovation and stakeholder engagement. But at its best it is only an enabler and will not of itself change hearts and minds.**

30

Case Examples

'Start by doing what's necessary; then do what's possible; and suddenly you are doing the impossible.'

(St. Francis of Assisi)

'We make our world significant by the courage of our questions and by the depth of our answers.'

(Carl Sagan)

30.1   An International Organisation – British Council

Bumping round Trafalgar Square in a black cab, balancing four large display boards and a 'magic benefits box' full of coloured cards and stickers wasn't where we imagined we'd be five months after attending one of Gerald Bradley's 'Benefits Realisation Management' seminars.

It was September 2007. We were taking our new benefits workshop equipment just a short distance from the British Council to a local hotel, to help facilitate a workshop for one of our change programmes. We'd come a long way in terms of our understanding of benefits, but were blissfully unaware at that point of how much further we still had to go.

This is the story of our journey – so far.

THE BACKGROUND

The British Council has worked for 75 years to build engagement and trust for the UK internationally. We work in 110 countries, where last year alone we connected with over 112 million people through programmes in the arts, education, science, sport and English language.

Our small unit of three has existed since 2003. It was set up as a Centre of Excellence for Programme Management to support the biggest change programme that the British Council had ever undertaken – a totally new way of working underpinned by a global restructuring and a new IT system.

We set out to deliver this change professionally using Managing Successful Programmes (MSP) methodology. We built a risks database, trained people, developed plans and a reporting process – we seemed well on track to deliver the benefits described in our various business cases.

We undoubtedly did deliver many of those benefits – but some we didn't deliver and some we could have delivered if we'd captured them properly in the first place. It was the most important part of what we were doing, but the part that, like so many organisations, we could have done so much better. As time went on, senior managers wanted to see evidence of benefits being delivered from this major initiative, but we were struggling to provide a full picture.

That's when Gerald, his company **sigma** and BRM came into our lives.

BACK TO THE DRAWING BOARD

We came across **sigma** by chance through an email forwarded by a colleague sympathetic to our benefits' plight. In April 2007 Barbara Stock, the Unit Head, went to a **sigma** workshop with two of our senior Programme Managers – all three came back full of enthusiasm for what they'd heard and inspired to reassess our approach to benefits.

Ideally of course new initiatives start with a mandate from senior managers – but in reality it's not always like that. Our senior managers were receptive to talking to Gerald about benefits when he came to brief them in May 2007. However, they were also still reeling from the weight of documentation and process that they had been subjected to through our first experience of using MSP. They were impressed by the BRM approach, but not yet ready to take on another major new initiative.

So Barbara decided that the unit would take a different approach. We'd work with our own constituency of Programme Managers to introduce BRM into the organisation through them. We'd take it slowly; see what worked and what didn't. Gerald calls it 'sowing seeds to change the culture'; Barbara describes it as 'lighting fires'. Our longer term hope was that the British Council's next major strategic initiative would start with some benefits mapping.

LIGHTING FIRES

From April 2007 we started to light the fires. We commissioned various **sigma** consultants to work with the change programmes that had already started to try and 'retro-fit' benefits. This worked better for some than for others. Much of it was frustrating and at times felt like wasted work. At the very least though, Programme Managers exposed to the approach were generally positive about using it in future. Significantly:

- our network of overseas Programme Managers was particularly enthusiastic – and overseas is where we deliver most of our work;

- we started work on benefits with two major programmes that were just beginning.

In October 2007 we contracted **sigma** Associate Julia Wall for three months to help us embed BRM in the organisation. Julia was to stay for much longer as she guided us through the next part of our journey.

HELP WITH LIGHTING FIRES

From October onwards we started a systematic 'fire lighting' programme with Julia which included:

- mapping the benefits we expected to get from our own project to embed BRM into the organisation (practice what you preach);

- nurturing our Programme Managers' network to bring them along with us;

- running benefits workshops in the UK with new programmes;

- building our reach overseas, including a workshop run by Gerald in Vienna and one by Julia in Ukraine;

- starting work on our BRM processes and delivery toolkit;

- building and training a small group of internal benefits workshop facilitators;

- attending Gerald's benefits forums and advanced workshops to learn more from him and from the BRM community of practitioners;

- updating ourselves on the place of BRM in the new version of MSP.

MAPPING AT STRATEGIC LEVEL

By April 2008 we'd covered a lot of ground. Then our Director of Strategy and External Relations, John Worne, asked Barbara to help support the team developing the British Council's next organisational strategy. Our hope that benefits mapping would be included in this process were fulfilled.

We did face an immediate challenge. It was impossible to get our key stakeholders (four busy members of our Executive Board plus various senior people based overseas) together in one room to develop a BDM. If we wanted to stay involved we'd have to be creative. Julia showed us how – creating maps from records of interviews, conversations and meetings then checking back with everyone to see if it looked right – lengthy but effective.

It would be wrong of us to claim that the development of this strategy was primarily driven by a classic BRM approach – it wasn't. But some important elements of BRM were involved – a big step forward.

TAKING THE BENEFITS INITIATIVE FROM JULIA

Julia stayed with us for longer than we had anticipated, mainly because of her involvement over a number of months in strategic mapping. Ominously as we entered the last few months of 2008 a weekly meeting began to appear in our diaries – 'Taking the benefits initiative from Julia'. This was to involve:

- making sure that our benefits facilitators had their final training sessions;

- getting our BRM toolkit finished;

- running a major benefits workshop for our East Asia region;

- getting over 'separation from Julia' anxiety;

- organising Julia's leaving party.

By early December we were on our own – but feeling more confident than we'd anticipated about taking the benefits agenda forward alone.

WHAT DID WE LEARN?

We learnt a huge amount of 'technical' things about BRM which were invaluable in making us more skilled and professional. Equally importantly though we learned:

- That it's not essential to have a specific senior management mandate for introducing BRM. It was enough to be allowed to have a go, to influence people to try BRM and to let it speak for itself. In fact that way round is arguably more, rather than less, powerful.

- How to tackle 'the lurch', the point after the 'intellectual conversion', when the hard work of thrashing out the practicalities begins and measures and ownership have to be agreed. A major benefit of BRM is it makes accountability very clear, but that's also a potential disbenefit – it's very exposing and potentially uncomfortable. We had to try and take people through that – we have to admit that we didn't succeed every time.

- The importance of having an embedded consultant for this work. Julia helped us at every stage to see how BRM theory could, without losing its underlying rigour, be adapted to work in a variety of real life situations.

- To be adaptable. We thought that we would be trained to run a series of standard BRM workshops. Instead we learned to adapt what we were doing at each stage so that we could take people with us.

- How to use our Programme Managers as BRM champions.

- To be patient – some people started the process, dropped it and then later came back to it.

- To deal with all the benefits equipment, including transport by cab and plane!

AND THE FUTURE?

We've now got a practical framework in place. We've won various hearts and minds and influenced people. We hear conversations couched in benefits language and see people using Benefits Maps as a standard part of what they are doing.

We would be the first to admit that the journey isn't over, although we've come a long way. We may even have to lay low for a while before our next 'push' to get BRM more firmly embedded within our organisation. We'll carry on being realistic and pragmatic and using our influencing skills and we're confident that we'll make even more progress.

For helping us get this far, we have to thank our local restaurant for letting us spread Benefits Maps all over the place during working lunches when we desperately needed a change of scene. Most of all we owe thanks to John Worne, to Jane Beecroft, our Head of Corporate Strategy and Performance, to our Programme Managers and to Gerald and Julia for supporting us in different ways on this journey. It's been a rocky road at times but it's been fascinating, fun and most importantly, beneficial.

30.2   Local Government – Royal Borough of Kensington and Chelsea

BACKGROUND AND INTRODUCTION TO THE ROYAL BOROUGH

With a population of ca. 170,000 and covering just 4.7 square miles, Kensington and Chelsea is one of London's smallest boroughs – but it is also the UK's most densely populated. Its community is diverse and cosmopolitan: over half of residents in the borough were born abroad, and over 100 languages are spoken in the borough's schools. Within its borders some of the most affluent neighbourhoods in England, however there are pockets of marked deprivation.

The Council has been consistently regarded as high performing for many years: it is one of only three Councils in the country to be awarded the coveted '4 stars and improving strongly' status by the Audit Commission in every year since such judgements were introduced in 2002. Moreover, residents' satisfaction remains high and has increased.

In order to sustain such high performance, councillors and managers have continued to seek opportunities to enhance services and value for money, and over the years a number of improvement and transformation programmes emerged, particularly in the customer services arena. These initiatives showed considerable successes but the organisation lacked the capacity to demonstrate unequivocally the benefits of the change.

RECENT CHANGES IN THE SCALE AND SCOPE OF CHANGE

During 2007 and 2008, the scale of the Council's transformational ambitions increased dramatically. New initiatives around the personalisation of adult social care, the implementation of flexible office space and new ways of working, far-reaching carbon emission reduction targets and service transformation in other areas all meant that the Council faced an era of significant and complex change, requiring significant investment in order to deliver it.

Moreover, the fiscal climate in which the Council operates poses immense challenges. The requirements to yield cashable efficiency savings under the 2007 Comprehensive Spending Review (set by central Government) and the looming shadow of recession, leading to reduced income, and long-term constraints on grant funding, will place a significant strain on Council resources. Meanwhile, residents' expectations for Council services remain very high – and a new inspection regime (the Comprehensive Area Assessment) needs to be accommodated, this time one which focuses more heavily on outcomes and risk.

So the drivers for change have multiplied, the need for change is more acute and it is more crucial than ever that the Council realises the benefits of the change it invests in.

THE PROGRAMME MANAGEMENT OFFICE

Keen to support and assure the successful delivery of programmes, in 2008 the Council agreed to establish a corporate Programme Management Office (PMO) with three members of staff. At the same time, the senior leaders of the organisation developed an overarching vision for the future of the Council, which united the ambitions of the various programmes under the heading of 'Royal Borough: Smartest Council': under this banner, the Council seeks to become 'Leaner, Greener and Keener'.

The 'Smartest Council' vision provided a key opportunity to develop the organisation's understanding of and appetite for benefits delivery. The Council's senior leaders and managers had articulated 'what' they wanted to achieve in broad terms and agreed on the programmes which should fulfil these expectations. The task for the PMO was to develop a mechanism and approach to make sure that the Council could be very specific about those ambitions and be able to monitor the delivery of the benefits of change.

In conjunction with Programme Managers, the PMO embedded a concept of 'Smartest Council Benefit Categories' (see Section 9.4b). These are an interpretation of the Smartest Council vision in everyday language – and they map directly back to the Smartest Council strapline of 'Leaner, Greener and Keener' as follows:

- improved customer satisfaction (keen);

- improved quality of life (keen);

- improved job satisfaction (keen);

- net cost reduction (lean);

- improved environmental impact (green).

All transformation programmes use these headings to express the benefits they are seeking to deliver. This enables the PMO to monitor their contribution to the delivery of the 'Smartest Council' vision and helps to ensure that benefits are not 'double counted'.

WORKING HANDS-ON WITH PROGRAMMES

Alongside this broad conceptual work, the PMO works closely with Finance colleagues to support individual programmes with their work on benefits. PMO and Finance staff have facilitated benefits workshops and offered hands-on assistance in identifying individual programme benefits and relating these back to the Smartest Council initiative. Although all of these programmes had already done some thinking on what their benefits were and how these contribute to strategic objectives, PMO and Finance assistance helped the programmes to be more precise in terms of what individual improvements and outcomes (benefits) they are seeking to deliver, and, crucially, how these benefits will be owned, delivered and measured.

Meanwhile the PMO has worked to strengthen the wider organisation's understanding of benefits and appetite for BRM. The PMO commissioned **sigma** for two days: one day's training for Business Change Managers and Finance Officers from different departments and a two hour presentation by Gerald Bradley to an internal Programme Management Community of Practice. For the remaining time within those two days **sigma**'s consultancy expertise helped to advance the Council's thinking on how BRM can fit in with a Business Process Redesign project and how benefits might be embedded into existing financial and service planning cycles.

From **sigma**'s suggested approach, tools and methodology, we have particularly adopted the concept of bounding objectives which clarify the scope of a programme's accountability. We are also beginning to use maps as a means of representing the complete benefits landscape of a programme in a logical manner, allowing Programme Team members and stakeholders to conceive of the programme as a cohesive whole with interdependent elements and a given lifespan.

WHAT PROGRESS HAS BEEN MADE?

As a result of the continuing hands-on support to individual Programme Teams and the training and consultancy input from **sigma,** the Council is confident that it is better equipped than ever to realise the benefits of its change programmes.

Programmes now actively seek help and support as they work to identify benefits, measures and baselines. Demand for workshops and input from the corporate PMO is strong, and the importance of benefits realisation is not questioned. Most programmes have an identified suite of benefits – and those that haven't are working towards this. The Council's Management Board is eager to see benefits delivered and has begun to apply pressure for 'quick wins' (particularly financial benefits, in the current climate). For the Management Board, BRM is a means to an end – the successful delivery of improvements and positive outcomes from the Council's investments in change. It seeks reassurance that benefits will be delivered and requests regular reporting on both progress so far and prospects for future benefits realisation.

Some of the programmes which make up the Smartest Council portfolio are still in their definition phase and are not yet delivering benefits. The programmes which have been running for longer are closer to benefit realisation. The Council expects to achieve the main cost savings arising from this portfolio from 2010/2011 onwards, with some programmes delivering savings earlier. Increased staff satisfaction will be measured through the Council's annual staff survey, and the Council's recently approved carbon management programme will shortly introduce valuable metrics for measuring reduced environmental impacts. The usefulness of the generic 'Smartest Council' benefits is being tested by applying them not only to the transformation programmes but to all significant improvement initiatives.

WHAT IS THERE TO LEARN ABOUT BRM AND LOCAL GOVERNMENT IN PARTICULAR?

Through practical experience and with the benefit of **sigma**'s extensive wisdom, the Council has learned some key lessons regarding how to make BRM a reality in local government.

Firstly, local Council managers are not always free to decide *what* improvements to make. This might be for political reasons – for it is ultimately local Councillors who have to determine the *right things to do*. Clear direction from members is needed – and this then empowers officers to define, deliver and measure the improvements that members seek. Kensington and Chelsea is fortunate in having strong and long-standing working relationships between leading councillors and officers. These are harder to develop in less politically stable local authorities.

Secondly, central Government (either directly or via its agencies and auditors) seeks to exert a strong influence over local councillors' choices of which things to do, and in some cases, it also prescribes *how* things should be done. For example, many of the recent structural changes in children's services and adult social care have been driven by central Government. Individual Councils must ensure that these changes:

- are translated in ways that meet local needs and circumstances;

- accord with local political priorities; and

- are implemented smoothly and in the right way so that the anticipated benefits can be realised, and any potential disbenefits minimised or avoided.

Whether the impetus for *doing the right thing* comes from central government or is generated locally, it is up to local authorities to ensure that they *do things right*. For Kensington and Chelsea, this means:

- Establishing clarity on objectives and programme scope – knowing for what the programme is accountable and not accountable; in particular understanding how any government-driven initiatives might be interpreted locally.

- Identifying the range of benefits, financial and non-financial, associated with the objectives.

- Ensuring local needs are met and benefits realised even when the *means* of achieving an objective has been pre-specified (for example, ContactPoint, the national database for children's services).

- Establishing a means of monitoring benefit achievement and embedding this within existing and very stable financial planning and performance management cycles.

WHAT IS NEXT?

The PMO's learning in relation to benefits increases daily, and every interaction with a programme, a stakeholder or the Management Board contributes valuable experience and helps inform a Council-wide approach. The Council is seeing a gradual shift across the board towards a culture which focuses on benefits, rather than project outputs – and the current financial climate at the time of writing in spring 2009 supports this.

Next steps include rolling-out our BRM approach to include projects as well as programmes, and further work with individual Programme Teams to help them to identify their benefits, ensure ownership and buy-in and plan for monitoring and realisation. It will be important to ensure that BRM aligns with familiar and well-established business and performance management cycles and does not create a bureaucratic, time-consuming and energy-sapping benefits 'industry'. The Council's adoption of BRM must offer challenge and add value to the delivery of councillors' and managers' priorities if it is to continue to succeed.

30.3   A National Government Agency – DVLA

A TRANSFORMING VISION

Over a period of three to four years DVLA[1] has transformed itself from an organisation focused on routine licence processing to a valuable crime prevention organisation. A key part of this transition is the way change is managed, where the focus has shifted from managing a set of projects delivering capabilities to managing a portfolio of change

---

1   DVLA is UK's Driving and Vehicle Licensing Authority.

programmes delivering benefits. These include benefits to the public, benefits to staff and benefits to other UK Government Agencies.

THE STARTING POINT – THE BASELINE

In 2002 change was managed through a set of projects which were largely uncoordinated and where the focus of Project Managers was on delivering capability (new systems, buildings and processes) to time, cost and quality. A number of projects were mandatory in response to UK or European Legislation.

Benefits were usually identified by the Project Manager in order to justify the expenditure but they were not always owned by stakeholders and were at times unrealistic.

In this environment, as no thorough evaluation took place, and given analysis of similar organisations, it is probable that most projects were delivering less than 20 per cent of the Business Case benefits.

BEGINNING THE TRANSFORMATION

Soon after the arrival of Clive Bennett as Chief Executive, all DVLA's projects (approximately 65 with an annual investment in excess of £100 million) were put into a single Change Programme with a clear Change Programme Plan. Clive then set up a Change Programme Board (CPB) to:

- direct this Change Programme;

- review new project proposals;

- monitor project achievements;

- plan and monitor the culture change in DVLA needed to facilitate delivery of the programme;

- allocate resources;

- monitor quality and ensure technical consistency.

This Board quickly recognised the need for greater emphasis on benefits and in particular the need to improve their identification, management and realisation, and commissioned the development of a Programme Management Framework to put greater emphasis on benefits. To bring about the necessary cultural change a corporate Benefit Facilitator function was established within a PMO. This PMO is similar to a corporate PSO but puts more emphasis on monitoring, compliance and quality assurance than on providing support.

The Benefit Facilitator function was responsible for defining the process for Benefit Management[2] and for promoting its adoption, through collaborative working with Project and Programme Managers. The function headed by Jacky Long (referred to as the Benefits Manager), working with two support staff (initially three) promoted and ensured compliance with the process.

THE TRANSFORMATION PROCESS

The Benefit Facilitator function utilised and promoted the use of many of the techniques described in this book including the fried egg model and the various mapping processes. These were customised and built into:

- a workshop training programme which was rolled out to about 80 Project Managers and other project and professional staff;

- the DVLA Benefit Life-cycle Model;

- The DVLA Project Life-cycle.

Disbenefits were taken very seriously and included any related increases in the running costs of the Business-as-Usual (BAU) state.

During this period, more programmes were added to the portfolio of change initiatives, including some which are focused more on broader business change and less on IT and process change. The role of the CPB has evolved into more of what I have referred to as a Portfolio Board (see Sections 6.5 and 24.5).

Initially Programme Managers had little authority and no budget (this lay with Project Managers and the CPB), but this is gradually changing as OGC's programme guidelines are gradually implemented.

THREE YEARS ON

Change is managed through an appropriate mix of programmes and projects. Programme Managers now have recognised authority and budgets and are increasingly taking responsibility for benefits – from programme scoping, through Business Case development to eventual realisation – though end accountability for their realisation lies with the business.

Benefits are now included in the Outline Business Case and there is a Benefit Delivery Plan[3] (BDP) to accompany the Full Business Case in at least 90 per cent of instances.

One large programme is a portfolio of 21 relatively discrete projects and for these it is appropriate to manage benefits at the project level and so BDPs have been developed for

2   Benefit Management is the term DVLA use for BRM.

3   BDP is the DVLA term for a BRP.

each project. In another instance for an HR Programme it is only meaningful to consider benefits at programme level; hence the BDP is for the programme.

The adoption of the Benefit Management process has successfully led to:

- engaging and securing the buy-in of stakeholders;

- allowing the Change Programme Board to make informed investment decisions;

- transferring Benefit Management skills to DVLA staff, especially Project and Programme Managers;

- the identification of additional benefits not previously envisaged;

- a reduction in duplicate benefit claims;

- accurate reporting on the success of projects and programmes – that is, the delivery of benefits;

- better management of disbenefits and monitoring to minimise new or increased operational costs.

As the number of projects which have BDPs and which regularly track and report benefits has increased, so has the load on the CPB. In response it was decided to split its function between two corporate Boards:

- an Executive Planning Board;

- an Executive Review Board.

HURDLES THAT WERE OVERCOME

Initially some Project Managers, who were very focused on delivering capability to time, cost and quality, were resistant to the increased focus on benefits. They felt that Benefit Management was unnecessary bureaucracy for which they did not have time – they knew that in the past little had happened as a result of any extra effort they had spent on benefits.

This time it was different. Jacky started with a big stick and Project Managers soon realised that the renewed focus on benefits was not going to go away. Re-enforcement from the top helped to ensure that the transition was successful. Over time the Project Managers also came to realise the value of the process and most are now committed and readily apply the process as standard. In fact, instead of being chased by the Benefits Manager for their plans, they often produce their draft plans before they are expected.

Quality has also steadily improved. Benefits are now much more realistic and the process for delivering them is much more effective so that over 75 per cent of planned benefits are now achieved.

LESSONS LEARNED

1. It is far better to start with the 'end in view' and to create the various route maps working right to left. Although this is now fairly well accepted within the culture there are still pockets of the more traditional 'cart before the horse' thinking, which is not helped by often having to respond to specific legislative directives in short timescales.

2. Business Case benefits are better understood when supported by a BRP including Benefits Maps (see Chapter 19).

3. The Benefit Manager would have preferred to have engaged with Programme Managers sooner, though, until the authority and accountability of Programme Managers became fully recognised, such involvement may not have been the best use of limited resources.

4. In the early application of the process, benefit forecasts were sometimes adjusted throughout the change life-cycle leading to over-favourable results. This has now been fixed by ensuring that benefit reporting is matched against the original or Business Case forecast in addition to any revised forecast.

5. One very important lesson was to avoid the temptation to give up in the face of resistance. At DVLA persistence has paid off with results now well ahead of industry norms.

30.4   The Results of One Man's Extraordinary Vision

Sometimes benefits are the avoidance of a negative and sometimes a vision can be of something bad – a forthcoming calamity. In this case the vision to be entertained and worked towards must be the avoidance of the calamity.

A wonderful example of such a vision was experienced by Rick Rescoria who, during the 1990s, had a vision of a terrorist plane flying into the Twin Towers in New York. Rick was the Head of Security for Morgan Stanley Dean Witter which occupied offices from floors 44 to 74 of Tower 2. Rick shared his vision with the Directors of Morgan Stanley[4] who bought into it and subsequently sponsored a programme of change.

The longer-term change was to relocate to another building, which was scheduled for 2003. Shorter-term plans included:

---

4   Rick also shared this vision with others including, I believe, the FBI.

- the appointment of fire wardens;

- fail-safe lighting;

- smoke extractors in the stair wells;

- regular fire drills, including complete and compulsory evacuation twice per year.

This programme involved considerable expenditure, meticulous planning, regular testing, significant stakeholder engagement and team working, no doubt in the face of opposition and resistance from sceptics.

Did this programme have a positive NPV? How was the ROI eventually measured? On 11th September 2001, the fact that only six of Morgan Stanley's 2700 staff didn't make it out of the Twin Towers I think says it all. That Rick was one of the six, shows his level of courageous dedication and commitment to the last.

In most programmes commitment costs but rarely will commitment demand the ultimate cost. This case is, however, a salutary reminder that though outcomes should be incredibly valuable, as in this instance, they are rarely perfect and 100 per cent of potential benefits are seldom achieved.

31

In a Nutshell

'You don't have to be great to start, but you have to start to be great.'

(Zig Ziglar)

'The tragedy of life is not that it ends so soon, but that we wait so long to begin it.'

(W. M. Lewis)

Critical Actions Summarised

So where do we go from here? Listed below are 20 critical actions which summarise the key messages of this book. Although all are important, applying any one of them should enable you to move forward on a voyage of discovery and success.

1.   APPLY BRM TO INCREASE PROGRAMME AND PROJECT SUCCESS

BRM is not simply about identifying and tracking a few benefits. It is a flexible and active process for:

- setting strategy and direction;

- creating a shared vision or end goal;

- determining and managing change;

- engaging and motivating stakeholders;

- managing risks;

- achieving success.

2.   START WITH THE 'END IN VIEW'

Don't start out without knowing where you are going, and ensure that the destination is of real value to the organisation and/or its customers. Both private and public sectors are plagued with the 'cart before the horse' mentality – projects which design and build solutions and then look for benefits to justify the investment. Begin with a vision or end goal congruent with the organisation's strategy and then determine how it can best be achieved.

3.   ENGAGE STAKEHOLDERS

It is vital to engage stakeholders throughout the change life-cycle and from the earliest possible stage, because:

- their knowledge and ideas will usually improve the quality of the end goal and the plan to achieving it;

- they can often throw a spanner in the works;

- benefit realisation and programme success will be dependent on business change within many of the stakeholder areas;

- they can become champions of change and ambassadors of success.

4.   ALIGN AND BALANCE THE CHANGE PORTFOLIO

The portfolio of change investments must be actively managed to ensure that, in a changing world, it remains aligned to the organisation's strategy and direction. The portfolio should be balanced in terms of:

- business impact;

- risk;

- reward;

- complexity;

- extent of business change – for each stakeholder;

- resource and funding requirements.

5.   IDENTIFY A COMPREHENSIVE SET OF BENEFITS

Use several different techniques with a good cross-section of stakeholders to determine a comprehensive set of benefits. For a large programme or for one of long duration this could result in 25–100 benefits. This may seem far too many, yet without identifying and managing a full set of benefits it is difficult to be effective in:

- motivating stakeholders;

- determining and driving the change agenda;

- monitoring progress over the whole change life-cycle – perhaps several years;

- realising the end benefits and ultimately the vision;

- attributing success to the programme.

6.   MAP THE ROUTE TO SUCCESS

Maps provide the best visual representation of the route to the end goal, linking key entities in cause-and-effect relationships. Three forms are recommended:

- At the highest level – Strategy Maps linking objectives;

- Benefits Maps linking benefits to one another and where appropriate to one or more of the objectives;

- Benefit Dependency Maps (BDMs) – the result of adding dependencies to a Benefits Map, especially required enablers and business changes.

Maps are particularly useful for:

- handling multiple relationships;

- communicating – aspirations, intentions and progress;

- reducing ambiguity and misunderstanding.

7.   MEASURE TO ENCOURAGE THE DESIRED BEHAVIOUR

Since measurement can be time consuming and costly it must have purpose. Its primary purpose should be that it leads to action. So it is important that the choice of measures and targets encourages desired behaviours and ultimately genuine realisation of the expected benefits.

Wherever possible measurement should be undertaken by those who are the most anxious to achieve the benefits.

The use of a Measures Dictionary avoids wasteful duplication of measurement and provides a cohesive higher-level view, which will also provide early warning of benefit overclaiming.

8.   USE MAPS TO DETERMINE REQUIRED CHANGES

Since the primary purpose of change is benefit realisation, benefits, and in particular Benefits Maps, should be the starting point for identifying and adding the dependent changes. The paths of the resulting maps (BDMs) can be weighted, working right to left, to give scores to the benefits and the changes, thus providing a mechanism for prioritising investment in change.

9.   BLUEPRINT THE FUTURE STATE

The model of the intended new business state, showing how the proposed enablers will integrate with the required business change to generate the intermediate benefits and ultimately deliver the vision, is called a Blueprint. The Blueprint will evolve and develop through the early stages of the change life-cycle as detail is added.

The Blueprint is the single comprehensive source of information about the future state of the organisation necessary to achieve the vision and could be referred to as the Solution. It needs to be of high quality and owned by the affected stakeholders as it is the basis for other key documents such as Requirement Specifications, ITTs and Supplier Contracts.

10.   STRUCTURE THE PROGRAMME TO MANAGE BUSINESS CHANGE

Successfully implementing the Blueprint is vital for the realisation of benefits and ultimately for programme success. This frequently requires business change from stakeholders outside the direct control or influence of the programme, it is therefore important that the programme is structured to facilitate this challenge.

Implementing business change requires at least the same dedication and meticulous care as the implementation of the enablers.

11.   USE BRM TO IDENTIFY AND MANAGE RISKS

The ultimate risk in any change initiative is the risk of non-realisation of benefits and the non-fulfilment of the vision. So the maps, particularly the BDM, provide a very relevant framework for identifying and assessing impact of risks.

12.   FOCUS GOVERNANCE ON BENEFIT REALISATION

The governance structure should both support and challenge the Programme Team. Its focus should be on benefit realisation and all other considerations should be driven by this emphasis. In this sense the Benefit Facilitator role is part of the governance structure.

Too often governance concentrates on cost management and procurement issues to the detriment of benefit realisation.

13.   OPTIMISE THE SOLUTION

Optimisation, focused primarily on benefit realisation, runs throughout the whole BRM process. Particular opportunities include:

- using weighted paths in the Strategy Map to determine the optimal bounding objectives;

- considering the portfolio of existing investments when selecting and approving additional initiatives, in order to optimise the whole portfolio;

- selecting highly weighted paths ('super highways') from the Benefits Map in order to optimise the route to the achievement of the vision;

- starting from a set of BDMs, designing an optimal Blueprint, to maximise realised benefits relative to cost and risk;

- partnering with stakeholders throughout the life-cycle to optimise their support and contribution;

- implementing the designed solution (Blueprint), in particular roll-out sequence, to optimise benefit achievement;

- responding rapidly with appropriate actions if and when shortfalls in benefit achievement occur.

14.   AVOID GIVING FINANCIAL VALUES TO NON-CASHABLE BENEFITS

While recognising the need to justify investment proposals, we advise against giving non-financial (non-cashable) benefits pseudo-financial values, for the following reasons:

- it distorts the truth;

- it leads to double counting;

- it can lead to loss of support from stakeholders;

- it usually results in non-optimal solutions.

15.   TRACK BENEFITS IN ORDER TO DRIVE ACTION

Tracking benefits is a form of intelligence gathering. This intelligence should be used to influence decision making and so determine and drive future actions. Identify and learn lessons, but use the information to look forwards and not backwards.

Report the information to those who can take action – generally those with the greatest interest in the realisation of the particular benefit. This may involve reporting different information to different stakeholders.

16.   REPORT BENEFITS TO PUBLICISE SUCCESS

The primary purpose for benefit reporting is to drive action; however, an important secondary purpose is to encourage and motivate stakeholders by publicising success.

17.   REWARD BENEFIT REALISATION

For many years now people have been rewarded for building enablers to time, cost and quality. It is high time that benefit realisation is similarly rewarded.

18.   CREATE A SUPPORTIVE ENVIRONMENT

To enable BRM to make the best contribution to business performance, a supportive environment is required, including:

- a supportive culture;

- an enlightened view of non-financial benefits;

- integration with other initiative and methodologies;

- establishment of a Benefit Facilitator role;

- software to support the process.

19.   SOW SEEDS TO BEGIN TO CHANGE THE CULTURE

Start now to sow seeds to change the culture. As an initial step, when asked about the benefits expected from a particular enabler – say none – and then explain the fried egg principle.

20.   START WHERE YOU CAN

Initially the complete BRM approach may seem too much. So start where it is most needed, then extend its application to where it is possible and continue until you find you are doing the impossible.

Bibliography

Achieving Efficiency Targets by Gerald Bradley (PSE Magazine – May 2007).

Achieving Maximum Value from Information Systems – A Process Approach by Dan Remenyi, Michael Sherwood-Smith with Terry White (Wiley – 1997).

How to Measure Anything – Finding the Value of Intangibles in Business by Douglas W Hubbard (Wiley – 2007).

Making it Happen by John Harvey Jones (Fontana – 1988).

Managing Successful Programmes (TSO – 2007).

P3O Portfolio, Programme and Project Offices (TSO – 2008).

Portfolio Management (TSO – 2009).

Realising Benefits from Government ICT Investment – A Fool's Errand? by Stephen Jenner (Academic-Publishing – January 2009).

Releasing Project Value into the Business by Michael Payne (Project Manager Today Publications – January 2008).

Seven Habits of Highly Effective People by Stephen R Covey (Simon & Schuster Ltd)

Strategy Maps by Kaplan and Norton (Harvard Business School Publishing Corporation – 2004).

Transformation – How to Make it Work by Gerald Bradley (Public Sector Review – Central Government 17).

Why Clinicians and Hospital Managers are Looking to Benefits not Cash as the Way Forward by Lawrence Hoare (PSE Magazine – February 2007).

Why More CEOs are Turning to Benefit Realisation Management (BRM) by Gerald Bradley (CEO Magazine – August 2006).

About the Author

After graduating from Oxford with a good honours degree in Mathematics, Gerald began his career teaching and university lecturing. During this time he obtained an MSc in Computer Science from London University and soon became Course Director for the Computer Science Degree Course at Kingston University. In 1974 Gerald left academia and joined BP where he successfully project managed two strategic computer projects. Following this success he joined a select team of internal management consultants where he worked on a restructuring of the BP Group, which inevitably involved significant change. After this broader experience he moved back into systems to become Head of Systems for the International Downstream Oil Business where he gained further much valued experience managing some major technology-enabled change. After several years in this role, he took on a roving international role with the purpose of encouraging senior managers worldwide:

- to see change as a vehicle to achieve their visions or end goals;

- to adopt a more creative and proactive approach to systems and change, in order to determine competitive edge opportunities and so increase the overall value of their investment portfolio;

- to focus, for each investment, on the measurable achievement of genuine business value.

It was at this time that Gerald recognised the need for, and subsequently began to pioneer, a fresh approach to benefit realisation. In recognition of the much wider potential of this new thinking, he left BP and founded **sigma**, to develop and promote this new approach, now known as Benefit Realisation Management (BRM). During the subsequent 20 years, by working with many major organisations from a cross-section of industries, Gerald has been able to prove and refine BRM and **sigma** has developed into an organisation which can provide a comprehensive range of benefit-related services. Initially clients were predominantly from the private sector, though in the past ten years there has been a swing towards the public sector and Gerald has recently been advising several major government programmes on their application of BRM.

The benefit-related services which **sigma** now provides cover the following application areas:

- the application of BRM to the setting and refining of business strategy;

- portfolio management;

- visioning and objective setting;

- benefit identification, classification and validation;

- programme and project scoping;

- establishing suitable organisation and governance structures;

- development of Benefit Realisation Plans and Business Cases;

- development of Business Change Plans;

- stakeholder management;

- measure determination;

- baselining, benchmarking and target setting;

- benefit tracking and reporting.

sigma is committed to skills transfer and so its primary service is partnership consultancy, whereby experienced **sigma** consultants work in collaboration with nominated client personnel to transfer skills through joint practical activity in any or all of the above listed areas. This consultancy is supported by training, coaching and mentoring and the availability of an integrated software tool to support all of the activity areas.

Gerald frequently addresses management and academic groups on benefit realisation issues, and has contributed to several MBA and other postgraduate courses, some on a regular basis. He has also written several articles on different aspects of BRM for journals and magazines.

Gerald is married with eight children, is an enthusiastic tennis player and very much enjoys travel and photography.

His contact details are: geraldbradley@talktalk.net; 01372 278512 or 07786 061662.

Index

If you have found this resource useful you may be interested in other titles from Gower

Making the Business Case:

Proposals that Succeed for Projects that Work

Ian Gambles

200 pages; Paperback: 978-0-566-08745-5

Training for Project Management:

Volume 1, 2 and 3

Ian Stokes

338 pages; A4 Looseleaf: 978-0-566-08869-8; 978-0-566-08870-4; 978-0-566-08871-1

Managing Project Uncertainty

David Cleden

140 pages; Paperback: 978-0-566-08840-7

Project Governance

Graham Oakes

288 pages; Hardback: 978-0-566-08807-0

Practical Schedule Risk Analysis

David Hulett

240 pages; Hardback: 978-0-566-08790-5

Images of Projects

Mark Winter and Tony Szczepanek

288 pages; Hardback: 978-0-566-08716-5

GOWER

If you have found this resource useful you may be interested in other titles from Gower

Managing Risk in Projects
David Hillson
126 pages; Paperback: 978-0-566-08867-4

Strategic Project Appraisal and Management
Elaine Harris
128 pages; Paperback: 978-0-566-08848-3

Stakeholder Relationship Management:
A Maturity Model for Organisational Implementation
Lynda Bourne
246 pages; Hardback: 978-0-566-08864-3

Systems Cost Engineering:
Program Affordability Management and Cost Control
Dale Shermon
328 pages; Hardback: 978-0-566-08861-2

Project Management 9th Edition
Dennis Lock
544 pages; Hardback: 978-0-566-08772-1

Go to:
www.gowerpublishing.com/projectmanagement for details of these and our wide range of other project management titles.

Visit **www.gowerpublishing.com** and

- search the entire catalogue of Gower books in print
- order titles online at 10% discount
- take advantage of special offers
- sign up for our monthly e-mail update service
- download free sample chapters from all recent titles
- download or order our catalogue